MONTANA COOKING

A BIG TASTE OF BIG SKY COUNTRY

GREG PATENT

ThreeForks®

GUILFORD, CONNECTICUT
HELENA, MONTANA

AN IMPRINT OF THE GLOBE PEQUOT PRESS

For Granny, Baba, and Edith Green

To buy books in quantity for corporate use
or incentives, call **(800) 962–0973**
or e-mail **premiums@GlobePequot.com**.

ThreeForks is a trademark of Morris Book Publishing, LLC.

Photos © Shutterstock.com

Design by Nancy Freeborn
Layout by Sue Murray

Library of Congress Cataloging-in-Publication Data is available on file.

ISBN 978-0-7627-4798-6

Printed in the United States of America

10 9 8 7 6 5 4 3 2 1

CONTENTS

ACKNOWLEDGMENTS

I relied on help and information from many people while working on this book. Erin Turner, who was instrumental in the book's editing; the late Tony Grace, who spoke so enthusiastically about his days as a chuck wagon cook at the turn of the century; the late Jo Rainbolt, for introducing me to Tony Grace and arranging a luncheon with him; Chu Chu Pham, for teaching me the rudiments of Vietnamese cooking; Gillian Malone, for introducing me to Sam Western; Sam Western, for expressing his feelings about hunting and for cooking a delicious meal of game with Asian flavors; the late Sam Arnold, for giving so generously of his time to relate the history of Native American and Western foods; John McCamant, for introducing us to black quinoa; Larry Evans, for generously sharing his wild mushroom harvests; Art and Nancy Callan, for educating me about apple growing in Montana and for making available little-known heirloom varieties at our local farmers' market; Don Spritzer, resource librarian at the Missoula Public Library, for directing me to historical diaries of emigrants; Rich and Lily Bumbaca, for sharing their enthusiasm for bison with us and introducing their beloved herd up close and personal; Roger, Carla, Leif, and Heidi Cox, for generous supplies of game; Ted and Peggy Christian, also for their generous gift of game; Mike Schwartz, for some of the best elk I've ever eaten; Dale Johnson, archivist at the Mansfield Library at the University of Montana, for opening his photographic files to me; the gardeners, foragers, millers, dairy owners, game purveyors, ranchers, fishermen, and poultry farmers, for caring enough to produce healthful, high-quality food products.

And my darling wife, Dorothy, who not only tasted, evaluated, and commented upon every recipe in this book, but helped me teach my computer to do what I wanted it to do.

I simply could not have done this without all of you.

INTRODUCTION

The West is not only a place, it is a state of mind—open, receptive, and welcoming. Perhaps the feeling of the West is best expressed by Cole Porter's song "Don't Fence Me In," which he based on a poem by Bob Fletcher, a Montanan. Although I spent my first eleven years in Shanghai, China, I have lived in the West most of my life—first in San Francisco, then in Missoula, Montana, where my wife and I raised our two sons and continue to live. Over thirty-five years, I've come to appreciate Montana's natural abundance—wild mushrooms and berries, all kinds of game meat, whole grains, and of course, the hard winter and spring wheats that are essential for making excellent yeast breads.

I began cooking shortly after my family emigrated to San Francisco in 1950. Each day I raced home from school to watch a live afternoon cooking show on KRON-TV hosted by Edith Green, who taught me the basics of baking powder biscuits, pies, cakes, and desserts. As a teenager, I branched out into preparing "real" food and helped my working parents by getting dinner ready before they came home. After I got married, Julia Child's early television shows taught me most of what I know today about cooking.

As I was growing up, it never dawned on me to pursue my passion for cooking as a career. It was just a hobby until 1979, when, at a friend's suggestion, I approached a local television station and proposed a weekly cooking show. At about the same time, I became a finalist in the National Pineapple Cooking Classic and won a trip to Hawaii to compete in a cook-off. That, coupled with my Pillsbury Bake-Off win as a teenager, convinced the management at KECI-TV in Missoula to make a pilot half-hour show called *Big Sky Cooking*—the beginning of my cooking career. We shot fifty-two episodes, and I published two cookbooks with the recipes. During that time I also wrote a weekly food column for the *Missoulian*, our local paper, while I continued my profession as a zoology professor at the University of Montana.

In 1982, the late Carl Sontheimer, then the president of Cuisinart, offered me a job I could not refuse. I left the university and began working as his company's national spokesperson. I traveled all over the country and taught food processor cooking classes for many years. Cuisinart also financed a twenty-six-episode food processor cooking show broadcast nationally on the

Learning Channel. I wrote a food processor cookbook, originally published by Cuisinart in 1985 as *Patently Easy Food Processor Cooking*. In 1992 Ten Speed Press reprinted the book as *Food Processor Cooking Quick and Easy*. For a number of years thereafter, I was a restaurant chef, and I had the good fortune of working with wonderful cooks in Switzerland and Bavaria as part of my training.

I now write about food from my home. Even though I've lived in the United States for more years than not, my early influences have always drawn me to the foods of other lands. My mother's mother, Granny, was Arabic. We lived with her for many years in Shanghai, and she cooked savory Middle Eastern dishes. Baba, my father's mother, cooked foods of her native Russia. I remember especially her superb pastries and desserts. And for a time in Shanghai, we even had a Chinese cook. I can still remember hanging around in the kitchen while she worked, begging for samples of her mouthwatering dishes. Later on after graduate school, my wife and I, along with our two young sons, lived in Naples, Italy, for a year. Our housekeeper there taught us to cook many specialties of the region.

What excites me today are the foods brought by new immigrants to Montana. Over the past thirty-five years, people from Asia, Mexico, Russia, and elsewhere have influenced public tastes by selling their homegrown herbs and vegetables at farmers' markets, getting supermarkets to stock ethnic cooking staples, and opening local restaurants. These flavors, when combined with traditional Western foods, create wonderful new tastes. For example, Asian-flavored marinades give smoked trout a new dimension, and adding cilantro to a sweet-and-sour sauce for buffalo meatballs brings out the flavor of the meat with newfound clarity. And an exciting variety of fresh herbs, now available in practically every market, add oomph and zest to almost any food.

The ongoing culinary renaissance in Montana has motivated me to write this book. In creating these recipes, I have been inspired by innovative chefs and local cooks who continue the tradition of living off the land—they hunt, forage for wild things, and love to try new foods. Cooking is much more than bodily nourishment. Good cooking satisfies the soul, and I am filled with wonder whenever a new flavor combination tells my taste buds that something extraordinary is happening. When I am cooking, I often think of how the character based on the painter Georges Seurat in Stephen Sondheim's musical *Sunday in the Park with George* approaches an empty canvas. "So many possibilities," he says.

Cooking is a dynamic part of culture and society. Its vitality depends upon a successful union of great ingredients with innovative cooks. The distinctive cuisines of France, Italy, and China, for example, have evolved over hundreds or thousands of years. And it is the precious gift of time that has helped shape these cuisines into what they are today. Thomas Jefferson believed it would take a thousand years to settle the West. Instead, it happened in just fewer than fifty years, by 1893. Because the history of the West's settlement has been so brief, its culinary potential is just beginning to be appreciated.

I do not believe that the West can claim a truly original cuisine, primarily because the region is so large and was settled by pioneers from so many different backgrounds. However, an extraordinarily wide range of foods, many unique to the region, are grown, farmed, raised, gathered, or hunted in the West. These vital staples, along with the diverse cultures the settlers brought with them, provide the raw materials from which Western cooks' imaginations have always taken flight. Buffalo, deer, elk, bear, moose, and all sorts of other game have played a significant role in Western cooking, and perhaps no other region in the country offers as many different kinds of edible wild mushrooms. The wild huckleberries that flourish in the mountains of Montana and Idaho are unique. They do not grow anywhere else, and they make the best pies, muffins, and jams imaginable.

The high-altitude Montana prairies and valleys are prime growing areas for wheat, barley, oats, lentils, and garbanzos. Large, juicy cherries grow along the shores of Flathead Lake. More familiar plants such as garden-variety rhubarb, strawberries, and raspberries grow in many parts of the country, but they thrive in the cool Rocky Mountain Montana air. Canning and preserving foods are important traditions, enabling farm families to put up the region's abundant harvest of fruits and vegetables to sustain them during the cold winter months. Montana cooks also smoke meats and fish to preserve them. In earlier times, the foods were cold-smoked for days, then stored in a cool place for months thereafter. Today, smoking remains popular, but hot-smoking is the preferred method because it is faster and virtually foolproof. All of these aspects of Montana cooking continue to define and distinguish the cuisine of the state today. This book is filled with recipes and anecdotes that celebrate and chronicle the people and landscape of the old and the new Montana.

Getting here by covered wagon from the East was arduous, and the trip could last several months. Trail food was not exciting—salt pork, beans, hardtack, dried fruit, and coffee made up the basic larder. Real cooking, with a home stove and a backyard garden, couldn't begin until the pioneers found a place to settle. When they did, they planted what grew best in the area, raised farm animals, hunted, fished, and gathered wild berries and mushrooms. Settlers from Europe knew how to identify edible wild mushrooms and were delighted to find these succulent fungi in their new Montana home.

Of course, those of northern European descent weren't the only pioneers. African Americans came to the West after the Civil War. Hispanics were already living in what is now New Mexico and Colorado before the area became states. Chinese came by ship to San Francisco and worked on the railroads and in mining and logging camps throughout the West. All came in search of a better life and all left their culinary mark.

Montana cooks are always looking for new ways to prepare familiar ingredients and to experiment with not-so-familiar foods. The ethnic lines have become blurred during the past two decades, engendering a more creative use of ingredients and the invention of new flavor combinations. Considering that the old West was the nation's second melting pot, it was only a matter of time before this happened. The only reason it has taken so long is that the region is so vast. The eleven Western states are the largest in the country, occupying almost half the area of the continental United States. The original pioneers who settled here wanted to re-create the foods of their homelands as best they could with the available resources. We, the new pioneers, create dishes that incorporate the tastes of native and traditional ingredients along with those brought here, grown, and harvested by the newest immigrants. May the parade of culinary delights never end.

BASICS

When we compare what we consider basic ingredients—sun-dried tomatoes, specialty cheese, Mediterranean olives, dried wild mushrooms, and shelled nuts—with what the pioneers considered essential when they trekked across the continent 150 years ago, the differences seem staggering. They, of course, relied on enormous quantities of flour, "parched" corn, cornmeal, sugar, bacon, dried beans, rice, dried fruits, and coffee to sustain them on a journey they expected to take several months. Any fresh food they encountered along the way—including game—was a special treat.

Yet, if we look over a list of the emigrants' basic food needs, we find many similarities between the items on their lists and those our pantries are always stocked with. Flour, cornmeal, sugar, dried beans, rice, dried fruits, coffee, and nuts are found in just about every American household on any given day. It's just the variety that has broadened over time. Today flour is available in more than a dozen different kinds. For the emigrant, the choice was limited to whatever was in the sack tucked in a corner of the covered wagon. And what about cornmeal? Then it was simply called "Indian meal." Today we have yellow, white, stone-ground, water-ground, hull-less, and so on. Sometimes we even call it polenta, even though it's still cornmeal.

Whatever you consider the core items in your pantry, take a look at the following ingredient descriptions and instructions for select basics called for throughout this book. With the addition of a few new basics, like cooked wild mushrooms, your pantry will hold the range of ingredients that generations of Montana cooks have relied on daily.

It's Still Mush

Lettice Bryan included a recipe for polenta, or "mush" as she called it, in her 1839 cookbook. Her method does indeed result in the smooth texture she claims:

> *Sift some fine Indian meal, make a smooth batter of it by stirring in a sufficiency of cold water. Having ready a pot of boiling water, throw in a handful of salt, and stir in your batter till it is like very thick soup. Boil it till of the proper consistence, and stir it frequently to prevent its being lumpy, and to keep it from burning on the bottom. Mush, made in this manner, will never fail to be thoroughly done and clear of lumps, which are two common failures. Cold mush may be sliced and fried brown in butter. They are very good for breakfast.*

Baking Soda

Travelers on the trek west were advised to pack several pounds of saleratus, or baking soda, for each adult. In many cases, this was not enough for the months-long trip, so more was often gathered at the edges of natural soda springs, where it dried into crusty white beds. One emigrant, Amelia Hadley, described the saleratus "as white as snow" and "3 or 4 inches deep," adding, "you can get chunks . . . as large as a pint cup just as pure as that you buy." As is true of modern-day baking soda, saleratus worked best when mixed into a batter and baked immediately in a moderately hot to very hot oven.

Butter

The recipes in this book call for unsalted butter. In the past, one had to hunt for it in the frozen foods section because the lack of salt means it has a relatively short shelf life of about 1 month. Because more and more people are using unsalted butter nowadays and the product's turnover is higher, it is commonly available in the refrigerated foods section. If you use *salted* butter, bear in mind that each stick ($1/2$ cup, or 4 ounces) contains the equivalent of about $1/2$ teaspoon salt and adjust accordingly.

Clarified Butter

Using clarified butter, which is butter with the milk solids removed, allows you to fry at high temperatures without much risk of the butter suddenly turning black and burning. Clarified butter is easy to make and keeps well in the freezer. One-half cup of butter makes about 6 tablespoons of clarified butter. To clarify butter, cut a stick into 6 or 8 pieces and place it in a small saucepan over very low heat. As it melts, the butter will bubble gently and foam will rise to the top. When the butter is completely melted, turn off the heat and let the butter stand for several minutes to allow the solids to settle. Carefully spoon off and discard the top foamy layer, then slowly pour the clear golden liquid into a container, and discard the milky white solids. Use as directed in recipes. Clarified butter keeps well in the refrigerator for 4 to 6 weeks.

Clarified Butter on the Trail

Clarified butter has been enjoyed for over a century and was even transported by covered wagon, as evidenced by these instructions, which Randolph Marcy included in his 1859 book:

Butter may be preserved by boiling it thoroughly, and skimming off the scum as it rises to the top until it is quite clear like oil. It is then placed in tin canisters and soldered up. This mode of preserving butter has been adopted in the hot climate of southern Texas, and it is found to keep sweet for a great length of time, and its flavor is but little impaired by the process.

Cream

Whenever whipping cream is called for, you may substitute heavy cream if you prefer. Although heavy cream contains a bit more fat, the results will be the same with either ingredient.

Duck Fat

Pull away pieces of fat from the body cavity and from under the skin of two ducks and chop the fat into 1-inch or smaller pieces. Put the fat in a heavy ovenproof 4-quart pot and add 1 cup water. Place in a 350° oven and stir once after 30 minutes. Cook until the fat is rendered (golden in color) and all of the water has evaporated, about 1 hour. The pieces of remaining fat, "cracklings," should also be golden brown. Strain the fat and cool to room temperature. Reserve the cracklings, which are delicious spread on French bread or chopped and added warm to salads or soup. Store the fat, covered, in an airtight container in the refrigerator for 2 to 3 weeks. It also freezes well and will keep up to 6 months. Small amounts of duck fat make roasted or sautéed potatoes taste sublime. Proper cooking assures that very little of the fat is absorbed. (For a great version of potatoes with duck fat, try Paula Wolfert's recipe for Potatoes in the Style of Quercy, in her marvelous *Cooking of Southwest France*.)

Eggs

Unless indicated otherwise, these recipes all use grade AA large eggs.

Flour

For general cooking I use all-purpose organic unbleached flour, which is what most of these recipes call for. It is a mixture of hard (high-gluten, high-protein) and soft (low-gluten) wheats and its gluten content is suitable for just about any type of cooking. Whenever I call for "flour" in these recipes, I mean all-purpose unbleached flour.

Cake flour is made from soft wheat and is much less likely to toughen during cake and pastry making; be sure to use it whenever it is specified. Bread flour has a higher gluten content than all-purpose flour and gives breads a pleasant elasticity and chewiness.

Hazelnuts

Hazelnuts, or filberts as they are sometimes called, grow abundantly in western Oregon, but are used in Montana a lot. They are usually sold shelled with their skins on. The skins, which taste bitter to some, should be removed before using the nuts by blanching or skinning them as follows. Spread the nuts in a single layer in a shallow baking pan and toast them in a 350° oven for 10 to 15 minutes. Stir the nuts occasionally until they are a toasty brown and have a delicious aroma. Transfer the nuts to a kitchen towel, wrap them up, and let rest. When the nuts are cool, rub them vigorously with the towel to remove the skins. If some skins refuse to come off, just leave them; there is no harm in including a few skins in the recipes.

Measuring Flour

(or, How did that flour get into that cup?)

The success of a recipe often depends on how flour is measured and whether it is sifted. The best way to measure flour is to weigh it. If you don't have a scale, however, just follow these simple guidelines. The weights given below apply only to all-purpose or bread flours.

In the old days, flour would sometimes get lumpy during storage, and sifting served two purposes: removing the lumps and aerating the flour. Both these procedures assured that the flour would be easily incorporated into recipes.

Most of the time, you will measure flour by stirring it in its container to aerate it slightly, spooning it into a measuring cup, filling the cup to overflowing, and sweeping off the excess with a metal spatula. A cup of flour measured this way weighs about 4 1/2 ounces. Sifted flour is called for in only a few recipes in this book. You can buy all-purpose presifted flour, but the flour gets packed down during storage and must be sifted again for accurate measurement. Sift the flour by placing more than you need in a sifter set over a sheet of waxed paper. Sift and then spoon the flour into a measuring cup, filling the cup to overflowing; do not pack or shake the cup. Sweep off the excess flour with a metal spatula or any straight-sided utensil. Sifted flour measured this way weighs about 4 ounces.

A third way to measure flour is to fill a metal measuring cup by scooping it into the flour container, filling the cup to overflowing, and sweeping off the excess with a metal spatula. This cup of flour will weigh about 5 ounces.

To be sure we're speaking the same language, recipes for baked items specify both the weight of the flour and how to measure it. Cake flour weighs less when measured by any of the three ways described above. Whole wheat flour tends to weigh a bit more. Generally speaking, accurately measuring flour for bread making is not as critical as for making cakes or delicate pastries.

Stocks

It is well worth making several quarts of chicken, beef, and fish stock and freezing them to have on hand. They keep perfectly for months. It isn't necessary to add salt to stocks while they are cooking. After stocks are degreased, I concentrate them by boiling and reducing, adding the salt at that stage. Whenever a stock is called for in this book, use one of the following stock recipes.

CHICKEN STOCK

The concentration of flavor is just right for recipes calling for chicken stock. For a stronger flavor or for use in recipes requiring a rich chicken stock, boil down the defatted and strained liquid until it is reduced by half. To make turkey stock, simply substitute turkey bones—fresh bones for a light-colored stock or bones from a roasted turkey for a brown turkey stock. The ginger adds a refreshing flavor and aroma, without giving the stock a gingery taste.

2 whole frying chickens with giblets
    (7 to 8 pounds total),
      or 7 to 8 pounds any combination
      chicken backs, necks, and wings
2 large carrots, scrubbed and cut into
    2-inch chunks
1 large yellow onion, peeled and
    cut in half
4 stalks celery with leaves
2 teaspoons black peppercorns
6 sprigs parsley
1 bay leaf
1 (2-inch) length fresh ginger
Water

1. Rinse the whole chickens inside and out or rinse chicken parts under cold tap water. Place the chicken and giblets in a heavy-bottomed 10- to 12-quart stockpot. (Reserve the livers for another use.) Add remaining ingredients, using enough water to cover the chicken by 1 to 2 inches.

2. Set the stockpot over medium heat. As the water comes to a simmer, skim and discard any scum or foam that rises to the surface. Continue to remove the scum as necessary. Don't allow the liquid to boil. As the stock gets hotter, decrease the heat to very low and cook slowly, partially covered, for 3 to 4 hours. Only a bubble or two should break the surface every now and then. Remove the chicken from the pot and set aside. Strain the stock, discarding the vegetables; cool, cover, and refrigerate overnight. The next day, remove and discard the solidified fat on the surface.

3. To make a more concentrated (rich) chicken stock, boil a measured amount until it is reduced by half. Cool, cover, and refrigerate. The stock keeps refrigerated for 1 or 2 days or up to 6 months frozen in an airtight container.

BEEF STOCK

The secret to good-quality beef stock lies in the bones. Oxtail is good because it is high in gelatin and provides a wonderful flavor. Veal bones are also high in gelatin and are good to include. (I tend not to use veal unless I know the animals have not been confined in pens.)

In this recipe, the bones are cooked twice. The first cooking gives you about 10 quarts of strained beef stock. After chilling, remove the fat and taste the stock. It can be used in this form for soups, or you can reduce it by half to concentrate the flavor and intensify richness. A second cooking produces several quarts of liquid that you will further reduce to about 2 cups of a very gelatinous meat glaze, which I use to thicken and enrich sauces. It is a joy to have cubes of meat glaze on hand in the freezer to produce extraordinary sauces in an instant.

15 pounds beef bones, including some shanks, marrow bones, knuckles, or oxtails

2 large leeks, washed thoroughly and cut into 3-inch pieces

6 to 7 stalks celery with leaves, washed and cut into 3-inch pieces

4 large carrots, washed and cut into 2-inch pieces

3 large yellow onions, with skins on, quartered

Water

½ pound white mushrooms, washed, cut in half if large

1 pound plum tomatoes, cut in half

3 bay leaves

8 sprigs parsley

2 teaspoons black peppercorns

1. Adjust two oven racks to divide the oven into thirds and preheat the oven to 400°. Arrange the beef in single layers in two large shallow roasting pans and place the pans in the oven. Roast for 1 hour. Place the leeks and celery in a heavy-bottomed 20-quart stockpot. Add the carrots and onions to the roasting pans, dividing them between the two, and roast for 30 minutes. Using tongs, transfer beef and vegetables to the stockpot. Pour off and discard the fat from the pans, add about 2 cups water to each, and heat on the stovetop, scraping the browned bits from the pan bottoms. Add the liquid to the stockpot along with the mushrooms, tomatoes, bay leaves, parsley, peppercorns, and enough cold water to cover ingredients by about 2 inches. (The pot will be almost full.)

2. Set the stockpot over medium-low heat and bring to a simmer. (This will take 1 hour or longer.) Simmer, uncovered, for 10 to 12 hours. Adjust heat if necessary so that the liquid bubbles very gently. If simmered over low heat, scum will not form. If you bring the stock to a simmer over higher heat, you will need to periodically remove the scum with a slotted spoon.

3. Remove the beef and vegetables from the pot and set them aside. Strain the stock through a fine-mesh strainer into another large pot and refrigerate it, uncovered, overnight. The next day, remove and discard the solidified fat on the surface.

4. Meanwhile, return the beef to the stockpot. (Some vegetables may cling to them and can be included.) Add about 6 quarts of cold water, or enough to cover the beef by 1 to 2 inches. Bring to a simmer as described above and cook slowly for about 10 hours. Strain the stock through a fine-mesh strainer into a 5-quart saucepan, cool, cover, and refrigerate overnight. The next day, remove and discard the solidified fat on the surface.

5. To make a more concentrated (rich) beef stock from your first batch of degreased stock, boil a measured amount until it is reduced by half. Cool, cover, and refrigerate. The stock keeps refrigerated for 3 to 4 days or up to 6 months frozen in an airtight container.

6. To make meat glaze, boil the second cooking of the meat and bones stock until the liquid becomes very thick and syrupy, darkens in color, has large bubbles, and measures about 2 cups. (Just estimate this amount, since much of it would stick to a measuring cup, resulting in waste.) Pour the thick liquid into an 8 x 4-inch nonstick loaf pan and let it cool completely at room temperature. It will become solid and have a rubbery texture. Meanwhile, add 1 cup of warm water to the saucepan and dissolve the meat glaze stuck to the sides and bottom by scraping and stirring with a rubber spatula. Reserve this to use as stock.

7. When the meat glaze is set, cut it into 1-inch cubes and transfer to an airtight bag. The meat glaze keeps frozen for 6 to 8 months.

DUCK STOCK

YIELD: 3 TO 4 QUARTS

2 duck carcasses, plus necks, hearts, wings, and gizzards

3 large carrots, cut into 1-inch pieces

2 large yellow onions, unpeeled and cut into quarters

3 stalks celery with leaves, cut into 2-inch pieces

1 large leek, washed, cut into 2-inch pieces

1 head garlic, cut in half crosswise

5 quarts plus 1 cup water

1 cup dry white French vermouth

6 sprigs parsley

6 sprigs oregano

6 sprigs thyme

1 teaspoon black peppercorns

2 bay leaves

1. Chop the carcasses into 3 or 4 pieces each. Place in a roasting pan along with the necks, hearts, wings, and gizzards. (Reserve the liver for another use.) Roast at 450° for 1 hour. Add the carrots, onions, celery, leek, and garlic. Stir well to coat the vegetables with some of the rendered fat and roast for 30 minutes at 400°. Transfer the duck and the vegetables to a 9-quart stockpot. Add the 5 quarts of water and the remaining ingredients to the stockpot.

2. Carefully pour off and discard the duck fat in the roasting pan, leaving the browned bits on the bottom. Pour in the remaining 1 cup of water and set the pan over high heat. Scrape the pan with a wooden spoon to release the browned bits. Add the liquid to the stockpot. Over medium-low heat, simmer the stock, partially covered, for 3 to 4 hours, allowing it to bubble gently while cooking. Strain the stock through a fine-mesh strainer. Cool, cover, and refrigerate it overnight. The next day, remove and discard the solidified fat on the surface.

3. For a more concentrated stock, boil until it reaches the desired strength. If you reduce the stock by half, you will have duck demi-glace (a concentrated, gelatinous stock packed with flavor). Both the stock and demi-glace keep refrigerated for 1 to 2 days or up to 8 months frozen in an airtight container.

Note: I usually use half the stock as is and boil down the rest to make demi-glace.

8 :: MONTANA COOKING

FISH STOCK

Unlike meat stocks, fish stocks cook for only 30 minutes. Be sure to use bones from non-oily fish, such as halibut, flat fish, or sturgeon. Unless you live near the sea or have a large fish market in your city, it can be difficult to find fish bones. Your best bet is to ask your fish market to save the frames (skeletons) from any whole fish they buy and fillet. Fish bones can be stored frozen until you have enough to work with.

6 pounds fish bones from lean fish, including heads and trimmings

1 large carrot, scrubbed and thinly sliced

1 large leek, thinly sliced

1 large yellow onion, peeled and thinly sliced

12 sprigs parsley

1 cup fresh white mushrooms, thinly sliced

1 teaspoon black peppercorns

2 cups dry white French vermouth

Cold water

Salt and pepper

1. Chop the fish bones into large chunks. Place the bones and the remaining ingredients except salt and pepper in a heavy-bottomed 10- to 12-quart pot, using enough cold water to just cover. Bring to a simmer over medium heat, removing any scum that rises to the surface. Lower heat to a gentle simmer and cook for 30 minutes. Strain through a fine-mesh strainer and discard solids. Season with salt and pepper and use as directed.

2. For a more concentrated stock, boil a measured amount of unseasoned stock until it is reduced by half. Cool, cover, and refrigerate. The stock keeps refrigerated for 1 to 2 days or up to 2 months frozen in an airtight container.

Wild Mushrooms

There are hundreds of species of wild mushrooms that grow in Montana. Late spring rains bring up the first mushrooms of the season. If there is a warm, wet June, more varieties pop up all over the hillsides. Early fall rains bring even more.

Many kinds of wild mushrooms are available in well-stocked markets all over the country at different times of the year. Or you may find there's a mycologist leading mushroom hunting expeditions in your area. (Check with local colleges and natural food stores.) Whether you buy your wild mushrooms at the market or forage for them with the guidance of a professional, *Mushrooms Demystified* by David Arora will help you identify hundreds of mushrooms. I suggest you buy wild mushrooms when they appear in your markets and cook them even if you have no immediate plans for them. You will be glad you did. The cooked mushrooms can be frozen for future use; see general instructions in the sections below.

Characteristics of Mushrooms

Wild mushrooms have distinct characteristics. Most spring up from the soil; some grow on tree trunks. Regardless of their different growth habits, the flavor and texture of each species is unique. Golden trumpet-shaped chanterelles have a subtle flavor. They are aristocratic and royal, and deserve to be treated that way. Pair them with cream, butter, and noble spirits such as cognac. The morel, on the other hand, is the king of the forest with its big, earthy taste. Even when morels are not the dominant ingredient, they lift the flavors of any dish. Oyster mushrooms grow in clumps on trees and are grayish, which gives them an oysterlike appearance.

They have a firm, somewhat chewy texture and a lusty, full taste. Shaggy manes stand alone, both in flavor and their growth habits. They inspire expediency because they remain in pristine condition for only a few hours before dissolving into an inky black mess. They are the blandest tasting of the four types described here, but cooking them in a healthy dose of butter imparts seductive flavor nuances that are difficult to beat.

Chanterelles

Carefully remove any dirt from 3/4 pound of chanterelles with a soft-bristled brush. Melt 4 tablespoons butter in a 12-inch skillet over low heat. Add the mushrooms, 1/2 teaspoon salt, and a few grindings of black pepper. Toss to coat the mushrooms with the butter, and cover the pan. Cook slowly, stirring occasionally, until the mushrooms are tender but have a slight firmness, about 15 minutes. Stir in 1 large minced shallot and 1 teaspoon chopped fresh tarragon. Cook, covered, 5 more minutes. The mushrooms should be lightly browned with no juice remaining in the pan. If there is juice, raise the heat and cook rapidly until the liquid has evaporated. Set aside to cool for use in recipes, or cool, cover, and refrigerate for a day or two. For longer storage, freeze in airtight bags for up to 6 months. Makes 2 to 2 1/2 cups.

Morels

Carefully brush away dirt from 1 pound of morels and trim away the stem tips if they are gritty. If the mushrooms are small (up to 1 1/2 inches long), leave them whole. If larger, cut them into 1-inch pieces. Cook no more than 1 pound at a time. Melt 4 tablespoons butter in a 12-inch skillet over medium-low heat. When the butter is hot and foamy and begins to turn a light nut brown, add the morels. Stir well to coat the mushrooms with the butter. Cover the pan and cook about 5 minutes, shaking the pan once or twice, until the morels are tender but slightly firm. Turn the mushrooms into a large wire strainer set over a bowl and let stand until they are completely cool and well drained. Store, covered, in the refrigerator for a day or two, or freeze in airtight bags and store for up to 6 months. The morel liquid may be frozen and used to flavor soups or stocks. Makes about 3 cups.

Oyster Mushrooms

Brush away any dirt clinging to 1 pound of oyster mushrooms and trim off tough ends. Cut the mushrooms into 1-inch pieces. For each pound of trimmed oyster mushrooms, melt 4 tablespoons butter in a 12-inch skillet over medium heat. When the butter foam begins to subside, stir in the mushrooms and season with 1/2 teaspoon salt and 1/4 teaspoon freshly ground black

pepper. Cover the pan and cook, stirring once or twice, for about 5 minutes, or until the mushrooms are tender but slightly firm. Cool and refrigerate, covered, for up to 2 days, or freeze in airtight bags and store up to 6 months. Makes about 3 cups.

Shaggy Manes or Inky Caps

These mushrooms have tall, domed white caps and white stems. They get their name from the fringes adorning the caps, giving them a shaggy, unkempt look. They appear along country roadsides right after a rainfall in spring and fall and have a life expectancy of less than 1 day. Within 24 hours, they literally dissolve into a black liquid, so you cannot delay in using them. Rinse 1 pound shaggy manes in a large basin of water as rapidly as you can, gently swishing them around to remove the dirt. Quickly transfer to a large colander. Squeeze a handful of mushrooms gently between your hands to remove excess water. Don't worry if the caps or stems crack. Cut off and discard the knobby stem ends and slice the mushrooms crosswise about 1/2 inch thick. Place them in an ungreased 12-inch-wide, 2-inch-deep pan (a 5-quart sauté pan is ideal). Cook over high heat, stirring occasionally at first, until the liquid released by the mushrooms has almost evaporated. Stir continuously during the last minute of cooking to prevent them from burning. Turn the mushrooms into a large wire strainer set over a bowl and allow to drain and cool completely. Freeze the liquid to flavor soups or stocks. Refrigerate the cooked mushrooms for 1 to 2 days or freeze in airtight bags for up to 6 months. Shaggy manes have very high water content; 1 pound will yield only 1 packed cup when cooked.

BREAKFAST

Perhaps the most important meal of the day, breakfast is often given short shrift because of time constraints. For this reason, the bread recipes here may either be made ahead or started the night before. The Sourdough English Muffins may even be baked beforehand and frozen. In the morning simply thaw them in the microwave and toast them.

Eggs, whether scrambled, poached, sunny-side up, over easy, or made into omelets, are always welcome with any of the breads or pancakes here. I've included a recipe for your very own homemade pork sausage patties because they're great with just about any breakfast food. And a Spanish omelet makes a perfect dish for a lazy weekend morning.

SOURDOUGH ENGLISH MUFFINS

Once you make your own English muffins, you won't want to buy them again. These call for a milk-based starter and are light and tender. As with most sourdough breads, the batter is started the night before. I made these every week for Sunday brunch to serve with eggs Benedict when I was a chef at a Montana guest ranch. The muffins are also delicious hot off the griddle, split, buttered, and eaten with slices of creamy Havarti cheese or preserves.

1½ cups warm whole or low-fat milk

¾ cup milk-based sourdough starter
    (page 31)

4 cups (1 pound 2 ounces)
    unbleached all-purpose flour

2 tablespoons sugar

1 teaspoon salt

¾ teaspoon baking soda

Cornmeal

1. Combine the milk and starter in a large bowl. Measure the flour by spooning it into a dry measuring cup, filling the cup to overflowing, and sweeping off the excess with a metal spatula. Stir 3 cups of the flour into the milk-starter mixture to make a stiff batter (the batter does not have to be smooth). Cover tightly with plastic wrap and let rest overnight at room temperature.

2. The next day, combine $^3/_4$ cup of the remaining flour with the sugar, salt, and baking soda, and stir it into the dough with a wooden spoon. Sprinkle a work surface with the last $^1/_4$ cup of flour. Turn the dough out onto the floured surface and knead it until smooth and no longer sticky, adding more flour if needed. Cover loosely with a towel and let it rest 15 minutes. Sprinkle two baking sheets with cornmeal. Roll or pat out the dough until it is about $^3/_4$ inch thick. Using a sharp 3-inch-diameter cookie cutter, cut out the muffins. Place them 1 to 2 inches apart on the prepared baking sheets. Gather, reroll, and cut the dough scraps to make a total of about 18 muffins. Cover loosely with dry kitchen towels and let the muffins rise in a warm place until they are puffy and light, about 45 minutes.

3. Heat an ungreased griddle to 275°. (If your griddle has no thermostat, adjust the heat to medium.) Cook the muffins for about 10 minutes on each side, or until they are nicely browned and cooked through. Test by splitting one with a fork to be sure the inside is cooked. Serve warm, or let cool, then split and toast. Leftover muffins freeze well; just thaw, split, and toast before serving.

SOURDOUGH WHOLE WHEAT WAFFLES

These waffles are ideal for a late and lazy Sunday brunch. The batter is started the night before and takes only a few minutes to complete the next morning. Once mixed, the batter can stand at room temperature for a few hours. It may not look as bubbly after an hour or so, but the results will be the same. The waffles are crunchy on the outside and light and tender on the inside. They are similar to Belgian waffles and can be enjoyed with sliced strawberries and whipped cream or with butter and maple syrup.

1 cup (4½ ounces) whole wheat flour

1 cup sourdough starter (use any on
    page 31)

½ cup warm water

1 cup plain nonfat yogurt

½ cup nonfat or low-fat milk

2 egg yolks

2 tablespoons melted butter

1 tablespoon pure vanilla extract

1 cup (4½ ounces) unbleached
    all-purpose flour

½ teaspoon salt

1 teaspoon baking powder

½ teaspoon baking soda

3 egg whites

3 tablespoons sugar

1. Measure the whole wheat flour by spooning it into a dry measuring cup, filling the cup to overflowing, and sweeping off the excess with a metal spatula. To make the sponge, combine the starter, water, and whole wheat flour in a large mixing bowl, beating with a wooden or rubber spatula until smooth. Cover tightly with plastic wrap and let rise overnight at room temperature.

2. The next morning, combine the yogurt, milk, egg yolks, melted butter, and vanilla in a small bowl and whisk the mixture into the sponge. Measure the all-purpose flour as described for the whole wheat flour, then sift the all-purpose flour, salt, baking powder, and baking soda together. Stir gently into the batter with a rubber spatula just until smooth. The batter will rise and bubble almost immediately.

3. In a small bowl, beat the egg whites with a handheld electric mixer until soft peaks form. Gradually beat in the sugar on medium speed; increase the speed to high and continue beating until the whites form stiff, shiny peaks. Carefully fold the whites into the batter.

4. Preheat a waffle iron and brush it lightly with vegetable oil or coat it lightly with nonstick cooking spray. Spoon in just enough batter to cover the bottom of the iron (about 1¾ cups). Close the iron and cook for about 6 minutes, or until the waffle is a deep golden brown. Serve immediately, repeating until all of the batter is used.

SOURDOUGH BUTTERMILK PANCAKES

My wife and I became sourdough pancake addicts while we were graduate students. A friend gave us some starter and a recipe, and we faithfully made the pancakes almost every weekend. Then we became parents, which quickly altered our routine. As a result, the starter fell into disuse and ultimately died. We still kept the recipe, though, and I was able to resurrect it many years later, using either the sourdough grape starter or milk-based starter. The pancakes are hearty but tender with the slightly chewy texture that is characteristic of sourdough starters. I use buttermilk for a rich, tangy taste. During blueberry or huckleberry season, I sprinkle the tops of each pancake with a few of the berries as the first side cooks. Serve with butter and maple syrup.

1½ cups grape- or milk-based
    sourdough starter (pages 31, 33)

1¾ cups (8¾ ounces) unbleached
    all-purpose flour

½ teaspoon salt

1 teaspoon baking powder

½ teaspoon baking soda

2 tablespoons sugar

1½ cups buttermilk

1 egg

2 tablespoons melted butter

1 teaspoon pure vanilla extract

2 cups fresh blueberries or
    huckleberries (optional)

1. Remove the starter from the refrigerator and let it stand overnight, covered, at room temperature. Measure the flour by scooping a measuring cup into the flour container, filling the cup to overflowing, and sweeping off the excess with a metal spatula. Sift the flour, salt, baking powder, baking soda, and sugar into a 2-quart bowl. In a separate bowl, whisk the starter with the buttermilk, egg, melted butter, and vanilla. Gently fold the wet ingredients into the dry ones with a rubber spatula, mixing just until the dry ingredients are thoroughly moistened. The batter will be bubbly and may have some lumps.

2. Heat the griddle to 375°. (If your griddle doesn't have a thermostat, adjust the heat to medium-high.) Lightly coat the griddle with nonstick cooking spray. For each pancake, lightly spoon about ⅓ cup batter onto the griddle. If using berries, sprinkle them over the pancakes. When the top sides are full of broken bubbles and start to lose their glossy look, flip the pancakes and cook until the undersides are golden brown, about 1 minute. Serve immediately.

BUTTERMILK-YOGURT PANCAKES

This recipe is for those who love light and tender pancakes that practically fly off the plate. The combination of buttermilk and yogurt gives the pancakes a taste that suggests a sourdough starter, but the texture tells you no starter was used. You can prepare the dry and liquid ingredients separately the night before and combine the two the next morning for breakfast or brunch. As usual, serve these cakes hot off the griddle with butter and syrup.

1⅔ cups (7½ ounces) unbleached
    all-purpose flour
¼ cup sugar
1¾ teaspoons baking powder
¾ teaspoon baking soda
½ teaspoon salt
1 cup buttermilk
⅔ cup plain low-fat yogurt
1 egg
1 tablespoon pure vanilla extract
2 tablespoons vegetable oil
1½ cups fresh huckleberries or
    blueberries (optional)

1. Measure the flour by spooning it into a measuring cup, filling the cup to overflowing, and sweeping off the excess with a metal spatula. Sift the flour together with the sugar, baking powder, baking soda, and salt into a medium-size bowl and set aside. In a separate bowl, whisk together the buttermilk, yogurt, egg, vanilla, and oil. Add the liquid mixture to the dry ingredients and fold both together gently with a rubber spatula just until the dry ingredients are thoroughly moistened. It is not necessary to break up any small lumps of flour.

2. Heat the griddle to 375°. (If your griddle doesn't have a thermostat, adjust the heat to medium-high.) Lightly coat the griddle with nonstick cooking spray. For each pancake, spoon about ¼ cup batter onto the griddle. If using berries, sprinkle them over the pancakes. When the top sides are full of broken bubbles and start to lose their glossy look, flip the pancakes and cook until the undersides are golden brown, about 1 minute. Serve immediately.

DAY-AHEAD APPLE AND HAZELNUT COFFEE CAKE YIELD: 12 SERVINGS

This coffee cake is unusual in that it defies one of the cardinal rules of baking: best when fresh. This recipe is best if made a day ahead. The apples need time to flavor and moisten the cake. Pioneer women would have loved the convenience of this recipe.

I fell in love with an Apple Baba recipe I baked from a superb Russian cookbook, Please to the Table, *by Anya von Bremzen and John Welchman. It was a huge tube cake with a special texture filled with apple slices. The memory of the cake has been with me ever since. In creating the batter for this coffee cake, I adapted the authors' method. Both hazelnut oil (to order, see pages 236–237) and toasted hazelnuts contribute to the cake's taste and texture. Be sure to use a firm-textured tart cooking apple, such as Granny Smith. We use one of our locally grown varieties—Sweet Sixteen, Lyman's Large, or Kidd Orange. If you like your cake warm, simply reheat it for a few minutes in a 300° oven while your coffee brews.*

Streusel Topping

¼ cup (1¾ ounces) unbleached
   all-purpose flour

½ cup granulated sugar

½ teaspoon pumpkin pie spice

¼ cup cold butter

Coffee Cake

2 cups (9 ounces) unbleached all-purpose flour

¾ teaspoon baking powder

¼ teaspoon salt

2 cups peeled, thinly sliced tart baking apples (about ¾ pound)

2 tablespoons granulated sugar

1 teaspoon ground cinnamon

2 eggs

1 cup firmly packed brown sugar

1 teaspoon pure vanilla extract

¼ cup hazelnut oil

¼ cup corn oil

Finely grated zest of 1 large orange

3 tablespoons freshly squeezed orange juice

1 tablespoon freshly squeezed lemon juice

½ cup blanched, toasted hazelnuts (page 3), chopped

1. To prepare the topping, measure the $^1/_4$ cup flour by scooping a measuring cup into the flour container, filling the cup to overflowing, and sweeping off the excess with a metal spatula. Combine the flour, sugar, and pumpkin pie spice in a small bowl. With a pastry blender, cut in the butter until the mixture resembles small peas.

   Refrigerate.

2. For the cake, adjust an oven rack to the center position and preheat oven to 350°. Grease a 13x9x2-inch baking pan and set aside. Measure the 2 cups flour by spooning it into a dry measuring cup, filling the cup to overflowing, and sweeping off the excess with a metal spatula. Sift the flour with the baking powder and salt and set aside. Combine the apples, granulated sugar, and cinnamon in a medium-size bowl, tossing to coat the apples well.

3. In the bowl of an electric mixer, beat the eggs, brown sugar, and vanilla together on high speed for 5 to 10 minutes, or until the mixture has tripled in volume and is thick and light colored. Combine the oils in a glass measuring cup. While beating on high speed, gradually add the oils to the egg mixture in a thin stream. Continue beating for about 1 minute after all the oil has been incorporated. Beat in the orange zest. Combine the orange and lemon juices in a glass measuring cup, then slowly drizzle them into the batter while beating on high speed. Scrape down the bowl. While beating on the lowest speed, add the sifted dry ingredients, mixing only until thoroughly incorporated, 1 to 2 minutes. Fold the apple mixture into the batter. Spread the batter evenly in the prepared pan. Sprinkle with the hazelnuts and scatter the streusel topping evenly over the top. Bake 40 to 45 minutes, or until the cake is golden brown and a toothpick comes out clean when inserted in the center of the cake. Cool on a wire rack and serve warm or at room temperature.

HUCKLEBERRY MUFFINS

These are light-textured, easy-to-make muffins that almost demand to be eaten with sweet butter. For many years, I made them nearly every weekend during huckleberry season and there were never any leftovers. Much of the preparation can be done the night before, leaving only the mixing and baking for the morning. Nonstick muffin pans work best. When huckleberries are in short supply, blueberries will work just fine. Wild Maine blueberries, sold frozen in many parts of the country, are excellent in these muffins.

1 cup sugar

1 teaspoon ground cinnamon

2 cups (9 ounces) unbleached
    all-purpose flour

2 teaspoons baking powder

¼ teaspoon baking soda

½ teaspoon salt

6 tablespoons cold butter, cut into
    6 pieces

1 cup buttermilk

1 egg

1 teaspoon pure vanilla extract

1½ cups fresh or frozen huckleberries
    or blueberries

1. Adjust an oven rack to the center position and preheat the oven to 350°. Lightly coat 12 standard nonstick muffin cups with cooking spray; set aside. Combine 2 tablespoons of the sugar with the cinnamon and set aside.

2. Measure the flour by spooning it into a measuring cup, filling the cup to overflowing, and sweeping off the excess with a metal spatula. Sift the flour with the remaining ³/4 cup and 2 tablespoons of sugar, the baking powder, baking soda, and salt into a large bowl. Cut in the butter with a pastry blender until the mixture resembles coarse meal. (The recipe may be prepared up to this point the night before; just cover tightly and refrigerate.)

3. In a small bowl, combine the buttermilk, egg, and vanilla and pour it evenly over the dry ingredients. Add the huckleberries (unthawed, if frozen), and fold everything together gently with a rubber spatula just until the dry ingredients are well moistened. The batter will be fairly stiff. Spoon into the prepared muffin cups, filling them almost completely. Sprinkle each muffin with about ¹/2 teaspoon of the sugar-cinnamon mixture.

4. Bake for 20 to 25 minutes, or until the tops are golden brown and spring back when gently pressed with a fingertip. Remove the pan from the oven and cool for 5 minutes. The best way to remove these delicate muffins is to invert the pan onto a baking sheet, wait a few seconds, then carefully lift the pan away. The muffins should fall out easily. If necessary, coax them out of the pan with the tip of a small sharp knife. Place the muffins in a large napkin-lined basket and serve immediately.

WHOLE GRAIN REFRIGERATOR MUFFINS

YIELD: 12 LARGE MUFFINS

These muffins, which are light and not too sweet, are made with whole wheat flour, wheat germ, and rolled oats. I like to use a food processor to chop the raisins and rolled oats into smaller pieces. You can store the batter for up to 1 month in the refrigerator and bake a muffin or a few whenever the mood strikes. If the batter separates, stir it thoroughly to recombine the ingredients. Serve with plenty of butter and/or fruit preserves.

1 cup whole wheat flour

2 tablespoons wheat germ, toasted
    or untoasted

1½ teaspoons baking soda

½ teaspoon salt

¼ cup firmly packed brown sugar,
    light or dark

¼ cup granulated sugar

½ cup raisins

4 tablespoons cold unsalted butter,
    cut into pieces

1½ cups quick-cooking rolled oats
    (not instant)

½ cup orange juice, boiling hot

1 large egg

½ teaspoon pure vanilla extract

1 cup buttermilk

1. Adjust an oven rack to the center position and preheat the oven to 375°. Line 12 standard-size muffin cups with paper liners or coat with cooking spray.

2. Measure the flour by scooping a measuring cup into the flour container, filling the cup to overflowing, and sweeping off the excess with a metal spatula. Insert metal blade into work bowl of a food processor and add the flour, wheat germ, baking soda, salt, sugars, and raisins. Process about 30 seconds until raisins are coarsely chopped. Add the butter and process 10 seconds. Transfer ingredients to a large sheet of waxed paper.

3. With the metal blade in the work bowl, add the oats and process until finely chopped, about 30 seconds. Transfer the oats to a large bowl.

4. Add the boiling orange juice to the oats and stir with a wooden spoon. Add the egg, vanilla, and buttermilk and stir well. Stir in the flour mixture—do not beat—only until moistened. Let batter stand at room temperature 20 minutes before baking.

5. Divide batter into prepared muffin cups (cups will be almost full) and place pan in the oven. Bake for 20 to 25 minutes, until the tops of the muffins are a rich brown color and spring back when lightly pressed. Cool in pans 5 minutes, then remove and serve warm.

6. Store leftover batter, tightly covered, in the refrigerator.

HUCKLEBERRY SCONES

These are my idea of the perfect scone—buttery and tender and loaded with wild huckleberries. If you don't live in Western Montana or Idaho where these particular huckleberries thrive at high elevations, use Maine wild blueberries, widely available frozen in markets nationwide, which are very similar in taste. You can mix all the dry ingredients together the night before and add the huckleberries and cream just before shaping and baking.

1½ cups fresh or frozen huckleberries

2 cups all-purpose flour, plus more
    for shaping

½ cup plus 1 tablespoon sugar

2 teaspoons baking powder

¼ teaspoon baking soda

¼ teaspoon salt

Finely grated zest of 1 lemon

½ cup (1 stick) very cold butter, cut
    into small pieces

1 cup plus 1 tablespoon heavy or
    whipping cream

1. Adjust an oven rack to the center position and preheat the oven to 425°. Line a large baking sheet with cooking parchment or silicone baking pan liner.

2. Pick over the huckleberries and discard any stems.

3. Measure the flour by scooping a measuring cup into the flour container, filling the cup to overflowing, and sweeping off the excess with a metal spatula. In a large bowl, whisk together the flour, $^1/_2$ cup sugar, baking powder, baking soda, salt, and lemon zest. Add the butter and work it into the flour rapidly with your fingertips, pinching the pieces to flatten them into flakes. Add the fresh or frozen huckleberries and toss to coat with the dry ingredients. Pour in 1 cup of the cream and fold into the berry mixture with a rubber spatula until just combined. The dough will look lumpy.

4. Dust your work surface with flour and scrape the dough onto it. Knead the dough a few times just until it holds together. Shape the dough into a disk measuring 7 inches in diameter and about 1 inch thick. Brush top of dough with the remaining 1 tablespoon cream and sprinkle with the 1 tablespoon sugar. With a sharp knife, cut the dough into 8 wedges. With a wide metal spatula, transfer scones to the prepared sheet, spacing them about 2 inches apart.

5. Bake 18 to 23 minutes, until tops and bottoms of the scones are golden brown. Cool 10 minutes before serving.

BREAKFAST SAUSAGE PATTIES

YIELD: SIXTEEN 2-OUNCE PATTIES

For top-quality sausage the meat should be ⅔ lean to ⅓ fat. The best readily available source for this is boneless pork shoulder, also called Boston Butt in some parts of the country. Making sausage with pork shoulder is easy: The whole piece of meat is used since it naturally contains the desired ratio of lean to fat. Do not skimp on this ratio if you want your sausage to be juicy. If you separately combine lean meat with fat, be sure to trim away all tendons and gristle from the meat for best results. To grind the meat you can use either a sausage grinder or food processor.

2 pounds boneless pork shoulder,
    well chilled

2 teaspoons salt

½ teaspoon freshly ground black
    pepper

1 teaspoon dried sage

1 teaspoon dried summer savory

½ teaspoon crumbled dried whole
    thyme leaves

¼ teaspoon allspice

¼ cup cold water

1. If using a meat grinder, cut meat into 4-inch-long strips about 1 inch wide and pass through the fine holes of a manual or electric meat grinder into a large bowl. If using a food processor, cut the meat into 1-inch chunks and arrange them in a single layer on a plastic wrap–lined baking sheet. Freeze for 20 minutes until the meat is firm but not at all frozen. Process in 4 batches in the work bowl of the food processor fitted with the metal blade. Simply chop the meat into very fine pieces by pulsing the machine until the texture is to your liking. Transfer the meat to a large bowl as each batch is done.

2. Add the seasonings and water and mix well with a wooden spoon. Cover tightly and refrigerate overnight for flavors to blend. Then cook a small portion to check flavor. Adjust seasonings if necessary.

3. Shape into 16 patties. Put the number you want to cook into a heavy medium-large skillet and set the pan over medium heat. Starting the cooking in a cold skillet keeps the meat juicy. Cook on both sides until patties are lightly browned and pork juices are a yellow color as they run from the patties, about 10 minutes. The meat itself may still be pink.

4. Freeze uncooked patties and store in a heavy-duty resealable plastic bag for up to 2 weeks. Patties may be cooked straight from the freezer. Adjust cooking time accordingly.

SPANISH OMELET

The Spanish omelet (called a tortilla in Spain) is one of the most versatile dishes of its kind because it can be a complete meal in itself. The omelet is cooked in a large skillet over very low heat and the eggs are not stirred at all during the cooking. For breakfast, serve it with biscuits, toast, or muffins and some fruit.

1 large potato, about 8 ounces, peeled and cubed (½-inch pieces)

½ pound zucchini, cubed (½-inch pieces)

2 tablespoons olive oil

3 scallions, thinly sliced

1 garlic clove, minced

¼ teaspoon ground cumin

¼ teaspoon dried oregano leaves, crumbled

¼ cup finely chopped parsley

5 or 6 large eggs

Salt and freshly ground black pepper to taste

1. Bring a large pot of water to a rolling boil over high heat and add the potato. Cook 2 minutes. Add the zucchini and cook 2 to 3 minutes more. Drain well in a colander and set the potato and zucchini on paper towels to drain further.

2. Heat the olive oil in a 10-inch skillet, preferably nonstick, over medium-high heat. Add the scallions and garlic and cook, stirring, for 1 minute. Add the partially cooked potatoes and zucchini, cumin, oregano, and parsley. Cook, stirring occasionally, about 5 minutes, until vegetables are lightly browned. Meanwhile, beat 5 of the eggs lightly with a fork just to combine the yolks and whites and season with salt and pepper.

3. Pour the eggs into the skillet. The eggs should just reach the top of the vegetables. If not, beat the last egg and add it to the pan. Cover the pan, and reduce the heat to very low. Cook 10 to 12 minutes, perhaps a bit longer, until the eggs feel firm on top. Shake the pan to loosen the omelet from the sides and bottom of the pan. If necessary, run a metal spatula around the sides and under the omelet.

4. Place a large platter over the pan and invert the two. Remove the skillet and slide the omelet back into the pan with the omelet's bottom side up. Cook 1 to 2 minutes more and serve hot.

Variations: You can cook some diced green, red, or yellow bell pepper with the scallions and garlic, add some diced cooked ham to the vegetables, or put in some mushrooms if you like. If you make a lot of additions, you may need to add the extra egg to make sure the liquid just reaches the top of the skillet contents.

BREADS

Yeast breads, especially those made with a sourdough starter, were a staple for the Western pioneers. The term "sourdough" even became eponymous, referring not only to the substance but to the person who made bread with it. This was long before the days of active dry yeast, and there was no way to transport highly perishable fresh yeast during the long journeys by covered wagon. Sourdough starters—firm or liquidy doughs containing living yeast cells—were the answer. All that was needed to transform them into bread-making yeast factories was more flour and water.

This chapter features many sourdough breads, not only because of their historical importance to Montana but because they have a taste unrivaled by any other leavening agent and stay fresh longer than breads made with commercial yeast. I began experimenting with sourdough starters about thirty-five years ago. I was fascinated by the notion that a mixture of flour and water or flour and milk would actually trap wild yeast cells when set out in the warm air. If properly nurtured, these cultures can be used to leaven all sorts of breads indefinitely, provided the starter survives. In addition to sourdough breads, English muffins, and waffles, this chapter includes recipes for breads made with commercial yeast and for quick breads.

As you will see, starters can be finicky. Sourdough bakers tend to have different experiences depending on where they live and in what season they collect the wild yeast cells, but all find that it's worth the effort to nurture a successful culture. More than any other kind of baking, bread making is a living, interactive process, uniting the baker with the dynamics of another living organism: yeast.

Most of the pioneer breads were made with white flour because of its long shelf life. I have kept the recipes in this chapter simple by using only two kinds of flour: white and whole wheat. Basic additions—carrots, beers, or grains—turn traditional fare into flavorful, nutritious, moist loaves and rolls. Once you've made some of these recipes, feel free to create your own variations.

I am a fan of heavy-duty electric mixers when making bread. For years I made bread by hand, and while I find the process satisfying, a mixer's power can knead more dough than my arms in a fraction of the time.

A Yeast Primer

In *The Bread Book,* Betsy Oppenneer writes,

> "More important than pigs, cattle, or sheep, starters were part of brides' dowries and were jealously guarded by pioneer wives as their caravans trundled across the country. These women kneaded the starter into a firm ball, nestled it in the flour barrel, and softened it with water when they needed to bake bread. The starter meant life, and as prospectors rushed to California and then to the Yukon and Alaska, they, too, carried a supply of starter for biscuits and other sustaining breads."

In America before the mid-1870s, the only way to make a yeast bread was with a sourdough starter, a batter containing live yeast cells. Although no one knows for sure how and when making sourdough breads with starters began, we do know that it is a very ancient technique that has existed for at least 5,000 years.

Yeast breads need yeast to rise, and there are many sources for that yeast. Packaged yeast wasn't known in America until the late nineteenth century, when the Fleischmann brothers, a pair of immigrants, perfected a method for a compressed yeast cake that reliably produced yeast breads. This yeast was perishable and required refrigeration, but by then ice boxes were common in American homes. The Fleischmann brothers, along with their business partner, James Gaff, introduced their revolutionary product to the world at the Centennial Exposition of 1876, in Philadelphia. A boom in home yeast baking began, and the use of homemade sourdough starters fell by the wayside. During World War II, the Fleischmann Laboratories in Peekskill, New York, developed active dry yeast for the armed forces. The yeast required no refrigeration and could be transported all over the world, thus furthering the popularity of commercial yeast. Most often, commercial yeast, usually in a dry form, is dissolved in warm water and mixed into doughs. When a small amount of sugar is added to the yeast and water, the mixture foams and bubbles, indicating the yeast is alive and active. This step is called "proofing."

In the following recipes, whenever dry yeast is called for, I simply measure 1 tablespoon from the large bag of yeast I keep in the refrigerator. If you bake a lot of bread, it's far cheaper to buy yeast in bulk and store it this way. If you use individual packets of active dry yeast, keep in mind that each one contains $2\frac{1}{4}$ teaspoons. It's easier to measure 1 tablespoon, and doesn't alter the results of the recipes, so I opt for that. Incidentally, be sure to use regular active dry yeast in these recipes and not the quick-rising type, which is a completely different strain and is handled in a different way.

Wild Yeast

Yeast cells live all around us, blown about by the wind. It is possible to rig various traps to capture wild yeast cells and create your own starter from them. Mix equal amounts of flour and water or flour and milk together in a container. After covering the container with cheesecloth to prevent insects, twigs, and leaves from taking up residence in the mixture, set it outdoors on a warm day—80° to 90° is ideal. After a few hours, bring the container back into the kitchen and leave it for 3 to 5 days in a warm place. During this time, if your trap was successful, the mixture will bubble and smell sour. If the mixture loses too much water due to evaporation or becomes too thick and doughy at any time, stir in tepid water to bring it back to its original thickness.

I spent two entire summers in different locations experimenting with various methods of trapping yeast cells. What I found was not always encouraging; the types of yeast cells and bacteria conducive to making great bread may not be available from one locale to another. When I worked as a chef at a guest ranch about 90 miles south of Missoula, I didn't have to add any commercial yeast to my wild sourdough starter doughs to produce fabulous breads. The starters were always potent. A starter made by boiling potatoes until tender, mashing them in their liquid, and whisking in flour while the potato mixture was warm seemed to work best there. After covering the container with cheesecloth, I set it outside. Potatoes are great yeast magnets, but sometimes they will attract the "wrong" kind, as they did at my home in Missoula during another summer. The starter I made there looked bubbly and very alive. It made my bread doughs rise spectacularly. But when I went to shape the bread, the dough became hopelessly gluey, wet, sticky, and impossible to use. I tried many times over a period of months using various starter mixtures: water and flour alone; potatoes, water, and flour; and milk and flour. Except for the milk-based starter, all my other starters failed at producing a decent loaf of bread—despite their appearance of bubbliness! Even when I added commercial yeast to my sourdough batters, the results were a disaster.

The reason for the mixed results is that milk-and-flour starters are consistently better than water-and-flour starters because milk is a better medium for growing many strains of yeast and bacteria that affect the bread's texture and flavor. The right balance of both organisms is needed to make a good starter. My water-based starters were apparently excellent at trapping wild yeasts or other microorganisms that altered gluten from its normally strong and elastic form to one that was wet, dense, and sticky.

Grape Starters

A few years ago, I read about starters that were made from yeasts growing on grape skins. I was intrigued. Here was a source of wild yeasts that didn't have to be lured into a liquid trap. The grapes were mixed with the flour and liquid and the yeast cells fed on the abundant supply of carbohydrates bathing them.

I have done countless trials using grapes for sourdough starters. The results have been far from consistent, but good enough to keep me trying. My last starter seems to be working just fine; it produces chewy, deliciously tangy bread.

Making an active grape starter takes 10 to 14 days, but if you're a die-hard bread fan, I urge you to try it. Expert Steve Sullivan, founder of Acme Bakery in Berkeley, California, uses wine grapes; master baker Nancy Silverton, founder of La Brea Bakery in Los Angeles, calls for red or black grapes. The grapes that produced my best starter were called "black grapes." They were organically grown and had a chalky bloom on their skins, which I took to mean that yeasts were living there happily. Be that as it may, the grape culture and resulting starter worked.

Choosing a Starter

Some of the following bread recipes call for one of the three starters I've given recipes for. For best results, use the starter recommended. In some cases, though, any of the above starters will work, so use whichever one you happen to have on hand.

About Sponges

Some of these bread recipes start off with a sponge, which is simply a mixture of sourdough starter, water, and flour that is allowed to ferment for a few hours or overnight in order to kick the starter into high gear. During this time, the sponge doubles or even triples in volume. The term "sponge" probably originated because the mixture is full of large holes and has the appearance of a sponge.

BASIC SOURDOUGH STARTER

1 tablespoon, or 1 package active
*   dry yeast*
¼ teaspoon sugar
1¼ cups warm water
1 cup (5 ounces) unbleached
*   all-purpose flour*

Combine the yeast and sugar with ¼ cup of the warm water in a small bowl or glass measuring cup. In a few minutes, the mixture will foam and bubble, indicating the yeast is alive and active. If it doesn't bubble, buy fresh yeast and start over. Transfer the yeast mixture to a 2-quart glass measuring cup. Measure the flour by scooping a measuring cup into the flour container, filling the cup to overflowing, and sweeping off the excess with a metal spatula. Add the flour to the yeast mixture along with the remaining 1 cup water and whisk to make a smooth batter about the consistency of pancake batter. Adjust the thickness with flour or water, if necessary. Scrape the side of the bowl and let the starter stand for a few hours at room temperature, loosely covered, until the mixture has almost tripled in volume. Stir the batter, cover with plastic wrap, and let rest overnight at room temperature. The next day, it will be ready to use.

WILD YEAST STARTER

2 cups whole milk
2 cups (10 ounces) unbleached
*   all-purpose flour*

Place the milk in a 2-quart glass measuring cup and let it stand at room temperature for 24 hours. Measure the flour by scooping a measuring cup into the flour container, filling the cup to overflowing, and sweeping off the excess with a metal spatula. Whisk the flour into the milk. Cover the mixture with cheesecloth and leave outside for several hours on a warm day out of direct sunlight. Bring the container back into the kitchen and let it rest uncovered at around 80° (near a pilot light or in a "cold" electric oven with the light on) for 3 to 5 days, or until the starter becomes bubbly and smells and tastes sour. If some of the liquid evaporates and the starter becomes too pasty, whisk in a bit of warm milk to return it to its original consistency. The starter is now ready to use. Every time you use some of the starter, replace it with equal amounts of milk and flour, whisking them in until smooth. Let the replenished starter rest at room temperature for several hours or until the starter becomes full of bubbles. Stir, cover, and refrigerate.

Maintaining a Healthy Starter

Starters gain character if you feed them with more flour and water over time and store them in the refrigerator. When the starter is stored in the refrigerator, a liquid layer ("hooch") will eventually separate from the flour mixture below it. Before using, always pour off the hooch. As long as the hooch is not pink or tinged with orange, it is all right to use. Sometimes the liquid layers of my various starters will be yellowish, gray, or even black, but they are fine. If your starter goes bad, simply begin again.

The day after you've made the basic Sourdough Starter, whisk in 1 cup each of flour and water and transfer the mixture to a larger glass or plastic container. Let the mixture stand at room temperature, uncovered, until it has again almost tripled in volume. Then stir the mixture, cover tightly with plastic wrap, and refrigerate overnight. Bring entire starter to room temperature before using. Each time you use some of the starter, replenish it with equal amounts of flour and warm water. For example, if you use 1 cup starter, replenish the remaining starter by whisking in 1/2 cup each of flour and water. Let the replenished starter rest, uncovered, at room temperature until it is bubbly and active; then stir, cover, and store in the refrigerator.

It is a good idea to refresh your starter every week or so. If you haven't used the starter in a few weeks or a couple of months, discard all but 2 cups of it and whisk in 1 cup each of flour and water. Let it stand at room temperature for a few hours until bubbly, then store as directed above. Sometimes you will need to feed it over a period of days before the starter comes back to life. The discouraging part is that after days of waiting, watching, and hoping, you may discover that the starter is dead (it will have very few or no bubbles in it), or the population of yeasts and bacteria in it may have changed so much that it is no longer capable of making bread. If you have the heart for it, begin all over again and keep your fingers crossed. I assure you that once you have made bread with your own starter you will be hooked on the whole experience.

GRAPE STARTER

5 cups (1 pound 9 ounces) bread flour

5 cups warm water

½ pound black grapes, stems
   removed

You'll also need 1 large square
   washed cheesecloth.

1. Measure the flour by scooping a measuring cup into the flour container, filling the cup to overflowing, and sweeping off the excess with a metal spatula. Whisk together 2 cups of the flour and 2 cups of the warm water in a 2-quart glass or plastic container. It's not necessary to break up any small lumps of flour. The remaining flour and water will be used several days later. Place the grapes on the cheesecloth and tie the ends securely to enclose grapes completely. Gently pound the grapes with a rolling pin to crush them a bit, then stir the bag of grapes into the flour-water mixture. Cover tightly with plastic wrap and leave at room temperature (75° to 80° is ideal) for 6 days. Every day, stir the mixture briefly and re-cover it. Over time, the mixture will bubble and then the bubbles may subside. A liquid layer will rise to the top and may have an odd purplish color. Leave it alone.

2. At the end of 6 days, the process of fermentation is complete, and the carbohydrate supply in the batter will have been exhausted by the multiplying yeast cells. You will have to feed the batter over a period of days to strengthen it. Remove the bag of grapes, squeezing the liquid back into the container; discard the grapes. Stir the starter with a rubber spatula and transfer it to a 3-quart glass bowl. Whisk in 1 cup flour and 1 cup warm water. Let the starter stand at room temperature, uncovered, for several hours, or until bubbly, then cover tightly with plastic wrap and refrigerate overnight. Repeat this procedure twice over the next 2 days, adding 1 cup each of the remaining flour and water at each feeding. At the end of the third feeding, and after the starter has stood at room temperature until bubbly, it is ready to use. It may have an odd grayish color, which is fine. Stir, cover, and store in the refrigerator. Replenish this starter in the same way as other starters. For a manageable quantity, discard all but 2 cups of the starter and feed the remainder with 1 cup flour and 1 cup water.

RANCH HAND SOURDOUGH LOAVES

These huge loaves are named in honor of the insatiable appetites of hard-working ranch hands. The loaves weigh 2 pounds each and make excellent ham, salami, and cheese sandwiches or toast. A heavy-duty electric mixer is highly recommended.

6 to 6½ cups (1 pound 14 ounces to
   2 pounds ½ ounce) bread flour
2 cups basic sourdough or grape
   starter (pages 31, 33)
1½ cups warm water
1 tablespoon or 1 package active
   dry yeast
½ teaspoon plus ¼ cup sugar
1 tablespoon salt
¼ cup vegetable oil

1. Measure the bread flour by scooping a measuring cup into the flour container, filling it to overflowing, and sweeping off the excess with a metal spatula. The night before baking, make the sponge. Beat the starter, 1 cup of the warm water, and 2½ cups of the bread flour in the bowl of a heavy-duty mixer with a wooden or rubber spatula until smooth. Cover tightly with plastic wrap and let rise overnight at room temperature.

2. The next day, stir the yeast and ½ teaspoon of the sugar into the remaining ½ cup of the warm water and let stand 10 minutes, or until the yeast is dissolved and mixture is very foamy. Add the yeast mixture, remaining ¼ cup sugar, salt, oil, and 1 cup of the bread flour to the sponge.

3. Using the flat beater of the mixer, beat on low speed to combine well. Increase the speed to medium and beat 3 minutes. Scrape down the bowl and beater. Replace the beater with the dough hook. Beating on low speed, gradually add the remaining 2½ to 3 cups bread flour to make a smooth, elastic, and slightly sticky dough. Knead 8 to 10 minutes on low to medium speed. Shape the dough into a ball. Lightly coat a 6-quart bowl with nonstick cooking spray. Transfer the dough to the bowl and turn to coat all surfaces. Cover tightly with plastic wrap and let rise at room temperature until almost tripled in volume, about 1½ hours. (It should rise nearly to the top of the container.)

4. Lightly flour a work surface. Turn the dough out onto the floured surface and gently pat it to a 15-inch square. Coat two 9x5x3-inch loaf pans with nonstick cooking spray or grease with vegetable shortening. Cut the dough in half with a sharp knife. Roll each piece tightly, jelly-roll style, to form a cylinder. Pinch the edges to seal. Turn seam side down and seal the ends, tucking them under the loaf. Place the dough seam side down in the prepared pans.

Cover loosely with lightly oiled plastic wrap and let rise at room temperature until the loaves are $1^1/2$ to 2 inches above the rim of the pans, about $1^1/2$ hours.

5. Meanwhile, adjust an oven rack to the lower-third position and preheat the oven to 400°. Remove the plastic wrap and place the loaf pans a few inches apart in the oven. Bake for 35 to 40 minutes, or until the bread is well-browned and the loaves sound hollow when removed from the pans and tapped lightly on the bottom. Cool completely on a wire rack before slicing. Use the bread within 2 days, or freeze in airtight plastic bags for up to 2 months.

Whole Wheat Variation: Substitute 2 cups of whole wheat flour for the $2^1/2$ cups of bread flour in the sponge. Complete the recipe as directed, using a total of 4 cups bread flour.

MILK-BASED SOURDOUGH LOAVES

This bread is light and tender but has real substance. It makes marvelous toast and is excellent for sandwiches. This recipe makes almost 5 pounds of dough, about the limit for a 5-quart heavy-duty electric mixer.

1 cup milk-based sourdough starter
 (page 31)

2 cups warm whole or low-fat milk

1 tablespoon or 1 package active dry
 yeast

1/2 teaspoon plus 1/3 cup sugar

1/2 cup warm water

5 cups (1 pound 9 ounces) bread flour

3 cups (15 ounces) unbleached all-
 purpose flour

1 egg

1 tablespoon salt

1/2 teaspoon baking soda

1. Combine the starter and warm milk in the bowl of an electric mixer. In a separate bowl stir the yeast and 1/2 teaspoon of the sugar into the warm water and let it stand about 5 minutes, or until the mixture is very bubbly and the yeast is dissolved. Measure the flours by scooping a measuring cup into the flour containers, filling the cup to overflowing, and sweeping off the excess with a metal spatula. Add the yeast mixture along with the bread flour, 1/3 cup sugar, egg, salt, and baking soda to the bowl of the mixer. Using the flat beater, beat on medium speed for 5 minutes. The dough will be ropy, elastic, and very sticky. Scrape down the bowl and beater. Replace the beater with the dough hook and gradually knead in the all-purpose flour to make a smooth, elastic dough that is only slightly sticky. If necessary, finish the kneading by hand.

2. To make the dough by hand, combine the starter and milk in a large bowl. In a separate container dissolve the yeast and 1/2 teaspoon of the sugar in the water as directed above and add it to the milk and starter along with 4 cups of the bread flour, 1/3 cup sugar, egg, salt, and baking soda. Beat with a sturdy wooden spoon or wooden spatula for about 3 minutes. Beat in the remaining cup of bread flour until the dough is ropy, elastic, and very sticky. Stir in 2 cups of the all-purpose flour to make a stiff dough. Sprinkle the work surface with the remaining 1 cup of all-purpose flour and turn the dough out onto the surface. Knead for about 10 minutes, adding more flour if necessary to make a dough that is smooth, elastic, and satiny.

3. Lightly coat a 6-quart bowl with nonstick cooking spray. Transfer the dough to the bowl and turn to coat all surfaces. Cover tightly with plastic wrap and let rise at room temperature until doubled in size, about 2 hours.

4. Coat three $8^1/_2$x$4^1/_2$x$2^3/_4$-inch loaf pans with nonstick cooking spray and set aside. Turn the dough out onto the work surface and divide it into 3 equal pieces. Pat each piece into an 8x12-inch rectangle. If the dough is sticky, dust it lightly with flour. Starting with a short end, roll each piece tightly, jelly-roll style, to form a cylinder. Pinch the edges to seal. Turn seam side down and crimp the ends, tucking them under the loaf. Place the dough in the prepared pans and cover loosely with lightly oiled plastic wrap. Let rise at room temperature until the loaves have risen about $1^1/_2$ inches above the rim of the pans, about $1^1/_2$ hours.

5. Adjust an oven rack to the lower-third position and preheat the oven to 375°. Remove the plastic wrap and bake the loaves for 35 to 40 minutes, until they are dark brown on top and sound hollow when removed from pan and tapped on the bottom. Cool completely on wire racks before slicing. Use the bread within 2 days, or freeze in airtight plastic bags for up to 2 months.

FRENCH SOURDOUGH BAGUETTE

Crusty French bread, which is normally full of large holes and has a tender yet chewy interior, is transformed into a sturdier loaf with more character when made with a sourdough starter. This bread is excellent for bruschetta or garlic bread. I prefer to use the Grape Starter because the taste is a bit sweeter and more subtle than the milk- or water-based starters, but use whatever starter you like. This dough needs to be made with a heavy-duty mixer; you will enjoy your results a lot more without an arm in a sling.

After the first rise, I shape this bread into a fairly fat baguette and let it rise again in a canvas-lined banetton— a basket specially made for rising bread. Banettons come in several sizes and shapes (see pages 236–237 for mail-order sources).

I have always used tiles to produce breads with crusty exteriors and moist interiors. I've also found that frequently spritzing the oven with water during the first 15 minutes of baking ensures a crisp and substantial crust. (Be sure to spritz only the walls of the oven and not the bread; if the bread is spritzed, the top of the loaf will be splotchy when removed from the oven.) I urge you to line an oven rack with a pizza stone or with square unglazed tiles. I leave my tiles on the lower-third rack all the time, so that I have a ready hearthlike surface for breads and pizzas.

1 cup grape starter (page 33)

⅔ cup warm water

3½ cups (1 pound 1½ ounces) bread
flour, plus more if needed

1 tablespoon or 1 package active
dry yeast

½ teaspoon sugar

2 teaspoons salt

Cornmeal

1. The night before baking, combine the starter and ⅓ cup of the warm water in a 1-quart bowl. Measure the flour by scooping a measuring cup into the flour container, filling the cup to overflowing, and sweeping off the excess with a metal spatula. Add 1 cup of the flour to the starter mixture, beating it in with a rubber spatula to make a smooth batter. Cover tightly with plastic wrap, and let rest overnight in a warm place.

2. The next day, stir the yeast and sugar into the remaining ⅓ cup warm water. Let the mixture stand until the yeast is dissolved and the mixture is very foamy, about 10 minutes. Transfer the starter mixture to the large bowl of an electric mixer. Stir in the dissolved yeast and 1½ cups of the remaining bread flour. Using the flat beater, beat on low speed until the dough is well mixed, then increase the speed to medium and beat for 3 minutes to form a smooth, creamy, thick batter. Scrape down the bowl and beater. Replace the beater with the dough hook and add the remaining 1 cup of bread flour and the salt. Knead first on low, then increase the speed to medium for 8 to 10 minutes to make a firm, elastic, nonstick dough. Add

a little more flour, if necessary. Shape the dough into a ball. Lightly coat a 3-quart bowl with nonstick cooking spray. Transfer the dough to the bowl and turn to coat all surfaces. Cover tightly with plastic wrap and let rise at room temperature until nearly tripled in volume, about 2 hours (it will nearly fill the bowl).

3. Sprinkle a work surface with flour. Turn the dough out onto the floured surface and shape it into a tapered loaf measuring about 16 inches long. Pat the dough into a 12-inch rectangle. Roll it tightly, jelly-roll style, to form a cylinder. Pinch the edges to seal. Turn seam side down and lengthen the cylinder by gently rolling it back and forth with your palms until it is the right length. If you have a baguette-shaped, canvas-lined banneton, coat it with flour and place the loaf in it seam side up. Enclose the banneton in a large plastic bag, leaving plenty of room to rise, and seal with a twist tie. Let it rise at room temperature until the loaf is slightly more than double in volume, about 2 hours. If you don't have a banneton, place the loaf seam side down diagonally on a large lightly oiled baking sheet. Cover loosely with plastic wrap and let rise as directed.

4. About 45 minutes before you expect the loaf to be ready for baking, line the lower third of the oven with a large pizza stone or unglazed quarry tiles. Preheat the oven to 450°. When the loaf is ready to bake, remove it from its plastic bag and carefully invert it onto a baker's peel or board lightly sprinkled with cornmeal. (If the loaf is on a baking sheet, simply remove the plastic wrap.) With a sharp razor, make four diagonal slashes about 4 inches long and $1/2$ inch deep along the top of the loaf, keeping the blade almost parallel to the loaf as you cut. Spray the oven generously with water and slide the bread off the peel onto the tiles (or place the baking sheet in the oven on the lower-third shelf). Close the oven door immediately. Spray the oven every 3 minutes for the first 15 minutes of baking, then lower the oven temperature to 400° and continue baking for another 20 minutes, or until the bread is well-browned and sounds hollow when tapped on the bottom.

5. Turn off the oven, and prop the door open a few inches. Leave the bread in the cooling oven for 45 minutes to 1 hour, then transfer it to a wire rack to finish cooling before slicing. Use the bread within 2 days, or freeze in an airtight plastic bag for up to 2 months.

SOURDOUGH SAGE BISCUITS

Sage grows very well in Montana. One summer, I decided to add some to sourdough biscuit dough to serve with a stewed chicken. We liked the biscuits so much, they have become a staple during fresh sage season in late summer and early fall. Dry sage will not give you the same results.

2½ cups (11¼ ounces) unbleached
    all-purpose flour

1 cup milk-based sourdough starter
    (page 31)

½ cup buttermilk

¾ teaspoon salt

1 tablespoon sugar

1 tablespoon baking powder

¼ teaspoon baking soda

¼ cup cold butter, cut into 4 pieces

1½ tablespoons chopped fresh
    sage leaves

1. Measure the flour by spooning it into a measuring cup, filling the cup to overflowing, and sweeping off the excess with a metal spatula. The night before, make the sponge. Combine the starter, buttermilk, and 1 cup of the flour in a medium-size bowl. Cover tightly with plastic wrap and let rest overnight at room temperature.

2. The next day, combine 1 cup of the flour, the salt, sugar, baking powder, and baking soda in a separate bowl. Cut in the butter with a pastry blender until the mixture resembles coarse meal. Stir in the sage. Add the sponge and stir to make a soft dough. Sprinkle a work surface with the remaining ½ cup flour. Turn the dough out onto the floured surface and knead for 2 to 3 minutes, adding more flour if necessary. The dough should be slightly sticky when properly kneaded. Cover loosely with a dry kitchen towel and let rest 15 minutes.

3. Preheat the oven to 450°. Pat or roll out the dough to a ³/4-inch thickness. Using a 2¹/2-inch-diameter cookie cutter, cut out the biscuits, dipping the cutter into flour as necessary to prevent sticking. Place the biscuits about 1 inch apart on a 15¹/2x10¹/2x1-inch jelly-roll pan. Gather, reroll, and cut the scraps. Place on the pan. Bake in the center of the oven until the tops are golden brown, 10 to 12 minutes. Serve hot with butter.

Variation: For a delicious breakfast biscuit, omit the sage and serve with honey butter (blend equal parts honey and softened butter with a fork until smooth).

BLACK QUINOA WHOLE WHEAT BREAD

YIELD: 2 LARGE LOAVES

Almost any bread can profit nutritionally from the addition of a whole grain. In this case, 100 percent whole wheat flour is combined with protein-rich cooked quinoa to make loaves that pack a nutritional wallop. I like to use the black quinoa because of its varied texture and color, but you can use regular quinoa if black is unavailable. This bread makes great sandwiches and is especially good toasted.

½ cup black quinoa

1 cup hot water

4 tablespoons butter, softened

⅓ cup firmly packed light brown
    sugar

1 egg

2 teaspoons salt

2 tablespoons or 2 packages
    active dry yeast

½ teaspoon granulated sugar

½ cup warm water

6 to 7 cups (1 pound 14 ounces to
    2 pounds 3 ounces) whole
    wheat flour

1½ cups buttermilk

1. Rinse the quinoa in a wire strainer under cold running water for about 1 minute. Shake off excess water and place the quinoa in a 2-quart saucepan with the hot water. Bring the mixture to the boil over medium-high heat. Cover the pan, reduce the heat to medium-low, and cook for 15 minutes, or until the quinoa is tender and the water is absorbed. Remove from the heat and stir in the butter. When the butter is incorporated, add the brown sugar, egg, and salt and stir to mix well. Set aside.

2. In a small bowl, combine the yeast and granulated sugar with the warm water. Set aside for a few minutes until the mixture is very foamy and bubbly. Meanwhile, measure the flour by scooping a measuring cup into the flour container, filling the cup to overflowing, and sweeping off the excess with a metal spatula. Place 4 cups of the flour in the mixing bowl of an electric mixer and stir in the yeast mixture and buttermilk. With the flat beater, beat on low to mix well, then increase the speed to medium and continue beating for 5 minutes. The mixture will be heavy, sticky, and elastic. Add the quinoa mixture (which may be warm), and beat it in on low to medium speed until thoroughly incorporated. Scrape down the bowl and beater. Replace the beater with the dough hook and gradually knead in 2 to 3 cups of the flour, waiting until each addition is incorporated before adding the next. Knead on low to medium speed for several minutes, or until the dough is firm, moist, and only slightly sticky. Do not add too much flour or the resulting bread will be dry and crumbly instead of moist and tender. (You have quite a bit of leeway in this regard, but be careful nevertheless.)

3. To mix the dough by hand, cook the quinoa and add the butter and other ingredients to it as described above. Dissolve the yeast as described above. Place 4 cups of the flour in a large bowl and add the quinoa mixture, dissolved yeast, and buttermilk. Stir well with a heavy wooden spoon or spatula and beat for several minutes until the batter is thick and elastic. (This takes a lot of arm power.) Cover the bowl loosely with a kitchen towel and let the dough stand at room temperature for 30 minutes. Beat again for about 1 minute. Gradually stir in about $1^1/2$ cups of the flour to make a firm dough. Sprinkle a work surface with the remaining $1/2$ cup of flour. Turn the dough out onto the floured surface and knead for 10 to 15 minutes, adding up to 1 more cup of flour as needed. If the weather is very humid, you may have to add more flour, but go easy. When properly kneaded, the dough should be smooth, moist, elastic, and slightly sticky.

4. Lightly coat a 6-quart bowl or casserole with nonstick cooking spray. Transfer the dough to the bowl and turn to coat all surfaces. Cover tightly with plastic wrap and let rise at room temperature until the dough triples in size and fills the container, about 2 hours. Sprinkle the work surface with flour. Turn dough out onto the surface and pat it into a 15-inch rectangle, flouring your hands as needed. Divide the dough in half and roll each piece tightly, jelly-roll style, to form a cylinder. Pinch the edges to seal. Turn seam side down and seal the ends, tucking the edges under the loaves. Coat two 9x5x3-inch loaf pans with nonstick cooking spray. Place the loaves in the prepared pans. Cover loosely with lightly oiled plastic wrap and let rise at room temperature until the loaves have risen about 2 inches above the rim of the pans, $1^1/2$ to 2 hours. They should look plump. The bread will not rise much more when baked.

5. About 30 minutes before the loaves are ready to be baked, adjust an oven rack to the lower-third position and preheat the oven to 400°. Remove the plastic wrap and bake the loaves for 40 to 45 minutes, or until they are well-browned and sound hollow when removed from the pans and thumped on the bottom. Cool completely on wire racks before slicing. Use within 1 day, or freeze in airtight plastic bags for up to 2 months.

WHOLE WHEAT CARROT BREAD

Montana hard wheat makes great-tasting breads with light but hearty textures. The high gluten content of the flour assures an expandable elastic fabric strong enough to contain the carbon dioxide bubbles that cause the bread to rise. This bread is a gorgeous orange color from the carrot juice. If you don't want to make it yourself, you can use 1 cup of canned carrot juice instead of the carrot and water in the recipe. The bread is excellent for making sandwiches or for toasting and spreading with butter and honey.

2 tablespoons or 2 packages
    active dry yeast

½ teaspoon sugar

⅓ cup warm water

1 large carrot, peeled and shredded

⅔ cup water

1 cup buttermilk

1 egg

⅓ cup unsulphured molasses

⅓ cup melted butter

1 tablespoon salt

4 cups (20 ounces) whole wheat flour

2 to 3 cups (10 to 15 ounces)
    bread flour

1. Stir the yeast and sugar into the warm water and let stand about 10 minutes, or until the yeast is dissolved and mixture is very foamy. Meanwhile, place the shredded carrot and the ⅔ cup water in a blender. Cover and blend on high speed until the mixture is a thick puree. Remove 1 cup for the recipe and combine it with the buttermilk in a small saucepan. (Reserve any leftover puree for another use, such as soup.) Heat the mixture just until it is warm to the touch.

2. In the large bowl of an electric mixer, combine the dissolved yeast and buttermilk-carrot mixture. Stir in the egg, molasses, melted butter, and salt. Measure the flours by scooping a measuring cup into the flour containers, filling the cup to overflowing, and sweeping off the excess with a metal spatula. Add the whole wheat flour to the mixer bowl. With the flat beater, beat on low until flour is moistened, then increase the speed to medium and beat for 3 minutes. Scrape down the bowl and beater. Replace the beater with the dough hook and gradually knead in 2½ cups of the bread flour on low to medium speed until the dough is soft, smooth, and elastic, about 8 minutes. If the dough is very sticky, knead in more flour as necessary.

3. Lightly coat a 6-quart bowl with nonstick cooking spray. Place the dough in the bowl and turn to coat all surfaces. Cover tightly with plastic wrap and let rise at room temperature until doubled in size, about 2 hours. Sprinkle a work surface with flour. Turn the dough out onto the surface and flatten it with your palms into a 15-inch square. Cut the dough in half and roll each piece tightly, jelly-roll style, to form a cylinder. Pinch the edges to seal. Turn

seam side down and seal the ends, tucking them under the loaves. Coat two 9x5x3-inch loaf pans with nonstick cooking spray and place the loaves in the pans seam side down. Cover loosely with lightly oiled plastic wrap. Let rise at room temperature until the loaves have risen almost 2 inches above the rim of the pans.

4. About 30 minutes before the loaves are ready to bake, adjust an oven rack to the lower-third position and preheat the oven to 375°. Remove the plastic wrap and bake the loaves for about 35 minutes, or until they are well-browned and sound hollow when removed from the pans and tapped on the bottom. Cool completely on wire racks before slicing. Use within 2 days, or freeze in airtight plastic bags for up to 2 months.

GREAT BIG HAMBURGER BUNS

YIELD: 12 BUNS

I first tasted these buns at a cookout for the board of directors of Missoula's farmers' market, and practically demanded the recipe on the spot. The buns are great with hamburgers, buffalo burgers, barbecued beef brisket, sloppy joes, or whatever else you want to put inside them.

2 tablespoons or 2 packages
   active dry yeast

⅓ cup plus ½ teaspoon sugar

⅓ cup warm water

2¼ teaspoons salt

⅓ cup vegetable oil

⅔ cup milk

3 eggs

4½ cups (1 pound 6½ ounces)
   unbleached all-purpose flour,
   plus more if needed

Sesame seeds

1. Stir the yeast and ½ teaspoon of the sugar into the warm water and let stand until the yeast is dissolved and the mixture is very foamy, about 10 minutes. Combine the ⅓ cup sugar, 2 teaspoons salt, oil, milk, and 2 of the eggs in the bowl of an electric mixer. Measure the flour by scooping a measuring cup into the flour container, filling the cup to overflowing, and sweeping off the excess with a metal spatula. Add the dissolved yeast and 3 cups of the flour to the bowl of the mixer and mix on low speed with the flat beater. Increase the speed to medium and beat for 5 minutes. Scrape down the bowl and beater. Replace the beater with the dough hook. Gradually knead in the remaining 1½ cups of flour on low to medium speed until the dough is soft, moist, elastic, and slightly sticky. The dough must be moist or the baked buns will be dry.

2. To make dough by hand, follow the directions above for dissolving yeast through adding the 3 cups of flour. Beat well with a sturdy wooden spoon or spatula for several minutes, or until the dough is smooth and elastic. Gradually add and stir in the remaining 1½ cups flour to make a soft dough. Sprinkle a work surface with flour. Turn the dough out onto the floured surface and knead until smooth and elastic, about 8 minutes. Add only enough flour to keep the dough soft and barely sticky.

3. Lightly coat a 3-quart bowl with nonstick cooking spray. Place the dough in the bowl and turn to coat all surfaces. Cover tightly with plastic wrap and let rise at room temperature until the dough almost reaches the top of bowl,

about 1 hour. Remove the dough from the bowl and knead it briefly on a lightly floured surface to redistribute the yeast cells. Divide the dough into 12 equal (3½-ounce) pieces. Lightly grease two large baking sheets with vegetable shortening so that the buns will adhere to the pans later when you flatten them. Shape each piece into a smooth ball and place the balls several inches apart on the prepared baking sheets, 6 per sheet. Cover loosely with dry kitchen towels and let rest for 10 minutes. With your fingers, flatten the balls of dough into 4-inch rounds. Cover them loosely with plastic wrap and let rise at room temperature until doubled in size, about 45 minutes.

4. Adjust two oven racks to divide the oven into thirds and preheat the oven to 350°. Lightly beat the remaining egg and remaining ¼ teaspoon of salt with

a fork. Brush the egg wash on the buns and sprinkle with the sesame seeds. Bake for 20 minutes, switching the top and bottom pans and rotating them front to back after about 10 minutes to ensure even baking. The buns should be well-browned. Using a wide metal spatula, transfer the buns to wire racks and cool completely before splitting. Unused buns may be frozen in airtight plastic bags for up to 2 months.

INDIAN FRY BREAD

Fry bread migrated up to Montana from the Southwest. It has become such a favorite here that vendors always sell out at fairs and expositions. Makers of fry bread are very secretive about their recipes. I once asked a vendor whether she used sugar in the dough and my question was met with stony silence. Two basic types are commonly made, one with baking powder and the other with yeast. I prefer the yeast version because of its chewy texture. After conversations with several Native Americans who were willing to share their hints for success with me, I came up with this recipe. Fry bread is delicious drizzled with honey or sprinkled with cinnamon sugar. Or you may use it like a taco shell and stuff it with any savory filling.

1½ teaspoons active dry yeast

1 tablespoon plus ½ teaspoon sugar

¼ cup warm water

1 tablespoon vegetable oil

½ cup evaporated milk

2 cups (9 ounces) unbleached
    all-purpose flour, plus additional
    for kneading

½ teaspoon salt

Vegetable oil for deep frying

1. Stir the yeast and ½ teaspoon of the sugar into the warm water and set it aside until the yeast is dissolved and the mixture is very bubbly, about 10 minutes. Add the 1 tablespoon of oil and the evaporated milk to the yeast mixture and stir to combine. Measure the flour by spooning it into a measuring cup, filling the cup to overflowing, and sweeping off the excess with a metal spatula. Place the flour, salt, and the 1 tablespoon of sugar in a medium-size bowl and stir well. Add the yeast-milk mixture and stir to make a soft dough.

2. Sprinkle a work surface with flour. Turn the dough out onto the surface and knead for several minutes, or until the dough is smooth and elastic. Lightly coat a bowl with nonstick cooking spray. Place the dough in the bowl and turn to coat all surfaces. Cover tightly with plastic wrap, and let rise at room temperature until it has more than doubled in volume, about 1 hour.

3. Divide the dough into 6 equal pieces and shape each into a ball. Cover with a kitchen towel and let the dough rest 10 minutes. Meanwhile, pour oil into an electric frying pan to a depth of ¾ inch. Set the thermostat at 375°. Roll out each piece of dough to form a circle or rectangle about ⅛ inch thick. Cover with a towel and let the dough rest for 10 minutes. Just before frying, make a 3-inch-long cut in the center of the dough with the tip of a small sharp knife. Fry one piece at a time until nicely browned on both sides, 1 to 2 minutes per side. Remove with a slotted spoon and set aside on paper towels to drain. Serve hot or warm.

Note: If you don't have an electric frying pan, heat the oil in a large skillet over medium to medium-high heat. Insert the tip of a wooden spoon into the oil, if bubbles form around it, the oil is hot enough to fry the bread.

48 :: MONTANA COOKING

BEER BREAD

This recipe is a tribute to the wonderful microbreweries that have sprung up everywhere. Beer gives bread a tenderness in texture that is usually associated with milk. It also contributes a unique taste, depending on the type of beer you use. Light beers give the bread a milder taste than dark beers. Consider what you are serving with the bread when selecting which beer to use. You will have two nice fat loaves with a beautiful rich-brown soft crust—ideal for slicing and eating with butter.

1 tablespoon or 1 package
    active dry yeast

2 tablespoons plus ½ teaspoon sugar

¼ cup warm water

2½ cups (12½ ounces) whole
    wheat flour

2 cups (10 ounces) bread flour

1½ teaspoons salt

12 ounces beer

2 tablespoons vegetable oil

1 egg white, lightly beaten

1. Stir the yeast and ½ teaspoon of the sugar into the warm water and let stand until the yeast is dissolved and the mixture is very foamy, about 10 minutes. Measure the flours by scooping a measuring cup into the flour containers, filling the cup to overflowing, and sweeping off the excess with a metal spatula. Combine the whole wheat flour with the salt and remaining 2 tablespoons sugar in the large bowl of an electric mixer. Add the beer, oil, and dissolved yeast and mix with the flat beater on the lowest speed just until the flour is moistened. Increase the speed to medium and beat for 5 minutes. With a rubber spatula, stir in 1 cup of the bread flour. Scrape down the bowl and beater. Replace the beater with the dough hook and gradually add the remaining 1 cup of bread flour while kneading first on low, then increasing the speed to medium until the dough is smooth, moist, elastic, and only slightly sticky, 6 to 8 minutes.

2. To make dough by hand, dissolve the yeast as directed and stir together with the salt, remaining 2 tablespoons sugar, beer, and oil in a large bowl. Add the whole wheat flour and beat with a sturdy wooden spoon or spatula for several minutes, or until the dough is thick and elastic. Stir in 1 cup of the bread flour. Sprinkle the remaining 1 cup of bread flour on a work surface. Turn out the dough onto the surface and knead until the dough is smooth, satiny, and only slightly sticky, 10 to 15 minutes.

3. Lightly coat a 3-quart bowl with nonstick cooking spray. Place the dough in the bowl and turn to coat all surfaces. Cover tightly with plastic wrap and let stand at room temperature until dough reaches the top of the bowl, 1 to $1^{1}/2$ hours. Punch down the dough and divide it in half. Cover loosely with a towel and let the dough rest for 10 to 15 minutes. Flatten each piece into a 12x8-inch rectangle and roll up tightly, jelly-roll style, beginning with a long side. Pinch the edges to seal. Turn seam side down and taper both ends. The loaves will be about 13 inches long. Grease a 17x14-inch baking sheet with vegetable shortening and place the loaves seam side down on the sheet, leaving about 5 inches between them. Cover loosely with lightly oiled plastic wrap and let the dough rise at room temperature until puffy, light, and doubled in size, about 45 minutes to 1 hour. Meanwhile, adjust an oven rack to the center position and preheat the oven to 375°. Before baking, make 3 or 4 slashes about 3 inches long and $^{1}/4$ inch deep down the length of each loaf at a slight angle with a sharp knife. Brush the loaves with some of the beaten egg white and bake for about 35 minutes, or until the bread is well-browned and the loaves sound hollow when removed from the pan and tapped on the bottom. Brush the tops again with egg white and transfer the loaves to wire racks to cool completely before slicing.

Variation: To make Beer and Cheese Bread, divide the dough in half after it has risen the first time. Work $^{1}/2$ pound of sharp cheddar cheese cubes ($^{1}/2$ inch) into each piece of dough, enclosing the cheese completely. Shape into loaves as directed above and continue with the recipe.

APPETIZERS

In nineteenth-century Montana, appetizers were served mainly in the homes of the wealthy and in fancy hotels. Those appetizers were commonly modeled on French foods because so many of the settlers were European emigrants who continued to value the principles and traditions of French cuisine when they came to the region.

The recipes in this chapter summarize my approach to Montana's new cuisine, with an emphasis on using traditional foods of the region with fresh, ethnic twists. Were it not for the large numbers of Southeast Asians now living in Missoula, I doubt that Gingered Buffalo Meatballs with Jicama in Sweet-and-Sour Sauce would have been created. Similarly, the flavors of Greece have influenced my cooking, thanks to the large Greek population residing here. The natural pairing of wild agaric mushrooms and feta cheese inspired the delicious and easy to prepare Greek-Style Stuffed Portobello Mushrooms. With the exception of the Vietnamese Seafood Imperial Rolls, none of these recipes is difficult or complicated to prepare.

GINGERED BUFFALO MEATBALLS WITH JICAMA IN SWEET-AND-SOUR SAUCE

YIELD: 40 MEATBALLS

Lean and mild-tasting ground buffalo lends itself to all sorts of seasonings, but any sauce you serve with the buffalo must not overwhelm the meat's mild taste. Ginger helps bring out the sweetness of the meat, and the slightly sour sauce makes you want to eat one after the other. Incidentally, the light soy is not a low-sodium product; it is simply lighter in color than regular soy sauce. Dark soy is a thicker soy and contains sugar.

Buffalo Meatballs

1½ pounds ground buffalo

1½ tablespoons peeled,
    minced fresh ginger

½ cup (2½ ounces) finely diced,
    peeled jicama

2 cloves garlic, minced

1 tablespoon dry sherry

2 tablespoons light soy sauce

1 teaspoon salt

¼ teaspoon freshly ground
    black pepper

1 egg

2 tablespoons water

1 tablespoon cornstarch

2 tablespoons vegetable oil

Sweet-and-Sour Sauce

1 cup sugar

1½ teaspoons salt

⅓ cup dry sherry

½ cup light soy sauce

1 tablespoon dark soy sauce

1 teaspoon chile paste with garlic (such as Lan Chi)

1 cup water

½ cup distilled white vinegar

½ cup ketchup

3 tablespoons cornstarch

2 tablespoons dark sesame oil

½ cup chopped fresh cilantro leaves

1. Place the ground buffalo in a large bowl. Add the ginger, jicama, garlic, sherry, light soy, salt, and pepper. Mix well with a fork. In a separate bowl, beat together the egg, water, and cornstarch with a fork to combine well. Mix in the oil. Add to the buffalo mixture and beat well with a fork until thoroughly combined.

2. Adjust the oven rack to the center position and preheat the oven to 350°. Lightly coat a large, rimmed 18x12x1-inch baking sheet with cooking spray. Using the palms of your hands, shape the buffalo mixture into 1-inch balls. Place the meatballs 1 inch apart on the prepared sheet. Bake for 20 minutes. Remove the pan from the oven and set aside while you make the sauce.

3. For the sauce, combine the sugar, salt, sherry, light soy sauce, dark soy sauce, chile paste with garlic, $1/2$ cup of the water, vinegar, and ketchup in a 4-quart saucepan. In a small bowl, combine the remaining $1/2$ cup water with the cornstarch and set aside. Bring the mixture in the saucepan to a boil over medium-high heat, stirring occasionally. Stir the cornstarch mixture well and quickly add it to the saucepan while stirring continuously but gently with a rubber spatula. Boil the mixture 1 to 2 minutes, or until it is clear and slightly thickened. Remove the pan from the heat and stir in the sesame oil. Drop the meatballs into the hot sauce and set aside until serving time. (The meatballs may be made hours ahead up to this point. Cover and refrigerate when cool.)

4. To serve, set the uncovered saucepan over low to medium heat and bring to a simmer slowly, stirring occasionally. When piping hot, add the cilantro and transfer the mixture to a serving dish. Serve with toothpicks.

GREEK-STYLE STUFFED PORTOBELLO MUSHROOMS

Field agarics, which are close relatives of the commercially available portobello mushrooms, grow abundantly in spring and summer in the Montana. The agarics and the portobello mushrooms look identical and have similar tastes and textures. I use the agarics whenever I can get them, but the portobellos do not suffer by comparison. The saltiness of the feta cheese and olives contrasts nicely with the mushrooms' sweetness. A good accompaniment is a salad of arugula or mixed baby lettuces dressed with olive oil and balsamic vinegar.

Mushrooms

6 field agarics or portobello
    mushroom caps (4 inches in
    diameter), stems removed

Marinade

2 cups Chicken Stock (page 5)

½ teaspoon salt, if using unsalted
    chicken broth

½ teaspoon freshly ground black
    pepper

½ teaspoon dried oregano leaves,
    crumbled

⅓ cup extra-virgin olive oil

Stuffing

¾ cup fresh fine bread crumbs, made from day-old crustless French or Italian bread or an
    English muffin

1½ tablespoons finely chopped fresh oregano

¼ teaspoon freshly ground black pepper

8 kalamata olives in brine, drained, pitted, and chopped

¼ cup (1 ounce) crumbled feta cheese

2 tablespoons extra-virgin olive oil

Salt to taste

1. Carefully look over the mushrooms and brush away any dirt. Combine the marinade ingredients in a 13x9x2-inch baking dish. Add the mushroom caps, turning to coat them well. Cover the pan tightly with aluminum foil and set aside to marinate for 2 to 3 hours or longer in a cool place. (This may be kept overnight in the refrigerator.) Turn the caps 3 or 4 times while marinating. Bake, covered, in the center of a preheated 400° oven for 30 to 40 minutes, or until the caps are tender. Cool, covered, in the pan. To stuff the mushrooms, remove them from the marinade and set them aside on paper towels to drain well.

2. To make the stuffing, use a fork to combine the bread crumbs, oregano, pepper, olives, feta cheese, and olive oil in a small bowl. The mixture will be moist but should not stick together. Add salt to taste if necessary. Place the caps upside down on a lightly oiled baking sheet. Sprinkle 3 to 4 tablespoons of the filling loosely and evenly over each cap. Pat in place very gently with your fingers, without packing the filling down. The mushrooms may be prepared hours ahead up to this point; just cover and refrigerate until ready to bake.

3. Preheat the oven to 375°. Bake on the center rack for 15 to 20 minutes, or until the filling is lightly browned in spots. Serve warm.

CHANTERELLE MUSHROOM AND ASPARAGUS TART

This is a special appetizer to make in spring, when both asparagus and chanterelles are plentiful. Serve it with a small salad of mixed baby greens. You can prepare this dish as a single tart or as individual tartlets in miniature muffin pans (see note at end of recipe).

Pastry

1½ cups (6¾ ounces) unbleached
    all-purpose flour
½ cup (1¾ ounces) cake flour
½ teaspoon salt
¾ cup chilled unsalted butter
⅓ cup ice water

Filling

18 to 20 asparagus tips, 2 inches long
3 large eggs plus 1 egg yolk
1 cup heavy cream
⅓ cup milk
½ teaspoon salt
⅛ teaspoon freshly ground
    black pepper
Pinch of freshly grated nutmeg
1 cup cooked chanterelles (page 10)
2 tablespoons grated
    Parmesan cheese

1. Measure the flours by spooning them into measuring cups, filling the cups to overflowing, and sweeping off the excess with a metal spatula. To make the dough using a food processor, place both flours and the salt in the work bowl with the metal blade in place. Cut the butter into 6 equal pieces and add it to the bowl. Pulse quickly 3 or 4 times to cut the butter into the flour. While pulsing very rapidly, add the water through the feed tube in a steady stream and pulse 20 to 30 times, or until the dough almost gathers into a ball. Carefully remove the dough from the work bowl, place on a piece of waxed paper, and shape it into a 6-inch disc. Wrap it securely, and chill for 30 minutes.

2. To make the pastry by hand, place both flours and salt in a mixing bowl. Cut in the butter with a pastry blender until the mixture resembles small peas. Toss with a fork, while gradually adding the water. Continue mixing with a fork until the dough gathers into a ball. Wrap and chill as directed above.

3. Roll the dough into a 14-inch circle on a lightly floured surface (a canvas pastry cloth works best). Transfer the dough to an 11-inch-diameter, 1-inch-deep tart pan with a removable bottom. Gently work the pastry into the corners, but do not stretch it. Use scissors to trim the overhanging pastry to ¹/2 inch beyond the edge of the pan. Fold the overhanging pastry back onto the pastry lining the sides of the tart, pressing the two together to make the sides double in thickness and extending about ¹/4 inch above the pan rim. Place the tart pan on a baking sheet and freeze for 20 to 30 minutes. Meanwhile, adjust the oven rack to the center position and preheat the oven to 400°.

4. Line the chilled pastry shell with aluminum foil and fill it with dry beans or rice. Bake for about 20 minutes, or until the edge of the pastry is light golden. Remove the foil and beans or rice and return the pastry to the oven for about 5 more minutes, or until it appears set and is only very lightly browned. If the pastry puffs up during baking, gently prick it with a fork to deflate. Cool the pastry until ready to use.

5. To make the filling, bring 2 quarts of water to a boil in a 3- or 4-quart saucepan. Drop in the asparagus tips and blanch uncovered for 3 to 4 minutes, or until they are crisp-tender. Drain well. Place the asparagus in a large bowl of cold water. Allow the tips to stand until they are cool, then drain well and set aside on paper towels. Preheat the oven to 350°.

6. In a medium-size bowl, whisk together the eggs and yolk to combine well. Whisk in the cream, milk, salt, pepper, and nutmeg. Scatter the cooked chanterelles over the bottom of the partially baked pastry shell. Arrange the asparagus tips on top. Carefully pour in the egg mixture and sprinkle the Parmesan evenly over the top. Place the tart on a baking sheet and bake for 30 to 40 minutes, until it is puffed, set, and light golden brown on top. Remove the tart from the oven and let cool in its pan for 5 minutes, then carefully remove the sides of the pan and slide the tart onto a serving platter. Cut into 12 wedges and serve on plates.

Note: To bake as individual tartlets or miniquiches, roll the pastry until it is quite thin, between $1/16$ and $1/8$ inch thick. To prevent sticking, lightly coat each miniature muffin cup with nonstick cooking spray before lining with pastry. Cut the pastry into 3-inch circles and fit them into the cups. The dough should make 24 to 30 tartlet shells. No prebaking is necessary. Cut the cooked asparagus tips into 3 or 4 pieces each. Place about 2 teaspoons of mushrooms and 2 or 3 pieces of asparagus into each shell, fill almost to the top with the egg mixture, and sprinkle with the Parmesan cheese. Bake on the center rack at 400° for 10 to 15 minutes, or until pastry is nicely browned and the filling is puffed and set. Carefully remove the pastries and serve immediately.

FAVA BEAN DIP

Fava beans, or broad beans, are commonly eaten in Asia, Europe, Africa, and South America. In China, favas have been part of the diet for about 5,000 years. Only recently, however, has the bean begun to catch on in the United States. Favas' bright-green pods contain beans that look much like limas, but the similarity ends there. They have a unique taste that is slightly bitter, but otherwise indescribable. Favas grow very well in cool climates and reach their peak in Montana in July, but you don't have to grow your own to enjoy this dip. Favas are becoming readily available in markets all over the United States. On the West Coast, they may be found from late March through early May. Because there is so much more pod than bean in each fava, and because each bean must be skinned before it is used, this exquisite dip takes a lot of pods and time to make, but is well worth it.

4 pounds fava beans in the pod

1 cup water

¾ teaspoon ground cumin

3 cloves garlic, peeled and sliced

½ teaspoon salt

½ teaspoon freshly ground
    black pepper

3 tablespoons extra-virgin olive oil

1 tablespoon freshly squeezed
    lemon juice

½ teaspoon paprika

Sliced crusty French bread or split
    and toasted pita triangles
    (see Note)

1. Shell the favas and place the beans in a large pot of rapidly boiling water to blanch for 15 to 30 seconds. Remove the beans with a slotted spoon and transfer them to a large bowl of very cold water. After 5 to 10 minutes, drain them well. Pierce the skin of a bean with a fingernail, then slip off and discard the skin; repeat for each bean. You should have 2½ cups of bright-green beans. Combine the favas, water, cumin, and garlic in a 2- to 3-quart saucepan. Bring the mixture to a boil over high heat. Reduce the heat to medium and cook, partially covered, about 20 minutes, or until the favas are tender. Most of the liquid should be gone. Transfer the favas to a wire strainer to drain excess liquid. Set aside for a few minutes to cool.

2. Place the favas in the work bowl of a food processor fitted with the metal blade. Add the salt, pepper, 2 tablespoons of the olive oil, and the lemon juice. Puree about 2 minutes, or until smooth, stopping to scrape the work bowl as necessary. If the puree is too thick, thin it with a little water. It should be thick enough to spread or use as a dip, not soupy. Transfer the dip to a serving dish and smooth the top. Drizzle the remaining 1 tablespoon of oil over the dip and sprinkle it with the paprika. Cover the dish tightly with plastic wrap and let it stand at room temperature for 1 hour or so before serving.

Note: To toast pitas, split them into individual rounds with a sharp knife and coat the inside surfaces lightly with olive oil cooking spray. Cut each round into 8 wedges and arrange them close together, oiled side up, on a baking sheet. Bake at 350° for about 10 minutes, or until lightly browned. They will crisp as they cool. Store them in an airtight plastic bag for up to 3 days.

GREEN TOMATO PIZZA

"Do you think the tomatoes will ripen before the frost comes?" We ask that question every year toward the end of August, when the tomatoes reach their peak in Montana. Even when Mother Nature grants us an abundant tomato harvest, there are always some laggards on the vine. This pizza is a great use for them. Incidentally, I like to dissolve the yeast in a glass measuring cup because the pouring spout makes it easy to add the mixture to the dry ingredients without spills. Instead of using a pizza pan, I prefer to bake free-form pizzas on unglazed quarry tiles or on a pizza stone, both of which are available at gourmet specialty stores or through the mail (see pages 236–237), because they create a crispier crust.

Dough

1 teaspoon active dry yeast

¼ cup warm water

1½ cups (7½ ounces) unbleached
all-purpose flour

¾ teaspoon salt

⅓ cup cold water

Topping

1½ ounces cream cheese

¼ cup (1 ounce) goat cheese

1 small clove garlic, minced

1½ tablespoons olive oil

3 firm green tomatoes

2 ounces fontina cheese, thinly sliced

1. To make the dough, stir the yeast into the warm water in a glass measuring cup and let stand about 10 minutes, or until the yeast has dissolved and the mixture is creamy. Meanwhile, measure the flour by scooping a measuring cup into the flour container, filling it to overflowing, and sweeping off the excess with a metal spatula. Place the flour and salt in the work bowl of a food processor fitted with the metal blade. Stir the cold water into the yeast mixture. Start the food processor and gradually add the yeast mixture through the feed tube in a steady stream. The dough will gather into a ball. Process for 1 minute. The dough should be moist and slightly sticky. Remove dough from processor and work it between your hands. It should lose some of its stickiness.

2. Place the dough in an ungreased 2- to 3-quart bowl, cover it tightly with plastic wrap, and set it aside to rise at room temperature until it is almost triple its original size, about 2 hours. If you're not ready to work with the dough after it has risen, deflate it, reshape it into a ball, and return it to the rising bowl. Cover tightly, refrigerate, and use within 24 hours.

3. Place the tiles or a pizza stone on an oven rack close to the bottom of the oven. Preheat the oven to 500° about 45 minutes before baking. If you use a pizza pan, brush it lightly with olive oil and preheat the oven just 20 minutes in advance.

4. To make the topping, place the cream cheese, goat cheese, garlic, and olive oil in a small bowl and mash thoroughly with a fork to make a smooth, creamy mixture. Slice the tomatoes $1/8$ inch thick and set them on paper towels.

5. Shape the risen dough into a ball, dust it lightly with flour, and set it aside, covered, about 20 minutes to allow the gluten to relax before shaping. If the dough was refrigerated, bring it to room temperature before shaping. Roll the dough into a 12-inch circle on a lightly floured surface. Lightly dust

a board or baker's peel with cornmeal and place the dough on it or in the prepared pizza pan. Spread the cheese mixture on the dough, arrange the tomato slices on top, and place the fontina over the tomatoes. Quickly slide the pizza onto the hot tiles or place the pizza pan in the oven. Bake for about 10 minutes, or until the edges of the crust are lightly browned and the cheese and tomatoes appear bubbly. Remove from the oven and let stand for 2 to 3 minutes before cutting into wedges.

ROCK CREEK TROUT IN TOMATO AND ONION SAUCE YIELD: 4 TO 6 SERVINGS

Rock Creek is a blue-ribbon trout stream located 45 minutes from my home in Missoula. Anglers from all over the United States are drawn there for the plentiful trout its waters hold. It is the first and only stream I've ever fished. The first time out, I landed a 14-inch brown trout—beginner's luck for sure. I learned quickly that I am not a fisherman by nature, and so now I buy fresh trout at the market. This is a quick, easy, and delicious way to enjoy it. I like to serve it with French or Italian bread to sop up the excess sauce. The recipe may be doubled.

1 pound boneless and skinless trout
    fillets, cut into 1½-inch pieces

¾ teaspoon salt

½ teaspoon freshly ground
    black pepper

¼ cup unbleached all-purpose flour

¼ cup extra-virgin olive oil

3 carrots, peeled and shredded

1 large sweet onion, peeled and
    finely chopped

1 (16-ounce) can tomato puree
    (2 cups)

¼ cup dry white wine or dry white
    French vermouth

1 tablespoon freshly squeezed
    lemon juice

Salt and freshly ground pepper,
    to taste

1. Sprinkle the trout lightly with the salt and pepper. Place the flour in a plastic bag, add the fish, and toss gently until all the pieces are well coated. Remove the fish, shaking off excess flour.

2. In a large skillet, heat 2 tablespoons of the oil over medium-high heat until very hot, but not smoking. Add the fish in batches and fry until golden and just done, about 1 minute on each side. (Don't crowd the pieces.) Use a slotted spoon to transfer the fish to paper towels to drain. Repeat until all of the pieces are cooked.

3. Discard the oil from the skillet and add the remaining 2 tablespoons of oil. Return the pan to medium-high heat and stir in the carrots and onion. Reduce heat to medium-low, cover, and cook 5 minutes. Stir in the tomato puree, wine, lemon juice, and salt and pepper to taste. Cover and cook another 5 minutes, or until the onion is barely tender. Add the cooked fish, very gently stirring it into the sauce. To serve hot, cover and cook 1 to 2 minutes, to heat fish through. To serve at room temperature, remove the pan from the heat after adding fish and let it stand, uncovered, until ready to serve. Adjust seasoning, adding salt, pepper, and lemon juice as desired.

New Flavors for the New West

When I was growing up in Shanghai, I loved eating all kinds of Chinese food, most of it prepared by our amah (female cook). In San Francisco, I could always find what I needed in Chinatown. By the time my family and I moved to Missoula, Montana, my cooking interests included the cuisines of Southeast Asia. But the only way I was able to get those ingredients was either by mail order or by having friends send me care packages. A few years after we moved here, new Asian products began appearing in our supermarkets. I was thrilled. I brought them home, but didn't know much about how to use them. Soon, a mutual friend introduced my family and me to Chu Chu Pham. That's when I discovered why and how Missoula supermarkets began stocking "exotic" Asian ingredients. Chu Chu tells the story:

When we first came here (in 1975), there weren't many Asian people. We were the second Vietnamese family. I went to the market and looked to see what I could find. There was carrot, and potato, and cabbage. I had no clue what celery was. For seasoning all they had was soy sauce, and my husband doesn't like it. So I decided that since I could speak the language, I'd be brave and stubborn. I went to the supermarket and said, "This is what I want. I want to see more Oriental food." But they didn't know what to do, where to buy it. So I said, "Okay, I see you have soy sauce. Where do you get it?" The man said it came from a supplier in Seattle. So I asked if he could get them to send a list of what they sold. And they did. I can still see the long list on that old computer paper with the thick green bars. I studied it. All I wanted was to get nuoc mam (Vietnamese fish sauce) for my husband. But then I thought while I'm here I might as well ask them to get some other stuff if they're willing to. I'll take the risk and promise to buy everything if they can't sell it. So they ordered rice paper and tree ear mushrooms, bean thread, and nuoc mam. Then more people came in and asked for other Oriental stuff and they got more and more. Other stores got it too as more and more Asians moved to the area.

FOLLOW-THE-SUN KOSHER DILL PICKLES

YIELD: 3 QUARTS

This recipe was given to me many years ago by Avis Olsen of Pinesdale, Montana, when I had a weekly cooking show on local television. I have made these pickles almost every summer since then. You should wait for a warm, sunny day to make them. I start them in the morning on the front porch, with direct sun shining on the jars. As the sun moves in its arc across the late summer sky, I move the jars accordingly, putting them on the bedroom porch at midday, moving them to the greenhouse in the late afternoon, and finally transferring them to the back porch, where the jars soak up the sun's last warming rays. If you like your pickles less sour, cut back a bit on the vinegar. But do try them this way first.

24 to 30 small firm pickling
    cucumbers

3 tablespoons salt

3 teaspoons pickling spices

6 tops fresh dill plants

3 to 6 cloves garlic, peeled

2 to 3 cups distilled white vinegar

Water

Alum

1. Wash three wide-mouthed, quart-sized Mason jars in hot soapy water, rinse thoroughly, and drain. Wash the cucumbers and pack them into the jars, leaving a bit of room at the top. Add 1 tablespoon of the salt, 1 teaspoon of the pickling spices, 2 tops of the fresh dill, and 1 or 2 of the garlic cloves to each jar. Fill the jars halfway with vinegar and add water up to the jars' necks. Put the lids and bands on the jars, but don't seal them tightly.

2. Place the jars in the sun for 8 hours or more, moving them during the day to follow the sun and turning them from time to time. The cucumbers will change from a bright green color to an olive green color by the end of the day. If there isn't enough sun in one day to do the job, or if you started the process late in the day, you can return the jars to the sun the next day and follow the procedure again.

3. After 8 hours of sun, bring the jars in, uncap them, and add a pea-sized bit of alum to each jar. (If the alum is powdered and not in a chunk, use a scant $1/4$ teaspoon.) Once the alum is added, replace the lids and seal tightly with the bands. Invert the jars 2 or 3 times to mix in the alum. Set the jars in a cool place for 3 days, at which point you can eat the pickles or store them in the refrigerator. They keep well for 3 to 4 months. Sometimes the lids seal all by themselves, creating a vacuum. Those that do should ensure that the pickles inside will keep even longer.

VIETNAMESE SEAFOOD IMPERIAL ROLLS

Called Cha Gio (jeye-YAW), these are, in the broadest sense, a Vietnamese version of Chinese egg rolls. My good friend Chu Chu Pham, who moved to Montana from Southeast Asia thirty years ago, taught me how to make them for a television program on the cuisine of Vietnam. We worked together on that show, Chu Chu doing most of the cooking while I did the talking. Rice paper, brushed with beer or water to moisten it and make it flexible, is wrapped around a filling of ground pork, crab, jicama, and other ingredients to make a small compact cylinder. After frying until very brown and crisp, the rolls are wrapped in a lettuce leaf along with cucumber, bean sprouts, cilantro, and mint. The Cha Gio is then dipped into Vietnamese fish sauce and eaten. Although there is a fair amount of work to the preparation, I assure you it's worth it. The bean thread, tree ear mushrooms, fish sauce, and rice paper are all available in well-stocked supermarkets or in Asian food stores. Vietnamese fish sauce has a strange smell and a strange taste to some. But please don't be put off by it, because it lends a delicious and special taste to these seafood rolls.

2 pounds lean ground pork

½ pound crab meat

half to whole 3.85-ounce package
    bean thread

½ ounce (⅓ cup) dried tree ear
    mushrooms

1 cup shredded jicama

1 large onion (8 ounces), finely
    chopped

½ to 1 teaspoon freshly ground
    black pepper

1 teaspoon salt

1 large egg

3½ tablespoons nuoc mam
    (Vietnamese fish sauce)

18 12-inch-diameter sheets rice paper

Beer or water for brushing rice paper

Oil for frying

1. Have the pork and crab ready and in the refrigerator. Place the bean thread in a medium-size bowl and cover it completely with warm tap water. Use from ½ to the whole package depending on how much you want. Place the tree ear mushrooms in another bowl and cover them with warm water. Let stand 20 to 30 minutes. During this time the bean threads will soften and lose their brittle consistency and the mushrooms will soften and swell a great deal.

2. Drain the bean thread and set it aside on paper towels. Drain tree ears and rinse them in fresh water to remove any sand or grit. Drain on paper towels. Cut the bean thread into 1-inch lengths and chop the tree ears coarsely.

3. Mix the pork and crab together in a large bowl. Add the bean thread, tree ears, jicama, onion, pepper, salt, egg, and nuoc mam, and combine thoroughly.

4. Place the beer or water in a bowl and have a pastry brush handy. Working with one sheet of rice paper at a time, brush the beer or water very lightly over both sides of it. Be careful; too much liquid will cause the rice paper to fall apart. After brushing, cut the rice paper circles with scissors evenly into quarters. Set 3 pieces aside on your work surface and place the fourth piece in front of you with its rounded edge nearest you.

5. Put about 2 tablespoons of the Cha Gio mixture in a horizontal strip 3 to 4 inches long about an inch from the rounded side of the paper. Fold both

sides of the rice paper over the filling, pressing firmly. Then fold the rounded edge over that and roll up the Cha Gio to form a tight, compact cylinder, measuring about 4 inches long. (The moistened rice paper will stick to itself.) Place the Cha Gio on a baking sheet. Continue making the Cha Gio until all the filling is used. If the rice paper tears, you can either place a piece of softened rice paper over the tear and pat it down firmly so that it sticks to the torn sheet, or you can overlap two quarter-sheets of rice paper to cover the damage. Usually a package of rice paper will have a defective sheet or two. I break these up and moisten them to use in emergency repairs. Completed Cha Gio may be refrigerated for an hour or so, or they can be cooked immediately, or they may be frozen (see Note on following page).

6. To cook the Cha Gio, pour cooking oil to a depth of $1/4$ to $1/2$ inch into a large electric frying pan or into a large skillet on medium heat. Set electric pan to 375°. To test if oil is hot in a regular skillet, stick the tips of a pair of wooden chopsticks into the pan. If bubbles form around the chopsticks, the oil is ready.

7. Place several Cha Gio about $1/2$ inch apart in the oil. Do not move them for at least a few minutes once they are in place, or else the rice paper might tear. When the Cha Gio have browned lightly, turn them over carefully (chopsticks work best). Continue cooking, turning them 2 or 3 times, for about 10 minutes, until Cha Gio are a dark brown color all over and the rice paper is crisp. Drain by propping cooked rolls on top of cooking Cha Gio and leaning them against the side of the pan for a moment. Transfer to paper towels to drain further.

8. You can add uncooked Cha Gio to the pan as cooked ones are removed. Keep adding oil to the pan, if necessary, to maintain a depth of about $1/4$ inch. So long as a temperature of 375° is maintained, the Cha Gio will not become greasy and will not absorb oil. So do not overcrowd the pan at any point.

9. When all the Cha Gio are done, leave them at room temperature until ready to serve. They should be served within an hour or two, with the vegetable platter and additional nuoc mam.

VEGETABLE PLATTER

The amount of fresh vegetables you prepare will depend upon how many Cha Gio are served. Here I've given the amount that goes with the above recipe. How you serve the vegetables is up to you. The instructions below explain how I present them.

6 dozen Boston or butter lettuce
    leaves
2 English cucumbers
2 cups fresh bean sprouts, rinsed
    and drained
2 cups fresh cilantro leaves, rinsed
    and patted dry
2 cups fresh mint leaves, rinsed and
    patted dry

1. Wash and dry the lettuce leaves and arrange them attractively in the center of a large round platter. Peel the cucumbers and cut them in half lengthwise. Cut each half crosswise into thin slices and arrange at the outer edge of the platter. Place the bean sprouts between the lettuce and the cucumbers. Arrange clumps of cilantro and mint leaves on top of the cucumbers and bean sprouts.

2. If the Cha Gio are being served at the dinner table, provide each diner with a small personal bowl of fish sauce. To put it all together, hold a lettuce leaf in your hand and place a Cha Gio on it. With chopsticks or a fork, pick up some cucumber, bean sprouts and cilantro and mint from the vegetable platter and put them on the lettuce leaf. Enclose everything in the leaf, dunk into the fish sauce, and eat.

Note: Cha Gio are best when freshly made and freshly cooked, but I've kept them frozen—either raw or cooked—and served them later with good results. The best way to keep Cha Gio is to freeze them right after they are shaped. Freeze them in single layers on baking sheets lined with waxed paper or plastic wrap. When solidly frozen, transfer them to airtight heavy-duty plastic bags and store them in the freezer for up to 2 weeks. To cook them, place the frozen rolls into cold oil. Then turn on the heat to medium (or set thermostat to 375° if using an electric frying pan) and fry for 10 to 15 minutes until they're crisp and well-browned. Drain and cool before eating. Cha Gio can be frozen after cooking, but they're not as good reheated. To reheat cooked frozen Cha Gio, place them on a baking sheet in the center of a preheated 375° oven and bake for about 10 minutes, or until thoroughly heated and crisp. Cool, then serve.

    Cha Gio may also be served in smaller pieces as a bite-sized appetizer. Snip each cooked Cha Gio into thirds with scissors, and arrange on platters. Serve with the vegetables and Vietnamese fish sauce.

FLATHEAD LAKE WHITEFISH CAKES

This makes an excellent appetizer for a formal dinner party because the fish cake mixture needs to be refrigerated for several hours after shaping and takes only minutes to cook. Whitefish are plentiful in lakes and streams of Montana. Because of an abundant food supply in Montana's Flathead Lake (see sidebar, page 150), the average size of whitefish has increased from just under 1/2 pound to more than 2 pounds. The flesh is firm and sweet, and holds its shape beautifully in these fish cakes. Since whitefish is usually sold frozen (for ordering information, see pages 236–237), I don't bother thawing them for this recipe. If you can't get whitefish, don't be concerned: Trout is an excellent substitute. Coating the fish cakes with untoasted wheat germ gives them a thin, crunchy crust, which contrasts nicely with the tender flesh.

1½ pounds boneless and skinless frozen or fresh whitefish fillets

1 cup water

½ cup dry white French vermouth

3 bay leaves

¼ cup finely chopped flat-leaf parsley

2 large shallots, finely chopped

1 clove garlic, minced

1 teaspoon Old Bay seasoning

½ teaspoon salt

¼ teaspoon freshly ground black pepper

¼ cup dry unseasoned fine bread crumbs

¼ cup mayonnaise

1 egg

2 teaspoons Dijon-style mustard

¾ cup untoasted wheat germ

¼ cup vegetable oil

½ cup sour cream

¼ cup buttermilk

1 tablespoon snipped fresh chives

1. Place the fresh or frozen whitefish in a 12-inch heavy skillet. Add the water, vermouth, and bay leaves. Cover the pan and cook for several minutes over medium-low heat until the liquid comes to a simmer. Do not let it boil. Carefully turn the fish with a wide metal spatula, cover the pan, and cook 2 minutes longer. If using fresh fish, remove the pan from the heat immediately after turning the fish. Remove the pan from the heat and let it stand, covered, for 15 minutes, or until the fish is cooked through. Test by separating the flesh with the tip of a sharp knife; the flesh should be opaque. Cover and let stand about 10 minutes before testing for doneness.

2. Transfer the fish to a dish lined with paper towels to drain and cool completely. Break the fish into large flakes and remove any small bones. Place the fish into a large mixing bowl. Add the parsley, shallots, garlic, Old Bay seasoning, salt, pepper, and bread crumbs. Fold gently with a rubber spatula to combine well and avoid breaking the fish into small pieces.

3. In a small bowl, combine the mayonnaise, egg, and mustard with a fork. Add to the fish mixture and fold in with the rubber spatula. Divide the mixture into 6 equal portions and shape each between the palms of your hands into a cake measuring about 3 inches in diameter and 1 inch thick. Press gently but firmly so that the cakes hold their shape. Place the cakes on a plate lined with plastic wrap. Cover loosely with more plastic wrap and refrigerate for several hours. (The fish cakes may be prepared up to 12 hours ahead up to this point.)

4. When ready to cook, spread the wheat germ on a large sheet of waxed paper, and coat each fish cake with wheat germ lightly on all surfaces. Heat the oil

in a 12-inch heavy skillet over medium to medium-high heat. When hot, add the fish cakes, leaving a bit of space between them, and cook on each side about 5 minutes, until nicely browned. Meanwhile, whisk together the sour cream and buttermilk. When the fish cakes are done, drain them briefly on paper towels and transfer to a serving platter. Spoon some of the sour cream sauce over them, sprinkle with the chives, and serve hot.

SOUPS

Soup is comfort food any time and in any season, but hot soups are especially welcome in cool mountain climates or in foggy and breezy coastal areas. At home in Montana I make soups often. Hearty soups like the Oyster Mushroom and Oyster Chowder bring to mind those days in Puget Sound. Lighter soups such as Summer Vegetable Soup and Tomato-Tarragon Soup satisfy during hot weather. The wild mushroom harvest during spring, summer, and fall provides abundant inspiration. Chanterelle Mushroom Soup is one creation inspired by a basket of plump mushrooms.

The best soups begin with the best stocks. When I was a teenager, I worked as an usher at a movie theater in San Francisco and Edna Allen, the telephone operator there, always said, "You have to put in good to take out good." That phrase has become a sort of mantra for me, and influences the way I cook, especially when it comes to soup making. Try the stock recipes in the Basics chapter (pages 5–9) and put some good into your soups.

CHANTERELLE MUSHROOM SOUP

It's hard to beat the combination of chanterelles and cream. This soup is easy to make and is a wonderful way to savor that special chanterelle taste. Make it once, and you'll have something to remember for an entire year.

3 tablespoons butter

2½ tablespoons unbleached all-purpose flour

3½ cups unsalted chicken stock (page 5), boiling

¼ cup sherry (see Note)

1 cup whipping or heavy cream

1 teaspoon salt

⅛ teaspoon freshly ground black pepper

1 cup cooked chanterelles (page 10)

1 teaspoon finely chopped fresh thyme leaves, for garnish

Melt the butter in a 3-quart saucepan over medium heat. When hot and bubbly, stir in the flour with a wooden spoon. Stir continuously for 2 minutes to cook the flour without browning. Remove pan from heat and pour in the boiling chicken stock all at once. Stir well with a wire whisk and return pan to heat. Bring the mixture to a boil and cook, stirring with the whisk, until it is only slightly thickened, just a minute or so. Stir in the sherry and simmer over low heat, partially covered, for 10 minutes. Add the cream, salt, pepper, and the chanterelles. Stir briefly just to heat through without boiling. Ladle into small bowls, sprinkle with a pinch of the thyme, and serve at once.

Note: I like to use equal parts dry sherry and cream sherry.

PORTOBELLO AND BACON SOUP WITH OYSTER SAUCE YIELD: 6 SERVINGS

This is a multinational soup that showcases classic flavors from several countries. The true Montana foods here are the bacon and mushrooms. The bacon adds a smokiness to the mushrooms, emphasizing their meaty taste, while the Asian oyster sauce contributes a slight saltiness. The garlic toasts and cilantro bring all the flavors together.

6 slices French or Italian bread,
    about ½ inch thick

Extra-virgin olive oil, for brushing

3 cloves garlic, peeled and cut in half,
    for rubbing

¼ pound thick-sliced bacon, cut
    crosswise into 1/4-inch strips

6 cups unsalted chicken stock
    (page 5)

1 pound portobello mushrooms

½ cup dry white French vermouth

2 cloves garlic, minced

1 tablespoon extra-virgin olive oil

1 teaspoon salt

¼ teaspoon freshly ground
    black pepper

1 tablespoon minced fresh oregano

4 teaspoons oyster sauce

3 tablespoons chopped fresh cilantro
    leaves, for garnish

1. Brush the bread slices lightly with olive oil and brown them under the broiler on both sides. While the slices are still hot, rub both sides with the 3 cut garlic cloves.

2. Cook the bacon slowly in a large skillet until most of the fat is rendered and the bacon is lightly browned and almost crisp. Drain on paper towels. Pour off the fat, leaving the browned bits in the skillet.

3. Place the chicken stock in a 3-quart saucepan. Remove the stems from the portobellos and trim off their sandy ends. Slice the stems and add them to the chicken stock. Simmer for about 10 minutes, then remove and discard the stems. Cut the caps into cubes measuring about $3/8$ inch. Add them to the skillet along with 1 cup of the chicken stock, the vermouth, and the minced garlic. Cook, covered, over medium heat for 5 minutes. Then uncover and cook over high heat, stirring often, until the liquid has almost evaporated, about 5 minutes. Add the tablespoon of olive oil and continue to cook, stirring and tossing for 1 to 2 minutes, to brown the mushroom pieces slightly. Remove from the heat.

4. Combine the cooked mushrooms with the remaining 5 cups of chicken stock in the saucepan. Add the salt, pepper, oregano, and oyster sauce. Stir well, then add the bacon pieces. Bring the soup to a simmer. Place a slice of prepared bread in each soup bowl. Ladle in the soup, sprinkle with cilantro, and serve.

Note: If you use salted chicken stock, decrease the amount of salt and oyster sauce as desired.

CURRIED BUTTERNUT SQUASH SOUP

At my house, we compost all vegetable trimmings in the backyard garden. Sometimes volunteer plants spring up, and we wonder what in the world they are. During one long and hot growing season, several intriguing-looking vines bearing blossoms that clearly belonged to the squash family spread all over the place. We didn't have the heart to uproot them, so we let them flourish and were rewarded with huge butternut squashes. This soup is one of the results of that bounty.

2 tablespoons butter

1 large or 2 medium yellow onions, coarsely chopped

1 large fresh jalapeño chile, seeded and finely chopped (about 2 tablespoons)

1 teaspoon curry powder

3 pounds butternut squash, peeled, seeded, and cut into 1-inch chunks (about 6 cups)

4 cups water

2 teaspoons salt

1 cup half-and-half

2 tablespoons dry sherry

Salt to taste

Melt the butter in a heavy 5-quart stockpot over medium heat. Add the onion and stir to coat it well with the butter. Cover and cook until tender but not browned, about 5 minutes. Add the jalapeño and curry powder and cook, stirring, 1 to 2 minutes more. Add the squash, water, and salt. Stir well and bring to a boil over high heat. Cover the pan, reduce heat to medium-low, and simmer slowly until the squash is very tender, 30 to 40 minutes. Puree in batches in a blender until very smooth. Return to the pot and stir in the half-and-half and sherry. Add the salt to taste, if desired. Heat slowly, stirring occasionally, until very hot but not boiling. Ladle into bowls and serve.

Squashes

Winter squash have wonderfully distinct flavors. Butternut squash is my favorite—it grows well in our garden, keeps for months in a cool place, and tastes terrific. That's why it is the squash of choice in the recipes here. Squashes and pumpkins are native to the Americas, where they have been cultivated for more than 9,000 years. Because squashes grow best during warm weather, they probably originated in Mexico and South America. And they are extremely promiscuous—we're always finding new scouts in our garden as a result of crossbreeding. The longer the summer, the more likely a different volunteer plant will reach maturity. We never know exactly what we are eating when we cook these garden volunteers, but for the most part they are very tasty.

SUMMER VEGETABLE SOUP

I make this sweet soup in the heart of summer when turnips are small and tender, the sweet white corn and vine-ripened tomatoes are bursting with flavor, and the fava beans and zucchini are ready to pick. The lemongrass adds a wonderful accent to the vegetable stock. You can prepare the broth a day or two ahead and refrigerate it. There will be enough stock for two batches of this soup. I suggest freezing the extra or using it to make the Cauliflower Soup with Roasted Red Pepper Puree (page 84).

Vegetable Stock

1 ear sweet white corn, husked

¼ pound fresh shiitake mushrooms

1 head garlic, separated into cloves,
    unpeeled

2 large carrots, cut into 1-inch pieces

3 stalks celery with leaves, washed
    and cut into 1-inch pieces

2 stalks lemongrass, cut into
    ½-inch pieces

½ pound small white mushrooms,
    cut in half

2 large leeks, split, washed well, and
    cut into 1-inch pieces

12 sprigs parsley

2 bay leaves

1 teaspoon black peppercorns

12 cups water

Vegetables

2 pounds fresh fava beans in the pod

2 tablespoons butter

1 large sweet yellow onion, peeled and coarsely chopped

1 large carrot, peeled and cut into ¼-inch cubes

5 small white turnips, peeled and cut into ½-inch pieces

Reserved shiitake mushroom caps, sliced ¼ inch thick

1½ teaspoons salt

1 large ripe tomato, peeled, seeded, and diced

1 small zucchini, cut into ½-inch cubes

Reserved corn kernels

4 cups strained vegetable stock

2 tablespoons minced fresh thyme leaves, for garnish

1. Cut the kernels off the corn with a sharp knife and reserve them for the soup. Place the corn cob in a heavy 6-quart pot. Cut off the stems from the shiitake mushrooms and add them to the pot, reserving the caps. Add the garlic, carrots, celery, lemongrass, white mushrooms, leeks, parsley, bay leaves, peppercorns, and water. Bring to a boil over medium-high heat, uncovered. Reduce heat and allow the stock to simmer slowly for 1 hour. Strain through a fine-mesh strainer and discard the solids. You will have about 8 cups vegetable stock. Cool, cover, and refrigerate. The stock keeps refrigerated for 2 days or up to 3 months frozen in an airtight container.

2. Shell the fava beans and place them in a large pot of rapidly boiling water to blanch for 15 to 30 seconds. Remove the beans with a slotted spoon and transfer them to a large bowl of very cold water. After 5 to 10 minutes, drain them well. Pierce the skin of a bean with a fingernail, then slip off and discard the skin; repeat for each bean. You should have $1^{1}/_2$ scant cups of bright-green beans. Set them aside.

3. Melt the butter in a heavy 5-quart saucepan over medium-low heat. Stir in the onion, carrot, turnips, mushroom caps, and salt. Cover and cook, stirring 2 or 3 times, until the vegetables are almost tender, about 15 minutes. Raise the heat to high and add the tomato. Cook, stirring, for 1 to 2 minutes. Add the zucchini, corn kernels, fava beans, and vegetable stock. Lower the heat and simmer a few minutes, or until the vegetables are slightly al dente. Ladle into soup bowls, sprinkle with the thyme, and serve.

TOMATO-TARRAGON SOUP

Because of a typically short growing season, vine-ripened tomatoes are a precious commodity in Montana. When we're fortunate enough to get them, there are usually three things we make: a fresh tomato salad drizzled with extra-virgin olive oil and sprinkled with chopped basil and shallots; Tomatoes Stuffed with Fresh Herbs and Bread Crumbs (page 188); and this incredible soup. The color is a bright orange-red, and the taste is sensational.

8 large cloves garlic, peeled

2 tablespoons extra-virgin olive oil

2 sweet yellow onions, coarsely
  chopped

1 large carrot, peeled and coarsely
  chopped

4 pounds ripe tomatoes

1½ teaspoons salt

¼ teaspoon freshly ground
  black pepper

¼ cup chopped fresh tarragon leaves

½ cup whipping cream or
  heavy cream

1 tablespoon minced fresh tarragon
  leaves, for garnish

1. Adjust an oven rack to the center position and preheat the oven to 300°. If the garlic cloves vary in size, cut them into equal fragments. Place the garlic in a small (6-ounce) heatproof custard cup and add the olive oil. Cover tightly with foil and bake for 1 hour, or until the garlic is very tender. Turn into a small wire strainer set over a 5-quart saucepan and allow the oil to drain. Reserve the garlic.

2. Set the saucepan over medium-low heat and add the onions and carrot. Stir well, cover the pan, and cook for about 15 minutes, or until the vegetables are tender but not browned. Stir occasionally.

3. Place half of the tomatoes in a large pot of rapidly boiling water and blanch for 30 seconds. Remove the tomatoes with a slotted spoon and transfer them to a large bowl of very cold water. Repeat with the remaining tomatoes. When the tomatoes are cool enough to handle, drain, stem, and peel them. Cut the tomatoes in half crosswise and squeeze gently to remove the juices and seeds. (Freeze the juices and seeds to use in stock.) Cut the tomatoes into large chunks.

4. Add the tomatoes to the onions and carrot along with the salt and pepper. Stir well, cover the pan, and continue cooking over medium-low heat for another 15 minutes. Add the ¼ cup chopped tarragon and cook, covered, another 10 minutes. Stir in the roasted garlic.

5. Puree in batches in a blender until smooth. Return to the pan and add the cream. The soup may be made ahead and refrigerated to this point. When ready to serve, heat gently, stirring often, until piping hot. Do not allow the soup to boil. Ladle into bowls and sprinkle with the minced tarragon.

BORSCHT

I loved borscht as a child growing up in Shanghai. My Russian grandmother prepared it often; and after we moved to San Francisco, my mother frequently made the soup. I have carried on the tradition and make this soup in Montana, especially during the first fall harvest when beets, leeks, carrots, and onions are ready to be picked at about the same time. This recipe makes a large batch because I've found that people usually want seconds. Leftovers can be refrigerated for several days or frozen for longer storage. The slight browning of the beets emphasizes their sweetness.

6 small to medium beets

2 leeks

¼ cup butter

1 large yellow onion, coarsely chopped

1 large carrot, peeled and cut into thin
    half-circles

3 cloves garlic, minced

1½ pounds Yukon gold potatoes,
    peeled and cut into ¾-inch cubes

1 large green bell pepper, cored,
    seeded, and cut into ½-inch
    pieces

3 quarts rich beef stock (pages 6–7)

1 (14½-ounce) can peeled, diced
    tomatoes with juices, or
    2 cups fresh

4 teaspoons salt

½ teaspoon freshly ground black
    pepper

6 cups shredded green cabbage
    (about 1 pound)

¼ cup freshly squeezed lemon juice
    plus additional to taste

Sour cream, for garnish

Chopped fresh dill, for garnish

1. Wash the beets and wrap them together in heavy-duty aluminum foil. Bake in the center of a preheated 350° oven about 1¼ hours, or until tender when pierced with a small sharp knife. When the beets are cool, peel and cut them into ⅓-inch cubes. Set aside.

2. Thinly slice the white part of the leek and about 1 inch of the green portion. Melt the butter in a heavy-bottomed 8- to 9-quart stockpot over medium heat. Add the onion and leeks. Stir and cook for 2 to 3 minutes. Add the beets and cook for about 10 minutes, stirring occasionally, until they begin to brown slightly. Stir in the carrot and garlic and cook for 5 minutes. Add the potatoes and bell pepper and cook for 2 minutes.

3. Add the beef stock, tomatoes and juices, salt, and pepper, and bring mixture to a boil, uncovered, over medium-high heat. Stir in the cabbage and bring the mixture back to a boil. Reduce the heat and simmer, uncovered, about 15 minutes, or until the cabbage and potatoes are tender. Stir in the lemon juice. Adjust the seasoning to taste with salt, pepper, and lemon juice.

4. To serve, ladle the soup into bowls and place a dollop of sour cream in the center. Sprinkle with chopped dill.

CAULIFLOWER SOUP WITH
ROASTED RED PEPPER PUREE
YIELD: 6 TO 8 SERVINGS

Cauliflower, like its relative broccoli, grows very well in the cool mountain air of the Rocky Mountains. Both make excellent soups, but cauliflower results in a rather sweet soup when used alone. Red bell peppers, which grow extremely well during our hot Montana summers, contribute an intriguing background acidity. When the pepper puree is swirled into the cauliflower soup, the look and the taste are tantalizing.

1 head cauliflower

2 large red bell peppers

1 tablespoon extra-virgin olive oil

1¾ teaspoons salt

1 tablespoon butter

1 large or 2 medium sweet yellow
　　onions, chopped

4 tablespoons unbleached all-
　　purpose flour

4 cups vegetable stock (pages
　　80–81) or chicken stock (page 5),
　　boiling

¼ teaspoon freshly ground
　　black pepper

1 cup half-and-half

2 tablespoons snipped fresh chives
　　(optional)

1. Break the florets off the cauliflower stem and cut them into 1-inch pieces. Discard the stem. Steam the florets for about 5 minutes, or until they are tender when pierced with the tip of a sharp knife. Set aside to cool. The cauliflower may be wrapped when cool and refrigerated for 1 day before using.

2. Roast the red peppers over a charcoal grill or under the broiler, turning them as necessary, until the skins are black and blistered all over. Place the peppers in a paper bag, seal the top, and set aside until cool. Using your fingers, remove the skins and stems and discard. Cut the peppers into sections and wipe away the seeds with paper towels. Do not rinse the peppers under water or you will wash away most of their flavor. Puree the peppers in a food processor until smooth, stopping to scrape the work bowl as necessary. With the machine running, gradually drizzle in the olive oil. Add ¼ teaspoon of the salt and process 1 minute longer. Transfer to a small bowl, cover, and set aside.

3. Melt the butter in a 5-quart saucepan over medium heat. Stir in the onion, cover the pan, and cook for 5 to 8 minutes, or until the onion is tender but not browned. Add the flour and cook, stirring with a wooden spatula, for 2 to 3 minutes, but do not let it brown. Remove the pan from the heat and add the hot stock. Stir well with the wooden spatula and set the pan over high heat. Bring the mixture to a boil and cook, stirring continuously, for 1 minute, or until the soup is slightly thickened. Add the cauliflower and cook, stirring for another 2 minutes.

4. Puree the soup in a blender in batches until smooth. Return the soup to the saucepan and stir in the remaining $1^{1}/_{2}$ teaspoons salt, the black pepper, and the half-and-half. Heat slowly over medium heat until piping hot, stirring occasionally; do not allow the soup to boil. Taste the soup and adjust seasoning. Ladle the soup into bowls and place a generous spoonful of red pepper puree in the center. Swirl the puree into the soup with the tip of a dinner knife, using two or three broad strokes. Sprinkle with the chives, if using, and serve.

FAVA BEAN SOUP WITH BASIL AND TOMATO PESTO YIELD: 6 GENEROUS SERVINGS

A friend who grows favas every year once went on vacation just as the plants were reaching their maximum production. She asked my wife and me if we'd like to harvest her garden while she was away. I picked so many pounds I lost track. If you are unfamiliar with fava beans, this soup will help you get acquainted nicely.

Soup

3 pounds fava beans in the pod

6 cups medium-strength unsalted chicken stock (page 5)

1 carrot, peeled and sliced into half-circles

¾ to 1 teaspoon salt

¼ teaspoon freshly ground black pepper

Pesto

3 cloves garlic, peeled

1 cup loosely packed fresh basil leaves

2 tablespoons chopped walnuts

¼ cup extra-virgin olive oil

½ cup grated Parmesan cheese

½ teaspoon salt

¼ cup tomato paste

2 tablespoons chopped flat-leaf parsley, for garnish

1. To make the soup, shell the favas and place the beans in a large pot of rapidly boiling water to blanch for 15 to 30 seconds. Remove the beans with a slotted spoon and transfer them to a large bowl of very cold water. After 5 to 10 minutes, drain them well. Pierce the skin of a bean with a fingernail, then slip off and discard the skin; repeat for each bean. You should have 2 cups of bright-green beans. Set them aside. The favas may be prepared up to this point a day ahead; cover and refrigerate.

2. Bring the chicken stock to a simmer in a 4-quart saucepan. Add the carrot and cook, partially covered, 5 minutes. Add the favas and simmer, uncovered, another 5 minutes. Season with the salt and pepper. Set aside until serving time.

3. To make the pesto, place the garlic in the work bowl of a food processor fitted with the metal blade. Process 15 seconds. Add the basil and walnuts and process 20 seconds. Add the olive oil, cheese, salt, and tomato paste and process another 10 seconds. The mixture will be a thick paste. Transfer to a small bowl.

4. To serve, reheat the soup over medium heat. Ladle into serving bowls, making sure each gets a generous amount of fava beans. Place a rounded teaspoonful of pesto in the center of each bowl (see the Note for ways to use the leftover pesto), and sprinkle the parsley around the pesto. Serve immediately. Before eating, stir the pesto into the soup.

Note: This pesto recipe makes enough to accompany 12 servings of soup, but it has many uses. For example, you can spread it on grilled bread, serve it as a topping for pasta, mix it into mashed potatoes, or add it to a potato salad.

OYSTER MUSHROOM AND OYSTER CHOWDER

This is a perfect soup for late spring, when wild oyster mushrooms are abundant. Although oyster mushrooms don't taste like oysters, their cooked texture matches that of barely poached oysters. The corn highlights the sweetness of the mushrooms and oysters. If you can get lemon thyme, by all means use it. The thyme provides a slight citrus background that acts as a welcome counterpoint to the sweet ingredients.

1 pound yellow Finn potatoes, peeled and cut into ½-inch cubes (2 cups)

2 tablespoons butter

1 large sweet yellow onion, finely chopped

1 carrot, peeled and finely chopped

½ pound oyster mushrooms

2 (10-ounce) jars oysters

1 cup fresh sweet corn kernels

1 teaspoon Worcestershire sauce

½ teaspoon salt

¼ teaspoon Tabasco sauce

2 cups milk

2 cups half-and-half

2 tablespoons dry sherry

¼ cup minced parsley

1 tablespoon minced fresh lemon thyme (optional)

1. Place the potatoes in a 3-quart pot of rapidly boiling, lightly salted water. Cover and cook over high heat for 5 minutes. Drain and set potatoes aside. In a heavy 5-quart saucepan, melt the butter over medium heat. Stir in the onion and carrot. Cover the pan and cook slowly until the vegetables are tender but not browned, about 5 minutes. Wipe away any dirt from the mushrooms and slice them about ½ inch thick. Stir them into the onion and carrot mixture, cover the pan, and continue cooking slowly for another 5 minutes.

2. Drain the oysters in a large wire strainer set over a bowl. Reserve the oyster liquor; quarter the oysters and set them aside. Add the oyster liquor, corn, Worcestershire, salt, Tabasco, milk, half-and-half, sherry, and potatoes to the saucepan. Stir well and bring the mixture almost to a boil; do not allow it to boil because the milk and half-and-half may curdle. Add the oysters and cook, stirring continuously, over medium-high heat for a few minutes, or until oysters are just cooked. They should remain soft and tender.

3. To serve, ladle about 2 cups into each of 6 large soup bowls. Combine the parsley with the lemon thyme and sprinkle the herbs over the soup. Serve immediately.

CHICKEN AND CORN SOUP WITH TEQUILA, JALAPEÑO, AND TOMATOES

YIELD: 6 TO 8 SERVINGS

This is sort of a Mexican-style chicken minestrone in the making. I say that because you could easily turn it into a full-blown minestrone by adding more vegetables such as shelled peas, diced cooked green beans, and potatoes. Then it becomes a meal in itself. The soup is only mildly hot, but feel free to increase the heat with more jalapeño if you're an el flamo. *This is a perfect soup for a hot summer day. Note that there are choices of last-minute green additions. Each will give a different taste to the soup, but whatever you choose, the results will be harmonious. I know I've said this before, but the secret to wonderful soup is a wonderful homemade stock. Make your own and you will never be sorry.*

1 pound boneless and skinless chicken breasts, cut into ½-inch pieces

1 jalapeño chile, seeded and finely chopped

2 garlic cloves, finely chopped

2 tablespoons tequila

1 tablespoon lime juice

¾ teaspoon ground cumin

1 teaspoon salt

¼ teaspoon freshly ground black pepper

1 teaspoon sugar

2 tablespoons olive oil

1 pound Roma tomatoes

3 ears corn, husked, kernels cut off the cob

6 cups unsalted chicken or turkey stock (page 5)

Salt, pepper, lime juice, if needed

⅓ cup snipped fresh chives, chopped scallions, chopped cilantro, or chopped flat-leaf parsley

1. Combine the chicken, jalapeño, garlic, tequila, lime juice, cumin, salt, pepper, sugar, and 1 tablespoon of the olive oil in a medium-size bowl. Set aside for 30 minutes. (May be prepared several hours ahead and refrigerated, covered). Drop the tomatoes into a large pot of boiling water. After 30 seconds, use a slotted spoon to transfer the tomatoes to a bowl of cold water. When cool enough to handle, remove stem ends and skin with a small, sharp knife. Cut tomatoes in half crosswise and squeeze gently to remove juice and seeds (Roma tomatoes have much less juice and seeds than regular tomatoes.) Dice the tomatoes and set them aside. Prepare the corn.

2. Heat remaining tablespoon of olive oil in a 12-inch skillet over medium-high heat and add the chicken mixture. Cook and stir for 3 to 4 minutes, until chicken is done.

3. Bring stock to the boil in a 5-quart saucepan over medium-high heat. Add the corn and cook 2 minutes. Stir in the tomatoes and the chicken mixture and heat briefly just until piping hot. Taste and add more salt (about 1 teaspoon), pepper, and a few drops of lime juice, if necessary. Ladle into serving bowls and sprinkle each with about 2 teaspoons of chopped chives, scallions, cilantro, or parsley.

SHAGGY MANE AND LEEK SOUP

This soup came about during a particularly rainy spring, when shaggy manes sprung up in profusion on nearby dirt roads. Pounds and pounds of them were everywhere. I gathered as many as I could, cooked some for freezing, and made this soup.

4 tablespoons butter

2 cups chopped white part of leek
    (6 ounces)

3 tablespoons flour

4 cups chicken stock (page 5), boiling

1 pound shaggy mane mushrooms,
    prepared and cooked (page 11)

¼ cup dry sherry

1 cup half-and-half

1½ teaspoons salt

¼ teaspoon freshly ground
    black pepper

Dash of freshly grated nutmeg

2 tablespoons finely chopped
    flat-leaf parsley

1. Melt 2 tablespoons of the butter in a heavy 3-quart pan over medium heat and add the leeks. Cook, stirring occasionally, until leeks are tender but not browned, about 5 minutes. Add the flour and continue cooking 2 more minutes, stirring constantly. Remove pan from heat and pour in the boiling chicken stock all at once. Stir well with a wire whisk and set pan over high heat. Boil for 2 minutes, stirring constantly with the whisk. Turn mixture into a blender with a heatproof container and puree until smooth.

2. Squeeze liquid from shaggy manes and set mushrooms aside in a strainer. Melt remaining 2 tablespoons butter in the same pan used to cook the leeks. When hot, add the mushrooms. Stir and cook for a minute or so to drive off excess moisture. The mushrooms may start to stick to the bottom of the pan and leave a brownish film; this is all right. Remove pan from heat and add the sherry. Stir thoroughly to deglaze the mushroom film. Add the pureed leek mixture to the mushrooms along with the half-and-half, salt, pepper, and nutmeg. Taste carefully and adjust seasoning if necessary. (May be prepared hours in advance and refrigerated.)

3. When ready to serve, reheat soup slowly over medium heat, stirring occasionally, until it is piping hot but not boiling. Ladle into warmed soup bowls, sprinkle with the parsley, and bring to the table at once.

MEATS

Because beef has become such an integral part of our diet since the West was settled, I've included many recipes featuring it. The difference between pioneer days and now is that instead of eating beef three times a day, which was typical at least for ranch hands, beef consumption has significantly declined. Beef is still the most popular commercially available meat in Montana; it's just that people eat less of it because of health concerns and because pork has gained in popularity. The beef recipes included here are lighter versions of such classic main dishes as beef stew and new combinations, as in Stir-Fried Beef with Asian Noodles and Mizuna.

I have also included several lamb recipes, partly inspired by the significant amount of quality lamb that is raised in Montana. Strangely enough, lamb is not widely popular in my region, perhaps because the beef industry is so dominant. If our lamb is shipped to your part of the country, I hope you'll take advantage of your good fortune and give the recipes a try.

ROASTED ARMAGNAC-MARINATED FILET OF BEEF

Some of the best-tasting beef in America is raised in Montana. I make this roast when we have something special to celebrate. You'll probably need to special-order the beef from your butcher, and it should be of even thickness. The Armagnac does something wonderful for the meat, but cognac will also work. Roasted potatoes and freshly shelled peas are an excellent accompaniment. The roast is also great served cold as part of a buffet.

⅓ cup finely chopped shallots

2 cloves garlic, finely chopped

1 teaspoon salt

½ teaspoon freshly ground
    black pepper

2 tablespoons finely chopped
    fresh tarragon

2 teaspoons finely chopped
    fresh thyme

½ cup extra-virgin olive oil

⅓ cup Armagnac or cognac

2½ pounds fully trimmed center-cut
    beef filet

Additional olive oil, for roasting

1. Combine the shallots, garlic, salt, pepper, tarragon, thyme, olive oil, and Armagnac in a 1-gallon resealable plastic bag. Add the beef, seal the bag, and let it marinate in the refrigerator for 4 to 6 hours.

2. Remove the meat from the marinade and pat dry. Adjust an oven rack to the center position and preheat the oven to 450°. Tie the roast with kitchen twine crosswise in 4 or 5 places along its length, then tie it once circling the length of the meat. This will keep the meat cylindrical in shape during roasting. Rub the meat lightly with additional olive oil and place it in a shallow roasting pan. Cook for a total of 30 minutes for medium-rare, turning the roast carefully every 5 to 7 minutes. The meat will feel slightly springy to the touch, and the internal temperature should be between 125° and 130° when an instant-read thermometer is inserted into an end of the roast. Let the roast sit at room temperature or in a warm oven for 10 minutes before removing the strings and carving: Cut the meat into ½-inch-thick slices and serve as soon as possible with any pan juices.

"During roundups we were often off a long time and a long distance from town, so we had to have everything we needed and plenty of it. In the spring, when we branded and castrated the males, we'd throw the testicles right on the coals where they'd roast and cook. Everybody loved those mountain oysters!"

—Tony Grace, on his days as a chuck wagon cook, beginning in 1913

NEW WEST BEEF STEW

This recipe clearly shows the difference between the new and old cooking of the West. In the old days, all the ingredients for a stew were cooked together for hours until everything was overcooked. Hungry ranch hands wanted nourishing food as soon as their work was done, so stews were put on the stove and cooked for a variable number of hours. Today, we cook each ingredient in a stew so that its integrity is maintained, making the dish all the more enjoyable.

3½ pounds trimmed beef chuck, cut
    into 2-inch chunks

Unbleached all-purpose flour, for
    coating

⅓ cup vegetable oil

1 cup water

4 cups beef stock (pages 6–7)

2 bay leaves

½ teaspoon dried whole thyme
    leaves or 1 tablespoon chopped
    fresh thyme

1 tablespoon salt

2 pounds boiling potatoes, such as
    yellow Finn, peeled and cut into
    1-inch chunks

16 small turnips (1 to 1½ inches in
    diameter), peeled and cut in half

4 large carrots, peeled and sliced
    ½ inch thick

Salt and freshly ground black pepper

1 cup shelled fresh peas

1 cup fresh corn kernels

¼ cup mixed chopped fresh parsley,
    thyme, and oregano

1. Coat the beef in flour. Place the oil in a 5-quart Dutch oven or a wide, deep ovenproof skillet and set the pan over medium heat. When the oil is hot, add the meat in batches and brown on all sides. Remove meat and set aside. Repeat until all meat is browned.

2. Remove the pan from the heat and discard fat and any burned pieces of meat stuck to the bottom of the pan. Add the water, and scrape the bottom of the pan with a wooden spoon to dislodge any browned bits. Strain and reserve the liquid. Return beef to pan, add the beef stock, the strained liquid, bay leaves, and thyme. The liquid should just reach the top of the meat without actually covering it. If not, add more water. Simmer slowly, covered, until meat is very tender, 2 to 3 hours.

3. Meanwhile, bring 3 to 4 quarts water to a rolling boil over high heat in an 8-quart pot. Add the salt and potatoes. Cover and cook until potatoes are just tender, 8 to 10 minutes. Test with the tip of a sharp knife. Remove the potatoes with a large skimmer and set aside. Add the turnips to the pot of water and boil until tender, about 5 minutes. Remove the turnips and set aside with the potatoes. Finally, add the carrots to the water and cook until tender, 5 to 8 minutes. Drain and add them to the potatoes and turnips. Set aside until ready to use. The recipe may be completed hours in advance up to this point.

4. When the beef is tender, taste the cooking liquid and season with the salt and pepper. Add the potatoes, turnips, carrots, peas, and corn to the beef and stir together carefully without breaking up the meat or the vegetables. Cover the pan and place it in a preheated 350° oven until piping hot and the peas and corn are cooked, about 30 minutes.

5. To serve, transfer beef and vegetables to large soup bowls with a slotted spoon and ladle some of the broth into the bowls. Sprinkle with the chopped fresh herbs and serve immediately. If you are not going to serve the stew right away, cool, cover, and refrigerate.

STIR-FRIED BEEF WITH ASIAN NOODLES AND MIZUNA YIELD: 4 TO 6 SERVINGS

Flank steak is the best meat to use in stir-fries because it is tender and cooks very quickly. Slice it fairly thin crosswise against the grain or it will be tough when you cook it. Placing the meat in the freezer for 15 to 20 minutes will firm it sufficiently to make slicing very easy. Fresh Chinese lo mein noodles are readily available in well-stocked supermarkets, as are the other Asian ingredients.

1 pound fully trimmed flank steak, cut crosswise into ¼-inch strips

4 tablespoons vegetable oil

2 tablespoons dry sherry

1 tablespoon nuoc mam (Vietnamese fish sauce)

2 cloves garlic, chopped

12 ounces fresh lo mein noodles

1 tablespoon dark sesame oil

2 tablespoons light soy sauce

2 tablespoons dark soy sauce

⅓ cup rich beef stock (pages 6–7)

⅓ cup water

1 tablespoon cornstarch

1 ounce dried shiitake mushrooms

2 bunches mizuna (about 1 pound total), washed and cut into 3-inch lengths

2 broccoli stems, peeled and sliced thin

1 large red bell pepper, cored, seeded, and cut into thin strips

4 scallions, trimmed and thinly sliced

1. Combine flank steak, 2 tablespoons of the oil, the sherry, fish sauce, and garlic in a bowl; cover and refrigerate. This step may be completed hours ahead or shortly before cooking.

2. Cook the noodles according to directions on the package. Drain well and cool briefly in a large bowl of cold water. Drain well again and return noodles to the cooking pot. Mix in the sesame oil and cover the pan.

3. Stir together both soy sauces, the beef stock, water, and cornstarch; set aside. Soak the mushrooms in hot water to cover until soft. Squeeze out excess moisture, cut away and discard stems, and cut mushroom caps into 1-inch pieces.

4. Place a large wok over medium-high heat. When hot, add the beef mixture. Stir and toss 3 to 4 minutes, or until the meat is just cooked. Remove and set aside. Add the remaining 2 tablespoons oil to the wok and heat. Add the mizuna, stir and toss for about 2 minutes, or until the leaves are wilted. Add the mushrooms, broccoli stems, and red bell pepper. Stir and cook for another 2 minutes. Add the noodles and scallions and toss well to heat thoroughly. Stir the sauce mixture to distribute the cornstarch evenly and add it to the wok. Add the beef mixture and stir well for about 1 minute, or until the sauce is slightly thickened and the stir-fry is heated through. Transfer to a large serving dish and serve immediately.

The Spicy Green

Mizuna is an all-purpose tender leafy green with a delightful spiciness that is not overwhelmingly hot. It loves the climate in Montana and grows well in any weather, hot or cold. Mizuna has attractive lacy leaves that look pretty in salads or in stir-fries. Buy mizuna that is young and tender, preferably at farmers' markets, or grow it yourself. The entire plant can be eaten as long as the stems are very thin, about 1/8 inch.

LEG OF LAMB STUFFED WITH GARLIC AND HERBS YIELD: 6 TO 8 SERVINGS

For this dish, I like to buy a boneless leg of lamb. Even so, you will need to trim the meat well to remove the outer membrane and inner pockets of fat. The garlicky herb puree is an ideal foil for this robust meat. The lemongrass powder, which is available in Asian markets, is a nice addition but it's not essential to the success of the recipe. Try to serve the lamb pink. Tomatoes Stuffed with Fresh Herbs and Bread Crumbs (page 188) and roasted potatoes are perfect accompaniments.

1 boneless leg of lamb (about
   6 pounds)
¼ cup chopped garlic
1 teaspoon salt
6 tablespoons extra-virgin olive oil,
   plus extra to rub on the lamb
⅓ cup finely chopped fresh oregano
¼ teaspoon ground cayenne pepper
1 teaspoon freshly ground
   black pepper
3 tablespoons freshly squeezed lemon
   juice
1 teaspoon lemongrass powder
   (optional)
1 tablespoon sweet paprika
1½ cups rich chicken stock (page 5)
½ cup dry white French vermouth
2 tablespoons butter

1. Carefully remove the outer membrane from the lamb with a sharp boning knife. Open the inside of the lamb leg (using the incision already made to remove the bones as a starting point) so that the whole leg lies flat on your work surface in a rough triangular shape. Cut away as much of the fat as you can, but don't be obsessive about it. Make shallow slashes in the thicker portions of meat so that the marinade can penetrate. You will wind up with about 4 pounds of meat from a trimmed 6-pound boneless leg.

2. Pound the garlic and salt to a puree in a mortar with a pestle or mash with a fork in a small bowl. Gradually stir in the olive oil. Add the oregano, cayenne, black pepper, lemon juice, lemongrass powder, and paprika and mix in well. Rub the mixture all over the meat. Roll the lamb into a cylinder and tie it securely in 4 or 5 places crosswise with kitchen twine. Tie one string lengthwise around the lamb. The meat should be an even cylinder shape. Rub the outside surface lightly with olive oil. Place the lamb in a shallow dish, cover loosely with plastic wrap, and refrigerate 4 to 6 hours.

3. To cook lamb, adjust an oven rack to the center position and preheat the oven to 450°. Place the lamb in a shallow roasting pan and cook, uncovered, for 15 minutes. Reduce the oven temperature to 350° and continue cooking until the internal temperature of the lamb is between 125° (rare) and 130° (medium-rare). After 1 hour of total cooking time, test for doneness by inserting an

instant-read thermometer about halfway into the lamb while it is in the oven. Immediately remove the meat from oven and wait about 15 seconds to read the temperature. If lamb is not ready, remove the thermometer, return the meat to the oven, and keep retesting every few minutes until the lamb is cooked to your liking.

4. When the lamb is ready, transfer it to a cutting board and cut away the twine. Create a loose tent with foil, place it over the lamb, and let it stand 15 minutes before carving so the juices can be reabsorbed into the meat. While the lamb rests, pour off any juice from the roasting pan and reserve it. Add the chicken stock and vermouth to the pan and set it over high heat. Scrape the bottom of the pan with a wooden spoon to dislodge any browned bits and boil briefly to reduce the sauce by about one-third. Swirl in the butter and add the reserved juices. Adjust the seasonings, as desired. Carve the lamb into thin slices and serve with the sauce.

VIETNAMESE BE-BOON

My Missoula friend Chu Chu Pham gave me this recipe. It is a Vietnamese version of barbecued pork served with rice stick noodles, fresh vegetables, and fish sauce. The secret ingredient is ground browned rice, which is easy to make. This is a spicy and exciting eating experience.

½ cup long-grain white rice

1 pound pork tenderloin

7 tablespoons nuoc mam
    (Vietnamese fish sauce)

2 teaspoons dry white
    French vermouth

¼ teaspoon freshly ground
    black pepper

1 tablespoon vegetable oil

¼ cup sugar

3 tablespoons water

2 tablespoons rice vinegar or
    apple cider vinegar

1 large lime

¾ cup finely shredded carrot

¾ cup peeled, finely shredded jicama

1 fresh hot chile pepper (such as
    serrano, jalapeño, or habañero)

4 cloves garlic, peeled and
    coarsely chopped

1 English cucumber, peeled and sliced

2 cups fresh bean sprouts

1 cup fresh cilantro leaves

1 cup fresh mint leaves, torn into
    small pieces

5 to 10 ounces rice stick noodles

1. Wash rice thoroughly in several changes of cool tap water, then drain and dry it well on a kitchen towel. Place the rice in a small, heavy skillet (cast iron is best) over medium heat. Do not add any oil to the pan. Stir occasionally with a wooden spoon until the rice grains begin to brown. Then stir almost continuously until all the rice is a deep caramel color. Do not allow the rice to burn. This whole process takes about 20 minutes. Transfer the rice to a bowl and allow it to cool. Grind to a fine powder in a blender, mini-grinder, or spice mill. Transfer it to an airtight container. It will keep in a cool cupboard for up to several weeks.

2. Slice the pork about ½ inch thick. In a medium-size bowl, combine the pork with 2 teaspoons of the nuoc mam, the vermouth, pepper, and oil. Cover and refrigerate 1 hour or longer. Mix the remaining 6 tablespoons and 1 teaspoon of the fish sauce, the sugar, water, and vinegar together in a medium-size bowl. Stir until the sugar is dissolved.

3. Remove the rind from the lime. The easiest way is to slice both ends off and stand the lime upright. Cut the peel and white pith away from the lime in strips with a small sharp knife. Hold the lime over a mortar or a small bowl and remove the sections by cutting them out between the membranes. Collect the sections and juice in the mortar or bowl. Squeeze the remains of the lime to extract all of the juice. Crush the lime sections in the juice with a pestle or mash with a fork. Add the juice and pulp to the fish sauce mixture and stir in the carrot and jicama. Cover and refrigerate.

4. Wearing protective gloves, stem and chop the chile coarsely. Leave in the seeds and ribs if you like ultraspicy foods. Combine the garlic and chile on the chopping board and finely chop both together, or crush them to a paste with a mortar and pestle. Place in a small dish and set aside, covered. Arrange the cucumber, bean sprouts, cilantro, and mint on a platter. Cover and refrigerate until serving time. The recipe may be made hours ahead up to this point.

5. Rice stick noodles come dried in packages of 3 to 4 stacks. Each stack weighs about 5 ounces. Fill a large stockpot with 12 cups of water and bring it to a boil. Place 1 or 2 stacks of the noodles in the stockpot. Use the amount you prefer. Cook, stirring occasionally, for about 3 minutes, or until just tender. Drain in a large colander and rinse under warm tap water. Drain well. To prevent the noodles from sticking together, divide them into small piles on a serving dish. Let them stand loosely covered until serving time. The noodles may be prepared 1 hour or so ahead.

6. When ready to serve, heat a large nonstick skillet over medium-high heat and sauté the pork on both sides just until done, about 3 minutes total. Remove from the pan and set aside to cool briefly. Cut the pork into thin strips and combine them in a serving bowl with 1 to 2 tablespoons of the ground browned rice.

7. To serve, set the pork, the vegetable platter, bowls of the fish sauce mixture, the garlic and hot pepper paste, and the rice stick noodles on the table. Provide each person with a bowl and a pair of chopsticks. Each diner places some rice stick noodles in the bowl and adds some of the vegetables, pork, fish sauce mixture, and a dab of the garlic-pepper paste, if desired. Mix well with the chopsticks (or a fork!).

Note: You can substitute hot boiled rice for the rice stick noodles, if you prefer. Plan on about 1 cup cooked rice per person.

ROASTED RACK OF LAMB WITH ROSEMARY AND THYME

Completely trimmed racks of lamb, marinated in wine, olive oil, and herbs, make a festive entree for a special party. You can ask your butcher to trim the lamb for you, making sure all of the fat is removed, even between the ribs, or you can perform the operation yourself with a sharp boning knife. Lamb racks prepared this way are sometimes referred to as "Frenched." This dish goes very well with the Green Bean, Sweet Onion, and Yellow Beet Sauté with Vinegar (page 185) and roasted potatoes.

2 racks lamb, 8 chops each,
    completely trimmed

1½ cups sauvignon blanc

⅓ cup extra-virgin olive oil

½ cup sliced shallots

3 cloves garlic, coarsely chopped

1 tablespoon chopped fresh rosemary

1 teaspoon chopped fresh lemon
    thyme

1 teaspoon chopped fresh thyme

½ teaspoon freshly ground black
    pepper

Salt to taste

⅔ cup rich beef stock (pages 6–7)

⅓ cup pinot noir

2 tablespoons butter

1. Place the lamb racks in a 9x5x3-inch glass loaf pan. Combine the sauvignon blanc, olive oil, shallots, garlic, herbs, and pepper and pour over the lamb. The liquid should just cover the lamb. If not, add more wine. Cover and marinate 4 to 6 hours, refrigerated. Turn the lamb 2 or 3 times while it marinates.

2. When ready to cook, adjust an oven rack to the center position and preheat the oven to 450°. Remove the lamb from the marinade and place it in a shallow roasting pan with the meat facing up. Sprinkle lightly with salt. Roast until medium-rare, about 25 minutes. An instant-read thermometer should register 130° when inserted in the roast. Transfer the lamb to a dish, cover it loosely with foil, and keep warm while you make the sauce.

3. Pour off and discard any fat from the roasting pan. Add the beef stock and pinot noir and cook over high heat, scraping the bottom of the pan with a wooden spoon to dislodge any browned bits. Reduce sauce by about half, or until slightly thickened. Add the butter and swirl it in. Strain the sauce through a fine-mesh sieve; there will be about ½ cup. Adjust the seasoning to taste and keep the sauce warm. Slice the lamb into chops and divide it among 4 heated dinner plates. Spoon the sauce over the lamb and serve immediately.

BEEF, TURKEY, AND PORK MEAT LOAF
WITH TOMATO-MUSTARD GLAZE

YIELD: 8 TO 10 SERVINGS

If you're going to make meat loaf, you might as well fix a big one, because the leftovers make terrific sandwiches. This loaf is exceptionally moist, despite the use of lean ground meats, because of the liquid in the tomato puree, milk, and cooked onion and green pepper. But the baking has something to do with it, too. I follow Sylvia Woods's and Christopher Styler's recommendation in Sylvia's Soul Food *and place a pan of hot water on the rack below the baking loaf. The constant humid atmosphere in the oven guarantees a moist meat loaf. The loaf is so moist, in fact, it needs no sauce. Serve with Roasted Garlic Mashed Potatoes (page 192).*

2 cups fresh coarse bread crumbs,
    made from day-old crustless
    French or Italian bread
½ cup milk
1 tablespoon butter
1 large or 2 medium sweet yellow
    onions, chopped
1 large green bell pepper, cored,
    seeded, and chopped
4 eggs
1 cup tomato puree
½ teaspoon Tabasco sauce
1 pound extra-lean ground beef
1 pound extra-lean ground turkey
1 pound ground pork
2 cloves garlic, minced (1 tablespoon)
1½ teaspoons rubbed sage
1 teaspoon dried oregano leaves,
    crumbled
½ teaspoon dried whole thyme leaves
2 teaspoons salt
1 teaspoon freshly ground black pepper
2 tablespoons Dijon-style mustard
1 teaspoon prepared horseradish

1. Combine the bread crumbs and milk in a large bowl and set aside. Melt the butter in a large skillet over medium heat and stir in the onion and bell pepper. Sauté, stirring occasionally, until the vegetables are tender but not browned, 6 to 8 minutes. Cool briefly.

2. Whisk the eggs, ¾ cup of the tomato puree, and Tabasco into the bread-milk mixture. Add the beef, turkey, pork, garlic, sage, oregano, thyme, salt, and black pepper and mix thoroughly with your hands, making sure to break up any clumpy lumps of meat. Put the mixture into a roasting pan and pat it into a loaf about 12 inches long and 5 inches wide. (The meat loaf may be made hours ahead up to this point; just cover and refrigerate. Bring to room temperature before baking.) When ready to bake the meat loaf, combine the remaining ¼ cup tomato puree with the mustard and horseradish and spread it evenly over the top of the loaf.

3. Adjust an oven rack to the lowest position and another to the center position, and preheat the oven to 350°. Fill a 13x9x2-inch baking pan halfway with boiling water and place it on the lower shelf. Place the meat loaf on the upper shelf. Bake for 1 to 1¼ hours, or until the juices run clear yellow when the loaf is pricked with a fork. Let it stand 10 minutes, then cut it into 1-inch slices.

104 :: MONTANA COOKING

For the Love of Pigs

I grew to love pigs when I worked as the chef at a guest ranch in southwestern Montana. We had a sow who suckled and reared almost a dozen piglets. She reveled in her motherhood, lolling contentedly on her side as her babies nursed. We fed the mother and piglets well with leftover vegetables and bread. As the piglets grew, they showed decidedly different personalities and their intelligence really impressed me. I grew to appreciate them so much that I couldn't eat them for quite a while. But pigs figured so prominently as a food source during the settlement of the West, and are still one of our mainstays. So, I decided that no matter how I felt about the animals, I needed to include some pork recipes in this book.

ROASTED PORK TENDERLOINS, POTATOES, AND APPLES WITH CALVADOS GINGER SAUCE

YIELD: 4 SERVINGS

The key to the success of this recipe is using the proper potatoes and apples. Potato plants love our warm summer days and cool nights. I like to use yellow Finn potatoes in this recipe, but any firm-textured boiling potato will work, including Yukon gold or red-skinned varieties. Using the right kind of apple is also important because you want the apple chunks to hold their shape during cooking. I prefer the locally grown antique variety Lyman's Large, which is a big apple with a pale greenish-yellow skin that resembles a cross between a Granny Smith and a Golden Delicious in taste and texture. If you can get mature Granny Smith apples, use them. If not, firm Golden Delicious will do just fine. Serve with steamed tender green beans tossed with a touch of butter.

2 pork tenderloins (about 1½ pounds total)

3 teaspoons salt

¼ teaspoon freshly ground black pepper, plus two pinches

3 teaspoons extra-virgin olive oil

5 yellow Finn potatoes (about 1 pound), washed but unpeeled, cut into 1-inch pieces

1 large firm cooking apple, washed but unpeeled, cored, and cut into ¾-inch pieces (about 2 cups)

3 tablespoons butter

¼ pound fresh shiitake mushrooms, stems removed, caps thinly sliced

Salt and freshly ground pepper to taste

⅔ cup rich beef stock (pages 6–7)

⅓ cup Calvados

1 tablespoon peeled, finely shredded fresh ginger

1 tablespoon minced flat-leaf parsley, for garnish

1. Adjust an oven rack to the center position and preheat the oven to 400°.

2. Remove any membranes and fat from the pork with a small sharp knife. Rinse the pork and pat dry. Season each tenderloin with 1 teaspoon of salt and a pinch of pepper. Heat 2 teaspoons of the olive oil in a 12-inch nonstick ovenproof skillet over medium-high to high heat. When hot, add the tenderloins and cook for 6 minutes, or until all sides are nicely browned. Remove the pork and set aside on a plate.

3. Add the potatoes, remaining 1 teaspoon salt, and the ¼ teaspoon pepper to the skillet. Stir well and cook for 1 minute over medium-high heat. Place the pan in the oven and roast the potatoes for 15 minutes. Combine the apples with the remaining 1 teaspoon olive oil. Add to the potatoes and roast for 10 minutes. While the apples and potatoes are in the oven, melt 1 tablespoon of the butter in a 10-inch skillet over medium-high heat. Add the mushrooms and salt and pepper to taste and cook until the mushrooms are lightly browned, about 2 minutes. Remove the mushrooms from the heat and add them to the potatoes and apples, which should be tender. Transfer to a dish, cover, and keep warm. (The recipe may be prepared several hours ahead up to this point. Just cool, cover, and refrigerate the pork, potatoes, apples, and mushrooms, then bring to room temperature before continuing.)

4. Place the pork in the skillet used to cook the potatoes and apples. Reserve any pork juices to make the sauce. Return the pan to the 400° oven and roast for 15 to 20 minutes, or until the pork is only slightly pink in the center. An instant-read thermometer should register between 150° and 160° when inserted in the pork. Add the pork to the potato mixture; cover and keep warm.

5. Set the skillet over medium-high or high heat and add the beef stock, Calvados, pork juices, and ginger. Bring to a boil, scraping the bottom of the pan with a wooden spoon to dislodge any browned bits, and reduce the liquid by almost half. Immediately add the remaining 2 tablespoons butter, swirling until it has melted into the sauce. Strain the sauce into a small bowl and taste for seasoning, adding salt and pepper if desired.

6. Slice each tenderloin at an angle into 8 pieces. Arrange 4 pieces on each dinner plate with some of the potato, apple, and mushroom mixture. Spoon the sauce over the pork, sprinkle with a little parsley, and serve immediately.

GAME

Hunting is a way of life in Montana. At least half of the adults who live here hunt, and it's often a family affair. Before children go on a hunting trip, they are trained in the proper use and care of firearms and how to survive in the wild.

The new interest in game as a food source has resulted in the growing industry of raising a variety of game animals, both in the United States and abroad. The animals are reared under strict conditions to make them as healthy as possible for the consumer; because of this, the meat is expensive. But game meats are far different in taste from domestic animals, and they are well worth the price.

It is important to remember that eating game is not new. It was the first meat our ancestors ate. As development occurred throughout the plains and mountain states and towns sprang up, game fell by the wayside as a food source and the cattle and poultry industries rose in prominence. Now, chefs all over the country feature game on their menus.

I never ate game until my wife and I moved to Montana. Now, with the generosity of friends who hunt and the availability of game through mail-order sources that offer overnight delivery, we enthusiastically embrace it as a regular part of our diet. During the various hunting seasons, many of our friends host game parties, giving everyone a chance to sample a variety of tasty meats. Many farm-raised game species are available to the home cook, including some exotic ones such as squirrel and rattlesnake, and more familiar animals such as deer, buffalo, and pheasant (see the mail-order sources on pages 237–239).

The key to game cookery is to not overcook the meat. This is especially true when preparing steaks or roasts.

Game and fruit are natural partners. That doesn't mean that every game recipe has to include a fruit, but a sweet element tends to highlight the game's natural flavor.

For more information on all kinds of game and how to cook it, read *American Game Cooking* by John Ash and Sid Goldstein or *Wild About Game* by Janie Hibler.

ELK TENDERLOIN STEAKS WITH CHANTERELLES AND CREAM

YIELD: 4 SERVINGS

Our friends Peggy and Ted Christian are avid hunters who generously shared some elk with us. Hunters in Montana will tell you that elk, a close relative of deer, is their favorite game meat. It has a wonderfully meaty taste without being heavy and lacks the gaminess that can be so off-putting if you're unfamiliar with wild meat. This combination of chanterelles, cream, and elk is too seductive to pass up. If you don't hunt, beg some elk from a friend who does, or order it (see pages 236–237). Keep the rest of the meal simple, and serve the steaks with roasted potatoes and steamed green beans.

4 elk tenderloin steaks (5 to 6 ounces each, about ¾ inch thick)

1 tablespoon vegetable oil

1 tablespoon butter

1 cup cooked chanterelles (page 10)

⅔ cup rich beef stock (page 6–7)

½ cup dry white French vermouth

⅔ cup whipping cream

¼ teaspoon salt

⅛ teaspoon freshly ground black pepper

1 teaspoon freshly squeezed lemon juice

2 tablespoons finely chopped fresh tarragon leaves

Pat the elk steaks with paper towels. Heat the oil in a large nonstick skillet over medium-high heat, add the steaks and cook 2 minutes on each side for medium-rare. Transfer to a plate; cover and keep warm. Pour off fat in the skillet and return the pan to medium-high heat. Add the butter, and after it has melted, stir in the chanterelles. When the mushrooms are hot, pour in the stock and vermouth. Cook at a brisk boil, stirring occasionally, until the liquid has reduced by half and is syrupy. Add the cream, salt, and pepper, and continue reducing for several minutes until the sauce has thickened and coats a metal spoon. Stir in the lemon juice and taste carefully. Adjust seasoning with more salt, pepper, and lemon juice, if desired. Stir in the tarragon and return the steaks to the pan. Cook briefly just to heat through, while spooning the sauce and mushrooms over the meat. Serve immediately.

ELK SIRLOIN WITH PORTOBELLO MUSHROOMS AND SOY-LEMON MARINADE

YIELD: 4 SERVINGS

A friend presented me with beautiful elk sirloins one fall and told me to make something wonderful with them. It was a challenge I couldn't refuse. If you can't get elk sirloin from a supplier, use tenderloin instead. The dark soy sauce called for is available in Asian markets. It is a thick, almost black soy with some sugar added. If you can't find it, use regular soy sauce and add 1 teaspoon sugar to the marinade. The elk is terrific with savoy cabbage (prepared as described on page 194) and Roasted Garlic Mashed Potatoes (page 192).

1½ pounds trimmed elk sirloins or tenderloin, cut into 2x1x1-inch strips

½ cup thinly sliced scallions

2 tablespoons dark soy sauce, or regular soy sauce plus 1 teaspoon sugar

5 tablespoons extra-virgin olive oil

2 tablespoons freshly squeezed lemon juice

2 cloves garlic, minced

½ teaspoon freshly ground black pepper

½ teaspoon crumbled dried whole thyme leaves

1 pound portobello mushrooms

Salt and freshly ground black pepper

1 cup rich beef stock (pages 6–7)

1 cup dry white French vermouth

1. In a bowl, combine the elk, scallions, soy sauce, 3 tablespoons of the olive oil, the lemon juice, garlic, pepper, and thyme. To marinate, cover and refrigerate 2 hours or longer.

2. Remove mushroom stems and save them for another use. Slice the caps about ½ inch thick. Heat the remaining 2 tablespoons olive oil in a large skillet over medium-high heat. Add the mushrooms and stir well. Sprinkle with salt and pepper and cook, stirring frequently, until the mushrooms are tender, about 5 minutes. Remove the mushrooms and any liquid from the pan.

3. Place the pan over medium-high heat and add about half the elk with any marinade that adheres to it. Separate the elk pieces, so they don't steam as they cook. For rare or medium-rare, brown on all sides for about 2 minutes total. Remove from the pan and keep warm. Repeat with the remaining elk.

4. Pour off any fat remaining in the skillet, leaving any browned bits of meat. Add the beef stock and vermouth to the pan and return it to medium-high heat. Stir well, scraping the bottom of the pan with a wooden spoon to dislodge the browned bits, and boil until the liquid is reduced and slightly thickened. Decrease the heat to medium or medium-low. Add the mushrooms and cook for a few seconds, while stirring, then add the elk with any juices and cook briefly, continuing to stir, just until the meat is heated through. Serve immediately.

BISON TENDERLOINS AU POIVRE WITH ZINFANDEL SAUCE

This is my version of the French classic Steak au Poivre. Lean buffalo meat is ideal in this dish since the quick cooking over high heat ensures it will remain moist and tender. I've added tart cherries to tame the sweetness of the meat, and I use butter instead of cream so the sweetness of the cream doesn't dominate the taste of the meat.

4 (6-ounce) bison tenderloins,
    trimmed
2 tablespoons whole
    black peppercorns
Salt
2 tablespoons corn oil
¼ cup minced shallots
¼ cup dried sour cherries
    (Montmorency), soaked in hot
    water to plump
⅔ cup red zinfandel
½ cup rich beef stock (pages 6–7)
1 teaspoon minced fresh thyme leaves
4 tablespoons butter
Thyme sprigs, for garnish

1. Pat the meat dry with paper towels and set it aside. Place the peppercorns on the work surface and crush coarsely with the bottom of a saucepan. Press pepper onto both sides of the steaks and refrigerate, covered, until ready to cook. This may be done several hours ahead.

2. Just before cooking, lightly season the bison with salt. Heat the oil in a large, heavy skillet over medium-high heat. Cook the steaks 2 to 3 minutes on each side, depending on whether you want the meat rare or medium-rare. Remove the meat from the pan, pour off the fat, and keep the steaks warm.

3. To make the sauce, place the shallots in the pan and return it to medium-high heat. Scrape the bottom of the pan with a wooden spoon to dislodge any browned bits while stirring the shallots. Drain the plumped cherries. Add the cherries, zinfandel, stock, and thyme to the pan. Boil the mixture and cook until it is reduced by half, then add the butter and any meat juices. Swirl the contents of the pan and cook until the liquid is thickened enough to lightly coat the steaks. Lower heat to medium-low, return the steaks to the pan, and baste continuously with the juices for about 1 minute, or just until the meat is heated through. Serve on warmed plates and garnish with the thyme sprigs.

STIR-FRIED PHEASANT WITH GINGER AND ORANGE YIELD: 4 SERVINGS

The leanness of game meats makes them ideal for the high-heat quick cooking of stir-fry dishes. I suggest you order two whole pheasants weighing about 2½ pounds each and bone the breast meat yourself. That way you'll also have 4 leg-thigh cuts, which you can use in the next recipe.

1 pound boneless and skinless
    pheasant breast, cut into ¾-inch
    pieces
6 tablespoons freshly squeezed
    orange juice
4 tablespoons dry sherry
4 tablespoons hoisin sauce
2 tablespoons soy sauce
2 teaspoons cornstarch
½ cup chicken stock (page 5)
¼ teaspoon salt
½ pound fresh shiitake mushrooms
¾ pound fresh snow peas
2 tablespoons peanut oil or corn oil
2 tablespoons freshly grated ginger
4 scallions, trimmed and sliced into
    ¼-inch pieces
4 cups hot cooked rice

1. Mix the pheasant with 3 tablespoons of the orange juice and 2 tablespoons of the sherry.

2. Combine the remaining 3 tablespoons orange juice and 2 tablespoons sherry, the hoisin sauce, soy sauce, cornstarch, ¼ cup of the chicken stock, and the salt in a small bowl.

3. Remove the stems from the mushrooms and save them to flavor stocks or soups. Slice the caps about ¼ inch thick. Snap the stems of the snow peas and pull gently toward the other end of the peas to "string" them.

4. Heat 1 tablespoon of the oil in a wok or 12-inch nonstick skillet over high heat. Add the mushrooms, snow peas, ginger, and scallions. Stir and toss everything together for 1 minute. Add 2 tablespoons of the chicken stock and continue tossing and cooking until the liquid evaporates, about 1 minute. Add the remaining 2 tablespoons of stock and cook again until it evaporates. Transfer the mixture to a large bowl.

5. Add the remaining 1 tablespoon oil to the pan and place it over high heat. Add the pheasant mixture and stir-fry about 3 minutes, until the pheasant is done. When the pheasant feels springy to the touch, stir the cornstarch mixture well and add it to the pheasant along with the vegetable mixture. Stir and cook about 1 minute, until the sauce bubbles and thickens. Immediately transfer to a serving bowl and serve with the hot rice.

PHEASANT THIGHS WITH TORPEDO ONIONS AND SAVOY CABBAGE

YIELD: 4 SERVINGS

This is a perfect dish for a nippy fall evening. The newly dug onions and just-picked savoy cabbage are at their best, and practically beg to be paired with pheasant. Torpedo onions are spindle-shaped purple onions; "red" onions may be used as a substitute. Savoy cabbage, however, has no substitute. Its flavor is milder than regular cabbage and it works perfectly with pheasant or other poultry.

1 clove garlic, peeled and sliced

1½ teaspoons salt

¾ teaspoon freshly ground black
    pepper

½ teaspoon dried juniper berries
    (6 to 8)

¼ teaspoon dried whole
    thyme leaves

1 tablespoon olive oil

4 pheasant leg-thigh combinations

1 pound torpedo onions, peeled and
    sliced ¼ inch thick

2 tablespoons cider vinegar

1 teaspoon sugar

1 pound savoy cabbage, cut into
    1-inch pieces

1 apple, such as Braeburn, peeled,
    cored, and shredded

¼ cup dry white French vermouth

½ cup chicken stock (page 5)

1. Using a mortar and pestle, crush the garlic, 1 teaspoon of the salt, ½ teaspoon of the pepper, the juniper berries, and thyme together, pounding them to a paste. Add the olive oil and work it in to form a pasty mixture. Rub over the pheasant, then cover and refrigerate several hours or overnight.

2. Adjust an oven rack to the center position and preheat the oven to 350°.

3. Place the pheasant, skin side down, in a large, ungreased ovenproof heavy skillet (cast iron works best) and set over medium-low heat. Cook the pheasant slowly on one side about 20 minutes, or until the skin is nicely browned. Remove and set aside. There should be about 2 tablespoons of fat in the pan; if not, make up the difference with olive oil. Add the onions, vinegar, and sugar to the pan. Raise heat to medium. Stir well and cook, covered, for 10 minutes. Add the cabbage, apple, remaining ½ teaspoon salt, remaining ¼ teaspoon pepper, vermouth, and stock and stir several minutes until the cabbage is wilted. Return the pheasant to the pan, placing the pieces skin side up on top of the vegetable mixture. Cover tightly and bake 1½ hours. The pheasant should be completely tender. If the cabbage mixture is soupy at the end of baking, set the skillet over high heat and boil rapidly until the juices are reduced and slightly syrupy. Adjust the seasoning with salt and pepper, if desired.

4. To serve, spoon the cabbage mixture onto 4 heated dinner plates and set the pheasant, skin side up, on top. Spoon pan juices over the pheasant and serve.

BUFFALO BURGERS WITH THYME IN TARRAGON CREAM SAUCE

This may be gilding the lily, but it works. The creamy tarragon-flavored sauce makes this dish suitable for company.

3 tablespoons corn oil

2 cups finely chopped sweet yellow onions

2 pounds ground buffalo

1 teaspoon salt

1 teaspoon freshly ground black pepper

2 teaspoons minced fresh thyme

2 eggs

Unbleached all-purpose flour, for coating

1/3 cup dry white French vermouth

1/2 cup rich beef stock (pages 6–7)

1 cup whipping or heavy cream

3 tablespoons minced fresh tarragon leaves

1/2 teaspoon freshly squeezed lemon juice, plus more if needed

Salt and freshly ground black pepper

1. Heat 1 tablespoon of the oil in a heavy 12-inch skillet over medium-high heat. Add the onion and stir to coat well with the oil. Cover the pan and reduce the heat to medium-low. Cook 5 to 8 minutes, until the onion is tender but not browned. Transfer onion to a large bowl, and set aside to cool slightly. Do not wash the skillet.

2. Add the buffalo, salt, pepper, thyme, and eggs to the bowl of onion and mix well with a wooden spoon. Shape the mixture into 6 patties about 3 1/2 inches in diameter and 1 inch thick. Place the flour on a large sheet of waxed paper and lightly coat 3 of the patties, dusting off any excess. (Do this just before cooking or the flour will become gummy.) Add 1 tablespoon of the oil to the pan used to cook the onion and set it over medium-high heat. When it is hot, add the coated patties, leaving 1 inch or so between them, and cook for 3 to 5 minutes per side. (Medium-rare patties take about 6 minutes total cooking time.) Transfer the cooked patties to a platter, cover and keep warm. Coat the remaining 3 patties in the flour and cook in remaining 1 tablespoon oil. Cover and keep warm.

3. Pour off the cooking fat, but leave any browned bits of meat in the skillet. Add the vermouth and stock to the pan and set it over high heat. Bring to a boil, scraping the bottom of the pan with a wooden spoon to dislodge the browned bits. Boil rapidly until the liquid is reduced by about half. Add the cream and tarragon and continue boiling another minute or so, stirring continuously, until the sauce is thick enough to lightly coat a spoon. Remove the pan from the heat and stir in the lemon juice. Adjust seasoning with more lemon juice and salt and pepper, if desired. Spoon the sauce over the patties and serve immediately.

Paunch Cooking

Before emigrants came to the Great Plains with their metal pots, and began to trade with the Native Americans, the tribes used makeshift cooking vessels. They had an ingenious system of using the stomachs of buffalo and other large game animals for this purpose. After washing out the stomach, they created a scaffold for it by driving sticks into the ground. The stomach was supported on this structure and water and chunks of raw meat were added to it.

Meanwhile, clean, smooth stream-bed rocks were heated in a fire. When the rocks were sizzling hot, they were carefully added, one by one, to the paunch.

After a half dozen or so of these rocks were in the paunch, the heat was sufficient to begin cooking the meat. As the rocks in the paunch cooled, they were removed and replaced with hot rocks from the fire. Wild onions, turnips, dried corn, or other vegetables were also added if available. In this way, soups and stews were cooked for hours, until the meat was very tender. After the contents of the paunch were consumed, the stomach was cut up and eaten as well. According to Western food historian Sam Arnold, eating the paunch meat was "rather like chewing on a tough car inner tube."

VENISON CHILI WITH SINGAPORE HOT SAUCE

This is a colorful and spicy chili with flecks of green and red in a reddish-brown sauce. The hot sauce I use is made in Singapore, hence the recipe's name. Buffalo meat is equally good in this dish.

2½ pounds venison stew meat, trimmed and cut into ¾-inch cubes

2 tablespoons corn oil

1 cup chopped red bell pepper

1 cup chopped green bell pepper

½ cup chopped, seeded poblano chiles

2 cups chopped sweet yellow onions

6 cloves garlic, finely chopped

1 teaspoon sweet paprika

1 teaspoon ground coriander

1½ teaspoons ground cumin

1 tablespoon chile powder

1 teaspoon fennel seed

½ teaspoon salt

1 teaspoon freshly ground black pepper

1 (14½- to 16-ounce) can peeled crushed tomatoes with juices

12 ounces dark beer

¼ to ½ cup Yeo's Hot Chili Sauce (or use any hot chili sauce)

1. Pat the venison dry with paper towels. Heat the oil in a 12-inch-wide, 3-inch-deep sauté pan over medium-high heat. Add the venison and brown on all sides, about 5 minutes. Add the red and green bell peppers, poblano chiles, onions, and garlic. Stir well, cover, and cook 10 minutes, stirring occasionally. Add the paprika, coriander, cumin, chile powder, fennel, salt, and pepper and cook 1 minute, stirring continuously.

2. Add the tomatoes and juices, beer, and hot sauce (use ½ cup if you like spicy chili). Bring the mixture to a simmer and cover the pan. Reduce heat to low and cook slowly until the meat is very tender and the sauce is slightly thickened, 1½ to 2 hours. If the sauce seems too thin, cook, uncovered, 10 to 15 minutes more. Serve hot.

POULTRY

In nineteenth-century Montana, chickens were raised on every homestead or farm. The animals took care of themselves, roaming around the yard scratching for seeds and insects. Their eggs provided the household with a ready source of protein, and the Sunday supper of roasted chicken was something the whole family looked forward to.

Today, most commercial chickens are grown in crowded cages in huge buildings and never see the light of day. Fortunately, free-range chickens, which are often available in health food stores and at some supermarket butcher counters, offer an alternative to these "factory" farm birds. Many people believe the free-range birds are juicier and taste better than their cage-raised counterparts, but I think a more important consideration is showing respect for the animals that feed us by raising them humanely.

In this chapter, you'll also find recipes for ostrich, duck, turkey, and quail. In general, poultry dishes can be flavored with delicate or robust ingredients without overpowering the distinctive taste of the meats. It's this versatility that has helped make all kinds of poultry favorites with Montana cooks and their families.

OSTRICH STEAKS WITH GREEN PEPPERCORN SAUCE, SHIITAKES, AND BRAISED SHALLOTS

YIELD: 6 SERVINGS

Ostriches are raised in many parts of Montana and they are justly praised for their great-tasting meat. When I first tried ostrich, I couldn't believe I was eating a bird: It tasted like prime-quality beef. The raw flesh has a deep purple-red color, similar in appearance to venison or bear. The meat is lean and extremely low in fat, yet it cooks up so tender you can cut it with a fork. For best results, serve rare to medium rare.

There are three grades of ostrich meats, defined by the tenderness of the cuts. Prime Cuts consist of the 5 tenderest muscles: top loin, tenderloin, inside strip, outside strip, and fan fillet. All are suitable for dry heat cooking such as roasting, broiling, or pan frying. Choice Cuts come from the tip, oyster, and round muscles of the back. They are good for roasting, grilling, fajitas, stir frying, or as kabobs. Select Cuts, the inside and outside drum muscles from the leg, are the least tender. They're good to grind up as ostrich burger. For more information, visit http://bigbirdusa.com/ostmeat.php3.

Ostrich is commonly sold frozen. Consequently, when you thaw and pat the meat dry, it will weigh several ounces less. You'll need close to 1¾ pounds of thawed ostrich for this recipe. It needs no trimming, except for removing a thin membrane on the outside, and is ideally suited to cutting into thin steaks (see pages 236–237 for mail-order sources). Any of the prime cut muscles are suitable for this recipe.

Serve small portions with a full-flavored sauce made from rich beef stock (pages 6–7) accented by a fine wine. The green peppercorns add a piquancy that rounds out the meat's sweet, clean taste.

Braised Shallots

1 tablespoon butter

12 large shallots, peeled

Salt and freshly ground black pepper

¼ cup rich beef stock (pages 6–7)

¼ cup dry white French vermouth

4 sprigs fresh thyme

Shiitake Mushrooms

½ pound fresh shiitake mushrooms

1 tablespoon butter

Salt and freshly ground black pepper to taste

Ostrich Steaks with Green Peppercorn Sauce

2 pounds (frozen weight) ostrich meat, thawed

Salt and freshly ground black pepper

3 tablespoons corn oil

3 tablespoons finely chopped shallots

1 cup rich beef stock (pages 6–7)

½ cup pinot noir

2 tablespoons water-packed green peppercorns, drained and patted dry

3 tablespoons butter

1 tablespoon chopped fresh thyme

1. For the shallots, adjust an oven rack to the center position and preheat the oven to 350°. Melt the butter in an ovenproof 10-inch skillet over medium-high heat and add the shallots. Cook, shaking the pan frequently, until the shallots are golden brown in a few spots, about 8 minutes. Season with salt and pepper and add the beef stock and vermouth. Bring the mixture to a boil and cook for 1 minute, shaking the pan occasionally. Add the thyme sprigs and cover the pan. Bake for about 45 minutes, or until the shallots are very tender. (The shallots may be made hours ahead and set aside. Reheat in the oven or over low heat before serving.)

2. To prepare the mushrooms, remove the stems and save them to flavor soups or stocks. Slice the caps thinly. Melt the butter in a 10-inch skillet over medium-high heat. Add the mushrooms, salt, and pepper. Toss and cook until the mushrooms are lightly browned and tender, 2 to 3 minutes.

3. Pat the meat dry with paper towels and cut it at an angle to make steaks about $\frac{1}{2}$ inch thick. You should have about 18 small steaks or scallops. Cover and refrigerate until ready to cook. Just before cooking, pat the steaks dry again with paper towels and sprinkle both sides lightly with salt and pepper. Heat the corn oil in a 12-inch skillet over medium-high heat and add half of the ostrich steaks. Cook briefly, 1 minute on each side. Set the cooked meat aside while you cook the remaining ostrich, then cover it all loosely and keep warm while you make the sauce.

4. Pour off the fat remaining in the skillet, leaving the browned bits in the pan. Add the chopped shallots to the pan and stir with a wooden spoon, scraping the bottom of the pan to dislodge any browned bits. Return the pan to medium-high heat and add the beef stock and wine. Cook briskly to reduce the sauce by about one-third. Strain the sauce and discard the chopped shallots.

5. Return the sauce to the skillet and add the green peppercorns. Mash the peppercorns into the sauce and return the pan to medium heat. Add any juices that have drained from the ostrich to the pan. Bring the sauce to a boil and swirl in the butter. When the butter is incorporated, add the mushrooms. Adjust the seasoning to taste with salt and pepper. Add the ostrich to the pan to reheat and baste it with the sauce. Sprinkle the chopped thyme over the ostrich. Serve immediately on heated dinner plates with two braised shallots accompanying each serving.

ROASTED HAZELNUT-MARINATED OSTRICH WITH GARLIC CHIVE SAUCE

YIELD: 4 SERVINGS

Make this for a special meal. You'll need a large, tender muscle, with no fibers or membrane, preferably the tenderloin or top loin. The meat marinates in a mixture of hazelnut and corn oils and vermouth for several hours. It is roasted quickly in a very hot oven and served with a sauce made from the browned bits in the roasting pan, rich beef stock, vermouth, and garlic chives. Be sure not to overcook the meat. It should be a nice reddish pink, or medium-rare, throughout. Tomatoes Stuffed with Fresh Herbs and Bread Crumbs (page 188) and steamed asparagus are perfect accompaniments.

1¾ to 2 pounds (frozen weight)
    ostrich roast, thawed

¼ cup plus 1 tablespoon hazelnut oil

¼ cup corn oil

3 cloves garlic, finely chopped

1 sweet yellow onion, thinly sliced

½ plus ⅓ cup dry white
    French vermouth

½ teaspoon salt

½ teaspoon freshly ground
    black pepper

1 tablespoon finely chopped
    fresh rosemary

⅔ cup rich beef stock (pages 6–7)

2 tablespoons butter

3 tablespoons finely chopped fresh
    garlic chives

Salt and freshly ground black pepper
    to taste

1. Drain the roast and pat dry with paper towels. Combine ¼ cup of the hazelnut oil, the corn oil, garlic, onion, ½ cup of the vermouth, the salt, pepper, and rosemary in an airtight plastic bag. Add the ostrich, seal the bag, and marinate for 6 to 8 hours in the refrigerator. While it marinates, turn the bag 3 or 4 times to redistribute the marinade. When ready to cook, adjust an oven rack to the center position and preheat the oven to 450°. Remove the ostrich from the marinade and pat it dry with paper towels. Place the ostrich in a small roasting pan and rub the roast all over with the remaining 1 tablespoon of hazelnut oil. Roast for 20 to 25 minutes, or until the meat reaches an internal temperature of 130°. Transfer the ostrich to a platter, cover, and keep warm while you make the sauce.

2. Add the beef stock and the remaining ⅓ cup vermouth to the roasting pan. Set the pan over medium-high heat and scrape the bottom of the pan with a wooden spoon to dislodge any browned bits. Boil the mixture until it is reduced by almost half. Swirl in the butter. When the butter is melted, remove the pan from heat and add the garlic chives and salt and pepper to taste. Slice the ostrich into ¼-inch slices, arrange it on heated plates, and spoon the sauce over the meat. Serve immediately.

Big Bird Ranching

Ostrich—the largest bird on earth—is the West's newest livestock species. It is being bred and raised for meat, leather, and feathers all over the United States, including Montana. The birds grow quickly and are slaughtered when they are 12 to 14 months old. They weigh between 230 and 275 pounds at processing, and each bird yields about 75 pounds of meat.

When ordering ostrich, be sure to tell the supplier what you are going to use the meat for. That way, you'll get what you need.

TWICE-MORELED CHICKEN BREASTS WITH SAGE

This recipe confirms the theory that there can never be too much of a good thing. If morels are unavailable chanterelles or porcini mushrooms would also be terrific.

2 tablespoons butter

1 yellow onion, coarsely chopped

2 cloves garlic, coarsely chopped

¾ pound fresh morel mushrooms

4 boneless and skinless chicken
    breast halves (5 to 6 ounces each)

Salt and freshly ground black pepper

24 fresh sage leaves

Unbleached all-purpose flour,
    for coating

1 egg

1 tablespoon water

1 cup fresh fine bread crumbs, made
    from day-old French or Italian
    bread, trimmed of crusts

½ cup freshly grated Parmesan
    cheese

3 tablespoons clarified butter
    (page 2)

2 tablespoons extra-virgin olive oil

¼ cup minced shallots

⅓ cup dry white French vermouth

½ cup rich chicken stock (page 5)

1 tablespoon finely chopped fresh
    sage leaves

½ teaspoon freshly squeezed lemon
    juice, plus more if needed

1. Melt the 2 tablespoons of butter in a 10-inch skillet over medium heat. Stir in the onion and garlic and cook for 5 minutes, or until they are tender but not browned. Coarsely chop one-third of the morels and add them to the skillet. Continue cooking about 5 minutes, stirring occasionally, until the mushrooms are completely tender and almost no liquid remains in the pan. Cool.

2. Remove the thin strip of breast meat from the underside of each half breast. Cut away and discard the tough white tendon from each piece. Cut the strips of chicken into 1-inch pieces and place in the work bowl of a food processor with the metal blade in place. Pulse 4 times. Add the cooled morel mixture, ½ teaspoon salt, and ¼ teaspoon pepper. Pulse about 6 times to chop everything evenly and to combine well.

3. Place each chicken breast half between sheets of plastic wrap and flatten the thicker parts slightly so that the meat is of uniform thickness, about ½ to ¾ inches throughout. Lightly salt and pepper both sides of the chicken and place the side that the skin was attached to down on plastic wrap. Arrange 6 sage leaves along the length of each piece of chicken and cover each with one-quarter of the mushroom mixture, flattening it into a thin even layer with your fingertips. Press firmly so the mixture adheres to the chicken. Cover loosely with plastic wrap and refrigerate 30 minutes.

4. Place the flour on a sheet of waxed paper and lightly coat the chicken with a thin layer of flour. Dust off excess. Beat the egg and water together in a shallow dish to combine well. In another shallow dish, mix together the bread crumbs and Parmesan cheese. Dip each piece of chicken into the egg mixture then coat with a thin layer of the crumb mixture, patting the crumbs gently to help them adhere. Place the chicken, mushroom side up, onto a rack set over a tray and refrigerate, uncovered, until ready to cook. (The recipe may be made several hours ahead up to this point.)

5. Melt the clarified butter in a 12-inch skillet over medium-high heat. When the butter is hot, add the chicken breasts, mushroom side down, and cook 3 to 4 minutes. Turn and cook the second side until the chicken is cooked and feels springy when pressed, about another 3 or 4 minutes. Transfer to a plate. Cover and keep warm while you make the morel sauce.

6. If the remaining morels are large, cut them into 1-inch pieces. If they are small, leave them whole. Heat the olive oil over medium-high heat in the same skillet the chicken was cooked in. Add the shallots and cook, stirring, about 30 seconds. Add the remaining morels and cook, stirring, about 5 minutes, until tender. Add ½ teaspoon salt, ⅛ teaspoon pepper, and the vermouth. Cook and stir until the liquid has almost completely evaporated. Add the chicken stock and chopped sage and cook briefly until the sauce is slightly reduced and has thickened a bit. Add the lemon juice and taste the sauce. Add more lemon juice, salt, or pepper, if desired. To serve, place the chicken, mushroom side up, on dinner plates, and spoon the morels and sauce on top.

CHANTERELLE-STUFFED CHICKEN BREASTS

This is a favorite of mine when the first chanterelles make their appearance in spring. If there is an abundant supply of them, I cook and freeze the golden mushrooms (page 10–11) to use later in the year. Perfect accompaniments are crisp fried potatoes and steamed spinach.

4 tablespoons butter

2 large shallots, minced

½ pound chanterelle mushrooms,
     minced

½ teaspoon salt

¼ teaspoon freshly ground black
     pepper

5 tablespoons cognac

½ cup chicken stock (page 5)

2 tablespoons minced fresh parsley

4 boneless and skinless chicken
     breast halves (5 to 6 ounces each)

2 tablespoons vegetable oil

Unbleached all-purpose flour, for
     coating

½ teaspoon freshly squeezed lemon
     juice, or more to taste

Additional salt and freshly ground
     pepper to taste

1. Melt 2 tablespoons of the butter in a large skillet over medium-high heat. When the butter is hot, add the shallots and mushrooms. Toss and stir the mixture almost continuously with a wooden spoon for several minutes until the chanterelles are cooked and lightly browned. The mixture will be pasty; use the spoon to break it up. Add the salt and pepper, 3 tablespoons of the cognac, and 2 tablespoons of the chicken stock. Cook 1 to 2 minutes over medium-high heat, stirring with the wooden spoon until the liquid evaporates. Remove the pan from the heat and stir in 1 tablespoon of the parsley. The mushroom mixture should hold together.

2. Using a sharp knife, make deep horizontal cuts in the breast halves, and stuff each with the mushroom mixture. Cover and refrigerate. (The recipe may be made hours ahead up to this point.)

3. When ready to cook, adjust an oven rack to the center position and preheat the oven to 400°. Heat the remaining 2 tablespoons butter and the oil in an ovenproof 12-inch skillet over medium-high heat. Place the flour on a sheet of waxed paper and lightly coat each piece of chicken with flour, dusting off the excess. When the butter foam begins to subside, add the chicken to the skillet and cook over high heat for about 1 minute on each side to brown lightly. Cover the chicken loosely with a round piece of waxed paper that just fits inside of the skillet and place the pan in the oven. Bake 8 to 10 minutes, or until the chicken is just springy to the touch. Don't overcook. Remove the chicken from the pan, cover, and keep warm while you make the sauce.

4. To make the sauce, add the remaining 6 tablespoons chicken stock and 2 tablespoons cognac to the skillet and boil over high heat while swirling the mixture until it is syrupy. (This happens quickly.) Remove the pan from the heat and add the lemon juice and remaining 1 tablespoon of parsley. Adjust seasoning to taste with more lemon juice and salt and pepper, if desired. The sauce should not have a pronounced lemon taste; it should just have an edge of tanginess. To serve, place chicken on heated dinner plates and spoon the sauce over. There will just be enough sauce to coat the chicken lightly. Serve immediately.

Son-of-a-Bitch Stew

"Sometimes when we slaughtered for meat I'd make something called son-of-a-bitch stew. The main thing that went in the stew was the marrow gut, the tube connecting the young cow's two stomachs. It's got to be free of grass or the taste isn't right. First I cut the marrow gut into small pieces, about 2 inches long, dredged them in some flour seasoned with salt and pepper, and then fried the pieces in beef suet or lard in a Dutch oven until crisp. Next I chopped up the heart, kidneys, sweetbreads, and brains. After dredging those pieces in flour I added them to fry with the marrow gut so that everything was cooked crisp. Then I added enough water to cover everything. All of this was cooked until tender. You can't believe how good this tastes. Some of the hands used to squabble over pieces of kidneys and brains! They'd never eaten kidneys cooked any other way."

—Tony Grace, on his days as a chuck wagon cook, beginning in 1913

ROASTED DUCK WITH SWEET MARSALA AND BALSAMIC VINEGAR

YIELD: 4 SERVINGS

Duck is a delicious but fatty meat. The best way to coax the fat out of it is to steam the bird before roasting. When brushed with a sweet-sour mixture of sweet marsala, balsamic vinegar, sugar, and herbs, the duck takes on a beautiful mahogany color and its skin will be crisp and virtually fat-free. The meat will be so succulent that no sauce is necessary. Serve it with Roasted Garlic Mashed Potatoes (page 192) and lightly buttered steamed green beans with summer savory. You will need a large canning kettle or an oval roasting pan with a lid.

1 (5-pound) Pekin duck

1 lemon, cut in half

1 teaspoon kosher salt

¼ cup sweet marsala wine

½ cup balsamic vinegar

2 tablespoons sugar

½ teaspoon dried whole
    oregano leaves

¼ teaspoon dried whole
    thyme leaves

¼ teaspoon salt

¼ teaspoon freshly ground
    black pepper

2 unpeeled cloves garlic, sliced

1 tablespoon olive oil

8 sprigs fresh oregano

8 sprigs fresh thyme

1. Remove excess fat from the body cavity and under the neck skin of the duck with your fingers. If there is a large flap of neck skin, leave it attached. Chop off the wing joints so that there is only one attached to each side of the body. Save the bones for duck stock (page 8). To make carving the bird easier, there are three simple steps to perform. Remove the wishbone with a small sharp knife and add it to the wing bones. Locate the joints at which the wings join the body and sever the tendons. Finally, grasp the thighs and bend them both toward the backbone until you hear a "snap," indicating that you have freed them from their joints. At this point, the duck will look quite floppy. Rinse the bird inside and out under running water. Shake off excess water and pat the skin and cavity dry with paper towels. Squeeze the cut half of lemon all over the skin, rubbing the juice in, and squeeze some juice into the cavity. Sprinkle the skin and cavity with the kosher salt and insert both lemon halves in the cavity.

2. To prepare the steamer, place about 2 inches of water into a canning kettle or oval roaster. Set the ring of a springform pan into the kettle or use several empty cans opened at both ends to act as support for a rack. Set a wire rack directly on the springform ring or cans. Place the duck breast side up on the rack, cover the pan, and bring the water to a boil over high heat. Cook for 30 minutes. Carefully turn over the duck, allowing the juices in the body cavity to drain into the liquid below, and steam for another 30 minutes. You'll notice the bird has firmed up and can be turned easily with potholders. Try not to tear the skin. During steaming, fat will melt out of the duck skin and some duck juices will flavor the boiling water; when defatted, this liquid can be used as a base for duck stock or soup.

3. While the duck is steaming, prepare the basting mixture. In a small saucepan, combine the marsala, balsamic vinegar, sugar, oregano, thyme, salt, pepper, and garlic. Bring to a boil and cook, stirring occasionally, for several minutes, until the liquid is reduced to about $1/2$ cup. You can tell when that point is reached because the mixture will bubble up near the top of the pan. Strain and discard solids. Stir in the olive oil and set the mixture aside to cool. When the duck is ready, remove it from the steamer and let it cool for a few minutes.

4. Adjust an oven rack to the lower-third position and preheat the oven to 375°. Remove the lemon from the duck and insert the oregano and thyme sprigs in the cavity. Place the duck, breast side down, in a 13x9x2-inch pan and baste it all over with some of the marsala mixture. Cook for 20 minutes, brushing the back and sides with a little more of the mixture after 10 minutes. Turn the duck breast side up and brush it with the basting liquid. Return the duck to the oven and cook for another 30 minutes, brushing it with the marsala mixture two more times at 10-minute intervals, using up the basting mixture. When cooked, the duck will be a rich mahogany color. The meat will be juicy and practically fall off the bone. Let the duck rest in the roasting pan 10 minutes before carving.

Note: Although the duck needs no sauce, you could spoon some of the defatted duck juices over the portions before serving. Save all bones, including the carcass, and add them to the bones you've already saved for duck stock. Leftover duck is excellent in salads.

ASIAN-STYLE MARINATED SMOKED DUCK

In this recipe, duck breasts and thighs are given a dry rub with a homemade version of Chinese five-spice powder and refrigerated overnight. The next day, the duck is steamed to partially cook it and to remove excess fat. After cooling, the duck is marinated in a hoisin sauce mixture and then roasted in the oven over a water bath to make it tender and moist. The cooked marinade is excellent spooned over the duck and it is especially good with steamed broccoli. All of the Asian ingredients are available in most supermarkets and in Chinese markets.

Dry Rub

2 tablespoons Sichuan peppercorns

4 whole star anise

2 teaspoons fennel seed

1 teaspoon ground ginger

1 teaspoon ground cinnamon

½ teaspoon ground cloves

2 teaspoons salt

4 whole Pekin duck breasts, with skin

4 Pekin duck thighs, with skin

Marinade

¾ cup strained freshly squeezed
   orange juice

¾ cup dry sherry wine

2 tablespoons coarsely chopped
   garlic

2 tablespoons dark sesame oil

2 tablespoons corn oil

⅔ cup hoisin sauce

⅓ cup water

1. Place the Sichuan peppercorns in a small, heavy skillet (cast iron or enamelware is ideal) and set the pan over medium heat. Stir occasionally for about 5 minutes, until the peppercorns are aromatic. Do not burn them. Cool the peppercorns and pulverize them in a spice mill or with a mortar and pestle. Pass the peppercorns through a coarse strainer to remove the larger pieces; place the strained peppercorns in a small bowl. Crush the star anise with a mortar and pestle and add them to the Szechwan pepper. Crush the fennel seed and combine it with the peppercorns and star anise. Stir in the ginger, cinnamon, cloves, and salt. You will have about 3 tablespoons of spice rub. Use all of it to coat both sides of the duck breasts and thighs. Rub the spice into the skin and flesh with your fingertips. Cover and refrigerate overnight.

2. The next day, set up a steamer and rack as described on page 130. Steam the duck pieces, skin side down, by placing the thighs on the rack about 2 inches above boiling water. After about 15 minutes, add the breast pieces and steam 30 minutes. Remove the duck and let the pieces cool.

3. For the marinade, combine all of the ingredients in a medium-size bowl. Place the steamed duck in a glass dish measuring 12 x 8 x 2 inches and pour in the marinade. Turn the pieces of duck to coat well and marinate, covered, for 2 to 4 hours in the refrigerator. Turn the pieces two or three times during the marination. If you're not going to cook the duck directly after marinating, remove the pieces from the marinade and refrigerate, covered, for up to 2 days. Refrigerate the marinade.

4. When ready to serve the duck, adjust an oven rack to the center position and preheat the oven to 375°. Pour about $1/2$ inch of boiling water into a 13x9x2-inch baking dish and set a rack over the top. Arrange the duck pieces skin side up on the rack and carefully transfer the pan to the oven. Bake for 1 hour, or until the skin is a deep brown color and the duck is very tender. While the duck cooks, strain the marinade and boil it in a small saucepan for 5 minutes, until it has reduced in volume and is slightly thickened. Pour into a small bowl and serve with the duck.

ROASTED ALMOST BONELESS TURKEY WITH PORK, TURKEY, AND PINE NUT STUFFING

YIELD: 10 TO 12 SERVINGS

Years ago I watched Julia Child bone a turkey, stuff it with a savory filling, and roast it. When she served it, there was no hassle carving the bird. She simply cut it crosswise and placed gorgeous slices on dinner plates. Years later I decided to do a similar recipe on my local television show, Big Sky Cooking, as a Thanksgiving special. I had the camera aimed over my shoulder so that viewers would get a cook's-eye view of the procedure. I also opted to do the boning in one continuous step without stopping. Since this was a half-hour show, I had about 10 minutes to accomplish what I needed to. We worked with only one camera, so cutting to different views was not possible. The producer kept a close eye on the time and kept signaling me to speed up. I was out of breath by the time I finished, but the deed was done and the viewers saw that it was possible to bone a turkey without spending a lot of time. I received more comments from that program than any other I have ever done. Men were particularly enchanted with the idea, and many stopped me in grocery stores and on the street to tell me how they adapted the recipe to suit their tastes.

If you can get a farm-raised turkey, or one of the heirloom breeds so popular today, your results will be superior to a conventional commercial bird. When prepared in the following way, the turkey and stuffing are so juicy you don't really need a sauce, except perhaps for some lightly seasoned rich chicken or turkey stock flavored with a bit of wine. If you've never done something like this before, think of it as a culinary adventure and proceed with courage and confidence. Leftovers are excellent thinly sliced and served cold with mustard and cornichons (small pickles).

1 (10-pound) turkey

Salt and freshly ground black pepper

1½ pounds ground pork

1½ pounds lean ground turkey

2 teaspoons salt

1 teaspoon freshly ground
    black pepper

1 tablespoon chopped fresh thyme

2 tablespoons chopped fresh oregano

2 tablespoons chopped fresh
    garlic chives

½ teaspoon ground allspice

3 eggs

⅓ cup cognac

1 teaspoon olive oil

½ cup pine nuts

2 cups cooked diced carrots

2 cups rich chicken or turkey stock (page 5)

⅓ cup dry white French vermouth

Salt and freshly ground black pepper, to taste

134 :: MONTANA COOKING

1. Remove the giblets from the turkey and pull away any lumps of fat from the body cavity. If using a frozen turkey, thaw it in its wrapping in the refrigerator for 2 or 3 days before proceeding with the recipe.

2. Turn the turkey so that its back is facing up. With a sharp boning knife (it's very important that your knife is sharp and has a fairly short, stiff blade), make a slit down the back of the turkey from the neck to the tail to expose the backbone. Cut away the turkey meat on both sides of the backbone so that the rib cage is stripped of meat. Working on one side at a time, scrape and cut the flesh away from the carcass of the bird, always scraping against the bone to avoid tearing the flesh. As the meat comes away from the carcass, pull it aside with your fingers. Eventually you will reach the point where the upper wing bone is joined to the carcass by a ball joint. Cut through the joint and continue scraping the breast meat away from the breast bone until you reach the ridge of the breast where skin and bone meet. Stop here, and proceed to sever the thigh bone from its ball joint on the carcass. (This part always seems to take the longest, since the thigh bone is well connected to the carcass. Just take your time and be patient.) At this point, you've deboned half the bird. Repeat the steps on the other side, being careful not to cut through the skin at any point.

3. When you're done with the second side, the carcass frame will still be connected to the ridge of the breast bone. To sever this connection, lift the carcass frame from the tail end of the bird and place your knife edge tightly against the ridge of the breast bone. Moving the knife slowly in a forward direction toward the head end of the turkey, cut the carcass away from the turkey's flesh. You now have a turkey with wings and legs attached to a mass of flesh, which consists mostly of breast meat. With a large sharp knife, chop off the tips of the wings. Save them and the carcass to make a turkey stock. (Substitute turkey for chicken in the chicken stock recipe on page 5.) Wash and dry the deboned turkey and set it flesh side up in front of you. Remove the strips of meat that had been attached to the rib cage and carefully cut away the white tendon running through each. Set these meat strips (fillets) aside. Season the turkey lightly with salt and pepper.

4. To make the stuffing, place the ground pork and ground turkey, salt, pepper, thyme, oregano, garlic chives, allspice, eggs, and cognac in a large bowl. Beat well with a wooden spoon or mix together with your hands until the ingredients are thoroughly combined. Heat the olive oil in a small heavy skillet over medium heat. Add the pine nuts and stir constantly until they turn a toasty brown color. Transfer them to a small bowl and set aside to cool. Mix the pine nuts and carrots into the stuffing. Pile about half the stuffing onto the center of the turkey and arrange the turkey strips on top. Cover with the remaining stuffing and pat the whole mass with your hands to form a loaf. Bring the turkey sides up over the loaf to cover the filling completely. Sew the two edges of skin together with a sharp needle and white twine or string. The best way to do this is to work from the tail toward the neck, looping the string through the skin as you move up the length of the bird. When you reach the end, secure the string to the skin with a tight knot. Turn the bird right side up. Push and pat the whole thing back into turkey shape. Secure the wings and legs to the turkey by encircling the bird 3 or 4 times with kitchen twine. The turkey is now ready to be roasted. (You can bone the turkey and prepare the stuffing a day ahead. Simply stuff the bird when you plan to roast it.)

5. Adjust an oven rack to the lower-third position and preheat the oven to 350°. Place the turkey on its side in a shallow roasting pan and cook for 30 minutes. Then turn the turkey onto its other side and roast another 30 minutes. Place the turkey breast side up and reduce the oven temperature to 325°. Continue roasting the turkey, basting it with the pan drippings every half hour or so, until an instant-read thermometer registers 180° when inserted in the center of the turkey. Total roasting time will be 4 to 4½ hours. When done, the turkey will be a beautiful rich brown color. Transfer the turkey to a serving platter and cover it loosely with aluminum foil to keep warm. Let the turkey rest 15 minutes before slicing into it. Meanwhile, pour off any fat remaining in the roasting pan, but do not discard the browned bits. Add the chicken or turkey stock to the pan along with the vermouth and set the pan over medium-high heat. Bring the mixture to a boil, scraping the bottom of the pan with a wooden spoon to dislodge any browned bits, and boil for 1 to 2 minutes. Adjust the seasoning with salt and pepper, if desired. Pass through a fine strainer and serve with the turkey.

TURKEY SCALLOPINI WITH LEMON AND VERMOUTH YIELD: 4 SERVINGS

Humanely raised veal is hard to come by where I live. But you don't have to use veal to get an almost identical taste. Craig Claiborne once called turkey "the great impostor," referring to its ability to trick the taste buds into thinking veal was being eaten. Now, whenever I make scallopini, I always use turkey. Fresh turkey is available year-round and is far cheaper than veal. If you can, buy a farm-raised turkey from a local supplier. That way you'll get far better meat and you'll have the satisfaction of knowing the birds were not cooped up in small cages with hardly any room to move. Serve this dish with steamed fresh green beans and Tomatoes Stuffed with Fresh Herbs and Bread Crumbs (page 188).

1¼ pounds boneless, skinless
  turkey breast

Salt and freshly ground black pepper

²/₃ cup flour

1 tablespoon olive oil

4 tablespoons butter

¼ cup dry white French vermouth

½ cup rich chicken stock (page 5)

2 tablespoons freshly squeezed
  lemon juice

Dash of Worcestershire sauce

1 tablespoon chopped flat-leaf
  parsley

1 lemon, thinly sliced, for garnish

1. With a sharp knife, cut the turkey crosswise into slices about ¼ inch thick at an angle. You should have 12 to 15 scallopini. Lightly season both sides of the turkey slices with salt and pepper. Place the flour on a piece of waxed paper or plastic wrap. Coat half the turkey slices on both sides with the flour. Do this just before cooking or the flour will get gummy. Leave the turkey resting in the flour momentarily while you heat the olive oil and 2 tablespoons of the butter in a 12-inch skillet over medium-high heat. When the butter foam begins to subside, quickly shake off the excess flour from the turkey slices and add them to the skillet without crowding. Cook about 1 minute on each side, until the turkey is very lightly browned and tender. While the first batch cooks, coat the remaining turkey with the flour. Transfer the cooked turkey to a plate, cover it loosely with foil, and set it aside in a warm place. Cook the remaining turkey and add it to the first batch. Cover and keep it warm while you make the sauce.

2. Pour off any fat remaining in the skillet, but leave the browned bits in the pan. Add the vermouth and chicken stock and set the pan over high heat; scrape the bottom of the pan with a wooden spoon to dislodge any browned bits as the liquid boils. When the liquid has reduced by about one-third, remove the pan from the heat and stir in the lemon juice, Worcestershire sauce, and the remaining 2 tablespoons of butter. Adjust the seasoning with salt and pepper, if desired. Place the turkey slices in the pan and set the pan over medium heat. Turn the scallopini and spoon sauce over them. When hot, sprinkle with the parsley and serve immediately. Garnish each serving with a few lemon slices.

BROILED QUAIL WITH DIJON MUSTARD AND TOASTED SOURDOUGH BREAD CRUMBS

YIELD: 4 SERVINGS

Much of the quail eaten today is farm raised, and the quality is excellent. You can order boneless quail with metal skewers strategically inserted to keep the birds flat as they cook (pages 236–237).

½ cup Dijon-style mustard

½ cup extra-virgin olive oil

2 shallots, finely chopped

½ cup dry white French vermouth

2 tablespoons chopped fresh thyme

1 teaspoon salt

½ teaspoon freshly ground
    black pepper

8 boneless quail

1 cup fresh fine sourdough bread
    crumbs, made from day-old
    sourdough bread, trimmed of
    crusts

2 tablespoons melted butter

1. Whisk together the mustard and olive oil in a medium-sized bowl. Stir in the shallots, vermouth, thyme, salt, and pepper, and combine well. Transfer the mixture to a 9-inch square glass baking dish. Add the quail, turning it to coat both sides. Cover and marinate for 2 hours or as long as overnight in the refrigerator.

2. When ready to cook, bring the quail to room temperature. Position an oven rack 5 to 6 inches from the broiler element and preheat the broiler. Line a shallow roasting pan with aluminum foil. Remove the quail from the marinade, leaving any marinade clinging to the quail. Set the quail about 1 inch apart on the foil. Broil 5 minutes, then turn the quail and broil another 5 minutes. Remove the pan from the broiler. Turn the quail again and spoon half of the remaining marinade evenly over the birds. (The recipe may be prepared hours in advance to this point and refrigerated.) Combine the bread crumbs and butter in a small bowl. Sprinkle about 2 tablespoons of the bread crumb mixture over each quail. Return the pan to the broiler and broil 2 to 3 minutes, or until the crumbs are nicely toasted. Turn the birds over, spoon the remaining marinade over them, and sprinkle evenly with the remaining crumb mixture. Return the quail to the oven and broil for another 2 to 3 minutes, until the crumbs are well-browned. Serve immediately.

FISH AND SEAFOOD

According to Montana Fish, Wildlife, and Parks, Montana has 56 native fish species, but some are battling for survival. Many of our state's most popular game fish are introduced—rainbow trout, brown trout, largemouth bass, and walleye—and attract fishermen from all over the country. Native cutthroat trout is one of our most coveted species. Fish hatcheries throughout Montana raise trout commercially, and they make fine eating. Our whitefish is prized for both its flesh and its golden roe. Sturgeon is another fine eating fish, and one of my very favorites. The recipes here showcase the best Montana has to offer.

STURGEON PROVENÇAL

Sturgeon interacts well with many different flavors. In this dish, salty olives and capers work with sweet onions, tomatoes, and bell peppers to bring out the sturgeon's rich taste. The fish's firm texture is a nice contrast to the vegetables and other ingredients in the sauce.

1½ pounds skinless sturgeon fillet, about 1 inch thick

Salt and freshly ground black pepper, to taste

Unbleached all-purpose flour, for coating

3 tablespoons extra-virgin olive oil

1 yellow bell pepper, cored, seeded, and cut into ½-inch pieces

½ cup thinly sliced sweet yellow onion

3 firm, ripe tomatoes, peeled, seeded, and coarsely chopped

2 cloves garlic, minced

½ cup fish stock (page 9)

½ cup dry white French vermouth

¼ cup pitted kalamata olives, coarsely chopped

2 tablespoons capers, rinsed and drained

1 cup loosely packed fresh basil leaves

1. Slice the sturgeon crosswise into twelve ¾-inch-thick pieces (2 ounces each). Lightly season both sides of the sturgeon pieces with salt and pepper and lightly coat each with flour. Do not season or flour the sturgeon until just before cooking.

2. Heat 1 tablespoon of the olive oil in a large nonstick skillet over medium-high heat until hot. Add the sturgeon pieces, shaking off the excess flour, and cook 1 to 2 minutes on each side until the fish is golden brown and just cooked. You may have to do this in batches to avoid crowding the fish. Add more oil, if necessary. Remove fish pieces as they are cooked and set them aside, cover, and keep warm.

3. To make the sauce, add the remaining 2 tablespoons of olive oil to the skillet and place over medium heat. When hot, stir in the bell pepper and onion. Cook 3 to 5 minutes, until semisoft, stirring occasionally. Add the tomatoes and garlic and cook another 5 to 8 minutes, stirring occasionally, until the pepper and onion are tender. Add the fish stock and vermouth. Raise the heat to high and cook for 1 to 2 minutes, or until the mixture is thickened and saucelike. Stir in the olives, capers, and basil and cook 1 to 2 minutes more. Taste and add salt and pepper, if desired. Divide the fish among 4 dinner plates and spoon the sauce over.

STURGEON WITH MOREL MUSHROOMS AND COGNAC   YIELD: 4 SERVINGS

I ate sturgeon many times as a child growing up in Shanghai, where it was one of the favorite zakuski, *or appetizers, of my father and his Russian friends. But the first time I had sturgeon in America was more than twenty years ago, when Andre Soltner prepared a dish for my wife and me at his legendary restaurant Lutece in New York City. He had just received some wild sturgeon from the Columbia River. During our meal, he stopped by our table to see how we had enjoyed the sturgeon, and I told him it was great. I particularly wanted to know how he made the sauce, since it had fresh caviar in it. "The sauce?" he said surprised. "What about the fish? Wasn't it fantastic?" At that moment, I learned it wouldn't have mattered how terrific the sauce was if the fish it was designed to complement wasn't of the highest quality.*

In the following dish, sturgeon plays the starring role. The sauce is a supporting player, helping to bring the fish's flavor to the fore. Oven-roasted potatoes are excellent with this.

*1½ pounds skinless sturgeon fillet,
     preferably of even thickness*

*Salt and freshly ground black pepper,
     to taste*

*Unbleached all-purpose flour, for
     coating*

*2 tablespoons corn oil, plus more if
     needed*

2 tablespoons finely chopped shallots

1 cup rich beef stock (pages 6–7)

¼ cup cognac

*¼ pound fresh morel mushrooms, left
     whole if small or cut into 1-inch
     pieces if large, or 1 ounce dried
     morel mushrooms, rehydrated in
     2 cups warm water then rinsed
     and cut into 1-inch pieces*

2 tablespoons butter

2 teaspoons chopped fresh thyme

1. Slice the sturgeon crosswise into twelve ¾-inch-thick pieces or 2-ounce sizes. Season the sturgeon pieces with salt and pepper lightly on both sides and coat each with a thin layer of flour. Do not season or flour the sturgeon until just before cooking.

2. In a large nonstick skillet, heat the oil over medium-high heat until hot. Add the sturgeon pieces, shaking off excess flour, and cook 1 to 2 minutes on each side until fish is golden brown and just cooked. Fry in batches to prevent crowding the pieces, adding more oil, if necessary. Remove the fish pieces from the pan and keep warm. Pour off any oil remaining in the skillet and remove from the heat.

3. Add the shallots and scrape the bottom of the pan with a wooden spoon to dislodge any browned bits. Return pan to medium heat and add the beef stock, cognac, and mushrooms. Cook briskly until the mushrooms are tender and the liquid is reduced by half. Add the butter and swirl the pan to combine it with the sauce. Stir in the thyme. Adjust the seasoning with salt and pepper, if desired. Return the sturgeon pieces to the pan and spoon the sauce over the fish. Cook very briefly, just to heat the fish through. There will only be about ⅔ cup sauce in the pan.

4. Serve immediately, placing **3** pieces of fish on each dinner plate, and spooning the mushrooms and sauce over the fish.

Sturgeon

Sturgeon live in the turbid waters of the Missouri and Yellowstone Rivers and their tributaries in the eastern part of Montana. Three species, the shovelnose, white, and pallid sturgeons, inhabit these waters. An ancient fish, the sturgeon has remained unchanged for 100 to 200 million years, and was practically fished to extinction by the late 1890s.

Sturgeon fishing is now severely restricted in Montana, but the fish is widely available from fish farms in California's Sacramento Valley. Sturgeon can grow to gargantuan size. According to *Sunset* magazine, the largest sturgeon on record was caught in 1912 in British Columbia and weighed 1,800 pounds! A sturgeon's lifespan is estimated at 100 years or more. It takes $3\frac{1}{2}$ to 4 years for these fish to reach 20 pounds, which is the size of most sold for our consumption.

Although sturgeon flesh is firm, moist, and delicious, most people associate sturgeon with caviar. It takes about 18 years for a female sturgeon in the wild to produce eggs. Farm-raised females can produce eggs in about 8 years, after they've attained a weight of about 100 pounds. At that age, considerable time and money have been invested in rearing and caring for the sturgeon. The monetary rewards for the caviar, not to mention the fish's fine eating quality, more than compensate the fish farmer.

STURGEON BURGERS

If you want to try something different that will wake up your taste buds, try this. Ground sturgeon makes excellent burgers because the fish cooks up juicy and tender. This recipe may be doubled or tripled successfully.

Burgers

1¼ pounds skinless sturgeon fillet

1 clove garlic, minced

1 teaspoon dark sesame oil

1 tablespoon minced Japanese pickled
    ginger (beni shoga)

¾ teaspoon salt

¼ teaspoon freshly ground
    black pepper

1 tablespoon dry sherry

Hoisin Mayonnaise

¼ cup mayonnaise

2 tablespoons hoisin sauce

1 tablespoon Dijon-style mustard

½ teaspoon freshly squeezed
    lemon juice

4 kaiser rolls, split and toasted

2 tablespoons corn oil

Arugula leaves or mixed baby lettuces

Thinly sliced tomatoes

Thinly sliced sweet onion or
    English cucumber

1. Cut the sturgeon into 1-inch strips and pass it through the fine die of a meat grinder or cut the sturgeon into small pieces and chop it on a cutting board until it is "ground," using a large, heavy, sharp knife. Do not use a food processor. Place the sturgeon in a mixing bowl and add the garlic, sesame oil, pickled ginger, salt, pepper, and sherry. Mix gently with a wooden or rubber spatula until thoroughly combined. Divide the mixture into 4 mounds and shape each into a 4-inch-diameter patty about ¾ inch thick. Wet your hands to shape the patties to prevent sticking, if necessary.

2. Whisk together the mayonnaise, hoisin sauce, mustard, and lemon juice in a small bowl. Toast the kaiser rolls and keep them warm.

3. Heat the corn oil in a large skillet over medium-high heat. When hot, add the patties. Cook 2 to 3 minutes on each side, or just until the fish is cooked through. Remove from the pan.

4. Spread Hoisin Mayonnaise on the tops and bottoms of the rolls, using all of the mixture. Place a few arugula leaves on the bottom of each roll, followed by tomato slices, sturgeon patties, and onion slices. Cover with the tops of the rolls. Serve immediately.

TROUT SCALLOPS

YIELD: 4 SERVINGS

We have many varieties of cold water river trout in Montana, and all make fine eating. But just about any kind of trout, including commercially available rainbow trout, is excellent in this dish. Just be sure to use large fish, so you'll be able to make "scallops" of the right size.

2 large whole trout, cleaned (about 1 pound each, dressed weight)

Unbleached all-purpose flour, for coating

3 tablespoons butter

2 tablespoons olive oil

⅓ cup finely chopped pitted niçoise or kalamata olives

2 tablespoons small capers, rinsed and drained

½ cup dry white wine or dry white French vermouth

2 tablespoons finely chopped fresh flat-leaf parsley

Salt and freshly ground black pepper to taste

1 lemon, cut into 4 wedges

1. To fillet the trout, lay the fish on its side on a work surface. With a sharp knife, make a cut behind the gill opening from the backbone down toward the belly. Turn the fish so that its back faces you. Make a long cut along the back from the gill opening to the tail, following the backbone closely as you cut. Press the knife against the bone and lift the flesh as you cut to make sure you're always following the backbone. When you get to the tail, cut from the back toward the belly side to release the fillet at that end. Lift the fillet away, and repeat the procedure on the other side of trout.

2. Each fillet will contain tiny bones called pin bones. Remove them with tweezers or with your fingernails. To skin each fillet, grasp it by the tail and make a small horizontal cut to separate the flesh from the skin. Now you'll have a piece of skin you can hold onto. As you hold onto the skin, work your knife, keeping it almost horizontal, along the length of the fillet from the tail end toward the head end, moving the knife from left to right as you move the skin right to left. Before you know it, the flesh will be free from the skin. Reserve the bones and skin for a fish stock (page 9).

3. To cut the fish into scallops, place each fillet so that it runs lengthwise from left to right on the work surface. Holding a sharp knife at an angle, cut each fillet into 3 scallops. (If not ready to use right away, cover and refrigerate for up to 1 day.)

4. Place the flour on a sheet of waxed paper. Heat 1 tablespoon of the butter and 1 tablespoon of the olive oil in a 12-inch skillet over medium-high heat until the butter foam begins to subside and the fat is very hot. Quickly dust half the trout scallops with the flour to coat lightly, shaking off the excess, and place the fish in the skillet. Cook only 1 to 2 minutes per side, or until the fish is just done. Adjust the heat if necessary so the cooking fat does not burn. Remove fish from the pan and keep warm. Repeat with the remaining trout, adding 1 tablespoon each of butter and olive oil to the pan before flouring and adding the fish. Set aside the cooked second batch of fish and keep warm.

5. To make the sauce, add the olives, capers, and wine to the pan. Boil the mixture, stirring, for about 30 seconds to thicken slightly. Add the remaining 1 tablespoon of butter and the parsley. Swirl the pan to combine everything well, add salt and pepper to taste, and return the trout to the pan. Spoon the sauce over the scallops; there will be just enough to coat the fish. Serve immediately with the lemon wedges, which should be squeezed over the fish before eating.

WHITEFISH FILLET ROULADES WITH WATERCRESS SAUCE

The firm texture and large size of whitefish fillets make them ideal for stuffing with a savory vegetable filling, but any firm-fleshed flatfish, such as sole, can be substituted as long as the fillets are 5 to 6 ounces. Peppery watercress leaves have been used in soups, salads, and sauces for centuries. Watercress grows wild in the damp spots of every state, including Alaska and Hawaii. (I find my watercress year-round alongside a nearby thermal spring.) To store, wash the leaves well, pat them dry, and keep in a plastic bag in the refrigerator, where they will keep for about 1 week. Serve steamed, lightly buttered small red potatoes or hot buttered rice with this dish.

4 (5- to 6-ounce) skinless, boneless whitefish fillets, thawed if frozen

1 large leek

1 large carrot, peeled

¼ cup butter

¼ teaspoon salt plus additional to taste

⅛ teaspoon freshly ground black pepper plus additional to taste

1 cup loosely packed watercress leaves, coarsely chopped

1 lemon, cut in half

2 large shallots, finely chopped

1 cup water

½ cup dry white French vermouth

1 tablespoon all-purpose flour

1. Rinse the whitefish fillets in cold water and pat them dry with paper towels. Remove any small bones.

2. Trim off the leek's root end and cut a 4-inch length, including the white part and some of the green. Cut the length crosswise into 2-inch pieces and then into ⅛-inch-thick strips (about 2 cups). Cut the carrot into 2-inch-long julienne (about 1 cup). Melt 2 tablespoons of the butter in a heavy ovenproof 10-inch skillet over medium-low heat. Add the leek, carrot, salt, and pepper. Stir well, and cover the pan. Cook about 10 minutes, stirring occasionally, until the vegetables are almost tender but not browned. Transfer the vegetables to a small bowl and set aside.

3. In a small saucepan, melt 1 tablespoon of the butter over medium heat. Add the watercress and cook 1 minute, stirring, just to wilt the watercress. Set aside.

4. Place the fish on a flat surface and squeeze lemon juice over both sides of the fillets, gently rubbing the juice into the fish with your fingertips. Season both sides of the fish with salt and pepper. With the side of the fillet that the skin was attached to facing you, spread each fillet with one-quarter of the leek-carrot mixture. Roll the fillets into cylinders. Sprinkle the shallots over the bottom of the skillet and set the fillets seam side down in the pan. (The recipe may be prepared hours ahead up to this point. Cover and refrigerate, then bring to room temperature about 1 hour before cooking.)

5. Adjust an oven rack to the lower-third position and preheat the oven to 350°. Pour the water and vermouth into the skillet. The liquid will come halfway up the fish rolls. Lightly butter a square of parchment paper and set the paper butter side down on the fish. Cover the pan and place it in the oven. Bake for 30 to 35 minutes, or until the fish is just cooked through and opaque when tested with the tip of a knife. Carefully remove the skillet lid and parchment paper. Slowly pour the liquid that has collected in the pan through a strainer set over a heavy 2- to 3-quart saucepan; there will be about 2 cups. Cover the fish in the skillet and keep warm.

6. Boil the fish cooking liquid over high heat until it is reduced to 1 cup. Melt the remaining 1 tablespoon butter in a small, heavy saucepan over medium heat. Whisk in the flour and stir continuously for 1 to 2 minutes, cooking the flour without browning it. Remove the pan from the heat and immediately add the reduced hot cooking liquid. Whisk well and return the sauce to medium-high heat. Cook, whisking continuously, for about 1 minute, or until the sauce is slightly thickened. Remove from the heat and stir in the watercress. Taste the sauce and adjust the seasoning with salt, pepper, and additional lemon juice, if necessary. Place the fillets on warm serving plates and spoon the watercress sauce over them, passing the remaining sauce at the table.

A Whitefish Story

Whitefish are found throughout Montana's mountain lakes and rivers and have always been popular, but not as popular as salmon. In an effort to please the sport fishermen and stimulate commercial salmon fishing, the Montana Department of Fish, Wildlife, and Parks attempted to increase the kokanee salmon population in the early 1980s by introducing mysis shrimp, a favorite kokanee food, into Montana's Flathead Lake, the largest freshwater lake west of the Mississippi. The theory was that if there were plenty of mysis shrimp for the kokanee to feed on, the salmon population would grown quickly.

The plan didn't work. Instead, the kokanee population plummeted over a period of years and remains quite low today. No one knows exactly why the project was unsuccessful, but one possible explanation is that the mysis shrimp and kokanee have different periods of activity. Mysis are active on the lake's surface at night. Kokanee, on the other hand, are active during the day.

In the mid-1980s, fishermen began landing lots of large whitefish in the lake. The fish weighed an average of 2 pounds, but some were almost 9 pounds, which was unheard of prior to that. Coincidentally, the hitch that prevented kokanee from feeding on the mysis shrimp may explain the whitefish boom. Whitefish are bottom feeders and typically eat small fry. As a result, the proliferation of mysis shrimp returning to the lake bottom every dawn was the equivalent of free food literally raining on the whitefish.

In 1991, Ron Mohn established Mountain Lake Fisheries at Columbia Falls, Montana, to process whitefish for sale to the public. Whitefish flesh is flavorful yet mild, but the bonus is the fish's caviar. The eggs have a beautiful apricot color and are mildly salty, with no fishy taste at all. The caviar has a surprisingly long freezer life of almost 2 years. Once thawed, the jars keep for 30 days in the refrigerator. Ron collects the fish in the Flathead River during their spawning run, which begins in late October or early November and lasts until mid-December. The fish is single-line caught by a crew of up to 70 fishermen. During a 6-week season, Mountain Lake Fisheries hauls in about 20,000 pounds of whitefish—roughly $\frac{1}{3}$ of 1 percent of the 6 million whitefish in Flathead Lake. Whitefish are virtually fat free and very high in protein. Mountain Lake Fisheries sells whitefish, caviar, and other products through the mail. See pages 236–237 for ordering information.

OUTDOOR COOKING

Cooking outdoors has existed since our ancestors first discovered fire. Wood provided the fuel, and the food could have been cooked on rocks or on a wooden spit. Before iron pots became available, pits dug into the earth itself served as vessels for the food. This ancient method is still used today by many cultures.

Today, camp stoves are an excellent option because they're portable and easy to use. But some outdoor cooks look upon such stoves with disdain, preferring instead to use wood, or wood charcoal briquettes, for fuel. A Dutch oven or cast-iron skillet are the preferred cooking vessels for the dedicated outdoor cook.

When I first camped, I must confess that I was a fan of the Coleman stove, and aluminum pots and pans were my cooking allies for many years. But once I tasted food cooked in a cast-iron pan over charcoal briquette coals, I discovered it tasted a lot better than food cooked over gas.

A Dutch oven allows you to cook just about anything, or even bake. The kind to have is one with "feet" on the bottom to set over coals and a lid with a depression to contain coals on top. Depending on your Dutch oven's size, each briquette adds between 10 and 20 degrees of heat. For an oven with a 10-inch diameter, for example, you'll need 8 to 10 briquettes on the bottom and 10 to 12 briquettes on top. For each 2-inch increase in the diameter of the Dutch oven, simply add 2 more briquettes to the top and bottom. Don't be tempted to add more or the food may burn. Cast-iron retains heat extremely well. Light the briquettes in a fire pit or in a chimney funnel with newspaper or a commercial fire starter cube. Never use lighter fuel because it gives foods an off taste. The briquettes are ready to use when they turn gray. Position briquettes carefully with tongs.

Once your Dutch oven is all set up with coals on the top and bottom, rotate the oven with oven mitts every 10 minutes or so to distribute the heat more evenly. If you also turn the lid a one-third rotation in the opposite direction, that also helps to keep the heat even. Happy cooking!

CAMPER'S OMELET

This makes a delicious and hearty breakfast. What makes it so good is the bacon and bacon fat. And if you're not camping, you can cook this on top of your stove at home.

½ pound sliced bacon

2 medium potatoes, unpeeled and
    diced ¼-inch (Yukon Gold is a
    good choice)

1 medium onion, chopped

½ green bell pepper, diced

6 large eggs, beaten fluffy with a
    whisk or rotary beater

Salt and pepper to taste

2 Roma tomatoes, sliced

8 ounces sharp cheddar cheese,
    shredded

1. Heat a 12-inch cast-iron skillet over 12 to 15 hot coals. Fry the bacon until crisp. Remove the bacon and pat dry on paper towels. Chop or crumble the bacon and set aside. Fry the diced potatoes in the bacon fat until tender and lightly browned, stirring occasionally. Add the onion and bell pepper. Cook, stirring occasionally, until the onion is cooked. Reduce the heat by moving the pan to the side of the firepit or turning down the campstove burner.

2. Season the beaten eggs with a little salt and pepper, keeping in mind that the cheese and bacon are salty. Pour in the eggs, give the contents of the pan a stir, and cook for 2 to 3 minutes, stirring gently. The eggs should be just set and moist looking. Sprinkle the cheese and bacon over the eggs and arrange the tomato slices on top. Cover the skillet for a minute or two until the cheese melts and the tomatoes are heated through. Cut into wedges and serve hot.

SPANISH RICE

3 tablespoons olive oil

1 green bell pepper, diced

6 garlic cloves, minced

1 (15-ounce) can crushed tomatoes,
    undrained

2 cups long-grain rice (converted rice
    is okay)

1 teaspoon salt

2½ cups water

⅛ teaspoon crushed saffron threads
    (optional)

Heat a 12-inch Dutch oven over 12 to 15 hot coals. Add the oil. When hot, add the green pepper and garlic. Cook, stirring occasionally, until the pepper is tender. Add the tomatoes with their juice. Cook 5 minutes more, stirring occasionally. Add the rice, salt, water, and saffron. Cook covered, at a simmer, 20 to 25 minutes, or until the rice has absorbed the liquid and is tender.

SOUTHWEST CHILI ROAST

YIELD: 6 SERVINGS

Roasting the ingredients on your outdoor grill gives this chili its full flavor and aroma for that great Montana taste. You'll need a blender or food processor to puree some of the vegetables, so this is a dish to cook outdoors at home. Total cooking time is 3 hours.

½ pound dried pinto beans

6 cups water

½ pound hamburger

½ pound bulk sausage

8 large New Mexico green chiles

1 large sweet yellow onion

Olive oil

8 cloves garlic, unpeeled

2 pounds Roma tomatoes

1 serrano chile

6 sprigs cilantro

1 lime, peeled of all skin and
　　white pith

2 tablespoons brown sugar

Salt and freshly ground black pepper
　　to taste

1. Heat sufficient charcoal briquettes to make a hot fire. Bring the beans and 3 cups of the water to the boil in a large Dutch oven. Move the pan slightly to one side of the coals so that the beans cook at a simmer. Cover the pot. While the beans cook, brown the hamburger and sausage in a cast-iron skillet over direct heat. Drain off the fat and add the meat to the cooking beans.

2. Roast the next five ingredients over hot coals. Adding hickory or mesquite wood chips during roasting will enhance the smoky flavor. Frequently turn the chiles on the grill until their skins are blistered and partially blackened. Put the chiles into a plastic bag and close tightly. Let the chiles rest while you roast the other vegetables.

3. To roast the onion, peel it, cut it into ¾-inch-thick slices, brush with olive oil, and set the onion directly onto the grill grate. Cook until the onion is just soft and has black grill marks, turning once. Roast the garlic in a skillet set on the grill grate, stirring occasionally, until the skins are light brown and the flesh soft, about 10 minutes. When cool, discard the skin. Frequently turn the tomatoes on the grill until their skins begin to crack and change color. When cool enough to handle, remove the tomato peels. Roast the serrano chile until the skin just begins to turn color. Discard the stem.

4. Remove the blackened skins, stems, and seeds from the green chiles. Coarsely chop the green chiles, onion, and tomatoes, and add one half of each of them to the beans. Put the remaining green chiles, onion, and tomatoes into a blender or food processor along with the garlic, serrano chile, cilantro, lime, brown sugar, and salt and pepper. Blend or process until thoroughly mixed and add to the beans. Add the remaining 3 cups of water and continue to simmer, covered, for a total cooking time of 3 hours from the time the beans were started.

GRILLED BUFFALO RIB-EYE STEAKS WITH ONION CONFIT

In this confit, onions are cooked with wine, vinegar, and a bit of sugar to make a tangy relish that goes especially well with mild, sweet-tasting game meat like buffalo. I recommend using Walla Walla sweet onions or Vidalias. The confit is wonderful with hamburgers and Buffalo Burgers (page 116). Serve with Roasted Garlic Mashed Potatoes (page 192).

½ cup butter

4 large sweet yellow onions, peeled
    and cut in half vertically

¾ teaspoon salt

¼ teaspoon freshly ground
    black pepper

1 tablespoon firmly packed light
    brown sugar

2 cups pinot noir

¼ cup sherry wine vinegar

2 tablespoons balsamic vinegar

2 tablespoons red wine vinegar

2 tablespoons cassis
    (black currant liqueur)

2 (4-inch-long) sprigs fresh rosemary

4 buffalo rib-eye steaks (8 ounces
    each and 1 inch thick)

1 tablespoon olive oil

1. Melt the butter in a small saucepan over medium-low heat and cook, without stirring, allowing the butter to bubble gently until it is lightly browned. Remove the foam layer with a spoon and discard. Carefully pour off clear butter into a wide, shallow 5-quart sauté pan.

2. Meanwhile, cut the onions crosswise into thin slices. Add them to the butter in the sauté pan and set over medium heat. Add the salt and pepper and stir to coat the onions well. Cover the pan and cook 5 minutes, until the onions begin to release their liquid. Stir in the brown sugar, cover the pan, and cook another 5 minutes. Add the pinot noir, the three vinegars, cassis, and rosemary and stir well. Bring the mixture to a boil, then cover the pan partially. Decrease the heat to low and cook about 1½ hours, or until the liquid is almost completely absorbed and the mixture is thick and slightly syrupy. Watch carefully toward the end of cooking and adjust the heat accordingly. Serve warm.

3. While the confit is cooking, prepare a charcoal grill. Pat the steaks dry with paper towels and rub their surfaces lightly with olive oil. Grill over hot coals about 4 minutes per side for medium-rare. Serve immediately on warm plates. Leftover confit will keep, refrigerated, for about a week.

BUFFALO BURGERS WITH SHIITAKE MUSHROOMS AND ONION-CILANTRO RELISH

YIELD: 4 SERVINGS

Because buffalo is so lean, care must be taken during cooking to keep it moist. In these burgers, hydrated shiitake mushrooms, vermouth, and oyster sauce all contribute moisture as well as flavor to the buffalo. The Onion-Cilantro relish adds acidity to complement the sweetness of the meat. If you cannot get buffalo, don't despair; ground beef chuck will do in a pinch.

½ ounce dried shiitake mushrooms

1 pound ground buffalo

4 tablespoons oyster sauce

½ cup dry white French vermouth

1 English cucumber, washed and
   unpeeled

2 large sweet yellow onions

1 tablespoon vegetable oil, plus more
   for grilling or sautéing

1 tablespoon sherry wine vinegar

½ cup chopped fresh cilantro leaves

4 sesame-seed hamburger buns

4 tablespoons mayonnaise

1. In a small bowl, soak the mushrooms in 1 cup warm water until softened, about 30 minutes. Squeeze out the excess moisture, and trim away and discard stems. Chop the mushrooms finely.

2. If cooking on a grill, prepare a hot charcoal fire. In a large bowl, combine the buffalo, mushrooms, 3 tablespoons of the oyster sauce, and ¼ cup of the vermouth. Mix well, taking care not to compact the meat. Divide the meat mixture into 4 equal portions, form the portions into round patties to fit the buns, and refrigerate.

3. Cut the cucumber into thin slices and refrigerate. Slice the onions crosswise about ¼ inch thick. Heat the oil in a 10-inch skillet over medium-high heat, add the onions, and cook about 5 minutes, stirring frequently until the onions are browned and slightly tender. Add the remaining 1 tablespoon oyster sauce, ¼ cup vermouth, and the sherry wine vinegar. Stir and cook several minutes until the onions are tender and the liquid is almost completely absorbed. Add the cilantro and remove pan from the heat.

4. If grilling the burgers, brush the grill rack lightly with vegetable oil and place the patties on the grill. Cook until browned on the bottom. With a wide spatula, turn the patties and cook to desired doneness, 4 to 5 minutes total cooking time for medium-rare to medium burgers. If sautéing the burgers, set a large skillet over medium-high heat and add 1 tablespoon oil. When the oil is hot, cook the burgers until they are browned on both sides, about 6 minutes for rare to medium-rare.

5. After turning the patties to cook on the second side, toast the buns, cut side down, on the grill or set them cut side up a few inches under the broiler until nicely browned. To assemble the burgers, spread ½ tablespoon mayonnaise on each bun half. Arrange about 8 cucumber slices on the bottoms of the buns. Place the patties over the cucumbers and spoon the onion and cilantro mixture on top. Cover with the bun tops and serve immediately.

GRILLED SMOKED QUAIL IN PORT WINE AND HUCKLEBERRY SAUCE

YIELD: 4 SERVINGS

The smokiness of the succulent quail and the sweetness of the port and huckleberries are a dream combination. If ever there was a dish for a seduction, this is it. A Bandol with this meal would be perfection.

½ cup plus 1 tablespoon port wine

¼ cup strained freshly squeezed orange juice

¼ cup extra-virgin olive oil

⅓ cup red wine vinegar

2 tablespoons firmly packed dark brown sugar

¾ teaspoon salt

¼ teaspoon freshly ground black pepper

2 tablespoons finely chopped fresh rosemary needles

8 boneless quail

1½ cups hickory chips

½ teaspoon cornstarch

½ cup fresh or frozen huckleberries

1. In a small bowl, whisk together ½ cup of the port, the orange juice, olive oil, red wine vinegar, brown sugar, salt, pepper, and rosemary. Transfer the mixture to a 12x8x2-inch glass baking dish and add the quail. Turn the quail to coat it well with the marinade. Cover and marinate 2 to 4 hours or as long as overnight in the refrigerator, turning the quail occasionally.

2. Soak the hickory chips in cold water for about 1 hour. Prepare a charcoal grill with a hot fire on one side for direct cooking. Keep the opposite side free of coals for indirect cooking.

3. Combine the remaining 1 tablespoon port with the cornstarch in a small cup and set aside. Remove quail from the marinade and place them on the grill rack over the coals. Cover and cook 5 minutes.

4. While the quail are cooking, boil the marinade in a 2-quart saucepan until it is reduced to ½ cup. Add the huckleberries and return the sauce to a boil. Stir the port and cornstarch mixture and add it to the pan. Swirl the pan and cook briefly until the sauce is thickened. Remove the pan from the heat and keep warm.

5. Turn the quail and grill, covered, another 5 minutes on the other side. Move the quail to the side of the grill without the coals. Drain the hickory chips and place them on top of the coals. Cover the grill and smoke the quail 8 to 10 minutes, or until completely cooked and tender. Serve immediately, spooning about 1 tablespoon of the huckleberry sauce over each quail.

COOKING BY SMOKER

Smoking foods has always been popular, especially before modern refrigeration became an everyday convenience. Smoking, unlike brining, pickling, or curing, doesn't preserve foods over a long period of time because the antimicrobial and antioxidant compounds created by smoking cling to the surface of the food being smoked; they don't penetrate completely. But smoking adds terrific flavor to foods, and that is its primary function.

There are two main types of smoking, hot and cold. In cold smoking, the food is not actually cooked, so it must be first treated with a brine solution or rubbed with a mixture of salt, sugar, and spices. Over a period of several hours or even days, smoke passes from the smokehouse to the food chamber, kept at a room temperature of 60° to 80°F. Examples of cold-smoked foods include lox (salmon), bacon, ham, and some cheeses. In contrast, hot smoking can last for many hours in a fire-heated hot chamber (180° to 250°F). The heat is sufficient to kill any microbes throughout the food, but smoke alone won't preserve foods. Barbecue (pork), fish, poultry, beef, and other meats are favorites for this method of smoking.

Many types of smokers are on the market today, and the choices can leave one in a state of bewilderment. I use an electric water smoker made by the Meco corporation (see mail-order sources, page 236–237). It is inexpensive, easy to use, and always gives me excellent results. For apartment dwellers, stove-top smokers are available, and they, too, are excellent. But you'll probably have to reduce quantities and use cut-up meats and poultry. Nevertheless, they're a fine option if you want to smoke.

HICKORY-SMOKED BARBECUED PORK LOIN

YIELD: 12 TO 16 SERVINGS

This recipe makes spicy, moist, succulent pork loin. After massaging in the dry rub, the meat is refrigerated for two to three days to allow the flavors to permeate it. During smoking, the meat is left uncovered for most of the time. Then it is wrapped in foil with a wet marinade for its final cooking. This two-step smoke cooking is what makes the meat so juicy. I like to make a lot of this at a time and either throw a big party or freeze half the pork for later use. Leftover barbecued pork is excellent in sandwiches. Or use it in Smoked Pork Lasagna with Salsa Verde and Red Pepper Puree (page 164). If you don't want to make this much, reduce all ingredients by half. The cooking time will be the same.

Dry Rub

1 tablespoon ground cinnamon

1 tablespoon rubbed sage

1 tablespoon dried whole
    thyme leaves

1 tablespoon dried oregano leaves

1 tablespoon ground cumin

1 tablespoon ground cayenne pepper

1 teaspoon ground cloves

1 tablespoon salt

1 tablespoon freshly ground
    black pepper

2 tablespoons granulated sugar

2 tablespoons firmly packed
    brown sugar

6 to 7 pounds pork loin roast

16 to 20 hickory chunks

Wet Cooking Marinade

6 cloves garlic, minced

4 tablespoons freshly squeezed lemon juice

4 tablespoons freshly squeezed orange juice

2 tablespoons extra-virgin olive oil

162 :: MONTANA COOKING

1. Combine all of the dry rub ingredients thoroughly. Rinse the pork and pat it dry. Sometimes a thin layer of fat is on one side of the pork. Don't remove it completely, but cut away about a 1-inch-wide strip of the fat and the attached tough membrane that runs the length of the loin, to prevent the meat from curling during cooking. Cut the whole pork loin crosswise into two even pieces. Sprinkle dry rub over all surfaces and rub it in gently with your fingers, covering the pork completely. Place in an airtight plastic bag, seal, and refrigerate for 2 to 3 days. Let it stand at room temperature while you soak the hickory chunks and prepare the smoker.

2. Soak the hickory chunks in cold water for at least 2 hours.

3. Prepare the smoker, preheating the chamber to between 200° and 220°. Add 4 hickory chunks and some water to the smoker, according to the manufacturer's instructions, and place the pork on the upper rack. Smoke for $2\frac{1}{2}$ hours, adding 2 to 3 hickory chunks and additional water as needed while maintaining the smoker temperature between 200° and 220°.

4. Meanwhile, combine the wet marinade ingredients in a small bowl. Remove the pork and test its internal temperature with an instant-read thermometer. It should register about 140°. Place each pork roast on a piece of heavy-duty aluminum foil, fold up the edges of the foil slightly to make a shell, and divide the marinade between the two pieces. Seal tightly and return the pork to the smoker. Continue smoking for another 1 to $1\frac{1}{2}$ hours, or until the internal temperature of the pork is 160°. (If you are not ready to serve, the pork can be held at this temperature for an hour or so.) Let the pork stand for 10 minutes after removing it from the smoker. Place in a rimmed dish and carefully remove the foil. Slice the pork about $\frac{1}{4}$ inch thick, arrange on dinner plates or on a large serving dish, and spoon the marinade over it. Serve immediately.

SMOKED PORK LASAGNA WITH SALSA VERDE AND RED PEPPER PUREE

YIELD: 8 GENEROUS SERVINGS

This dish is my Montanan tribute to Italy, the land that gave the world lasagna. The three colors of the Italian flag—red, white, and green—are represented by the red pepper puree, lasagna noodles, and salsa verde, respectively. The tangy tomatillos in the salsa and the sweet taste of the pork and red pepper are a wonderful combination. All you need with this is a salad of tomatoes in an herb-and-garlic vinaigrette.

Salsa Verde

2 pounds tomatillos, with husks

8 cups water

3 teaspoons salt

2 cloves garlic, minced

4 jalapeño chiles, cut in half, seeded, and minced

½ cup loosely packed cilantro leaves, chopped

1 large yellow onion, finely chopped

1 tablespoon chopped fresh oregano

¼ teaspoon ground cumin

Red Pepper Puree

3 large red bell peppers

¼ teaspoon salt

⅛ teaspoon freshly ground black pepper

Lasagna

12 dried lasagna noodles

1 pound Hickory-Smoked Barbecued Pork Loin (pages 162–163)

4 ounces cream cheese, regular or Neufchâtel (⅓ less fat)

1 cup (4 ounces) freshly grated Parmesan cheese

½ cup finely chopped flat-leaf parsley

1 egg

1 tablespoon extra-virgin olive oil

3 cups (12 ounces) pepper jack cheese, shredded

1. To make the salsa, remove the thin husks from the tomatillos and place the tomatillos, water, and 2 teaspoons of the salt in a 4- to 5-quart saucepan. Cover and bring to a boil over high heat, then uncover, lower the heat to medium, and simmer the tomatillos just until they become soft, 6 to 8 minutes. (Their color will fade from bright green to olive drab.) Drain well and puree the tomatillos in a food processor or a blender. Transfer the puree to the saucepan and stir in the remaining 1 teaspoon salt and the rest of the salsa ingredients. Set the pan over low to medium-low heat and simmer the sauce, stirring every few minutes with a wooden spoon to prevent it from sticking to the bottom of the pan, about 40 minutes. You should have about 4 cups of sauce. Cool, cover, and refrigerate until ready to use. (The sauce keeps well in the refrigerator for several days.)

2. For the red pepper puree, roast the peppers over a gas flame, charcoal grill, or under the broiler, until all sides are charred black. As soon as they are ready, place them in a paper bag and close the top securely. Let them cool slightly, then remove the skins. Core and seed the peppers using a small sharp knife. Do not rinse the peppers to wash away the seeds or you will also wash away most of the flavor. Pat peppers dry on paper towels and puree them in a food processor until very smooth, about 2 minutes. Season with the salt and pepper and set aside, covered, until needed. Makes about $1\frac{1}{4}$ cups. (The puree may be made a day ahead and refrigerated.)

3. Cook the lasagna noodles in a large pot of boiling water until they are just tender. Drain, rinse in cold water, and set aside in a single layer on kitchen towels to drain further. Chop the pork into small pieces with a heavy chef's knife or cut it into 1-inch chunks and use a food processor to pulse-chop it into very small pieces. You will have about 4 cups of chopped pork. Place the pork into a large bowl and add 2 cups of the Salsa Verde, the cream cheese, $\frac{1}{2}$ cup of the Parmesan, the parsley, and egg. Beat well with a wooden spoon until thoroughly mixed. Combine $\frac{1}{2}$ cup of the Salsa Verde with the olive oil in the bottom of a 13x9x2-inch baking dish and spread the mixture into an even layer. Place 3 lasagna noodles lengthwise over the salsa in a single layer. The strips should just cover the bottom of the pan. Spread with one-third (about $1\frac{1}{2}$ cups) of the pork mixture, and sprinkle with one-third (1 cup) of

the pepper jack cheese. Layer another 3 lasagna noodle strips over the cheese and spread with half the remaining pork mixture. Cover with 3 more lasagna strips, the remaining pork mixture, and 1 cup of the remaining pepper jack cheese. Arrange the last 3 lasagna strips lengthwise on top, spread with all the remaining Salsa Verde, and sprinkle with the remaining 1/2 cup Parmesan and the pepper jack cheese. (The lasagna may be made in advance up to this point; just cover and refrigerate. Bring to room temperature before baking.)

4. Adjust an oven rack to the center position and preheat the oven to 375°. Bake the lasagna, uncovered, until it is piping hot throughout and top is lightly browned, about 50 to 60 minutes. When the lasagna is almost ready, warm the pepper puree over very low heat in a small saucepan, but do not let it boil. Remove the lasagna from the oven and let it stand 10 minutes, then cut it into portions. Spoon a stripe of the red pepper puree diagonally over each serving of lasagna.

SMOKED BEEF BRISKET WITH
TAMARIND BARBECUE SAUCE

YIELD: 10 TO 12 SERVINGS

This is what barbecue is all about—long, slow cooking at a low temperature until the meat is so tender it practically falls apart. Allow 8 to 10 hours, or longer, to smoke and cook the brisket. Start early in the day when you've got someone to share cooking duties and chat with.

Beef brisket comes from a well-exercised part of the chest muscle of a steer. It is an ideal cut to barbecue because it starts out tough; slow cooking breaks down the fibers and tenderizes the meat. It is also fairly high in fat. But this is desirable, because during cooking the fat melts out of the beef, basting it with flavor. This results in meat that is tender, moist, and ultimately low in fat. You will probably have to special-order the brisket at your market. Ask for a whole brisket with about 1/2 inch of fat covering most of one side. It should weigh 7 to 8 pounds. Brisket known as a "packer cut" is larger, weighs about 12 pounds, and has a thicker layer of fat and a tougher end. If you have a choice, opt for the former cut. You'll waste a lot less, and the results will be moist, juicy, and tender. According to Charlie and Ruthie Knote in Barbecuing and Sausage Making Secrets, *brisket and other tough cuts of meat require prolonged cooking at an internal temperature of 160° to become tender. Since that temperature is an internal one, I start cooking the brisket wrapped in foil for 3 hours, then unwrap the beef and continue cooking it for 5 to 7 hours, or until it is very tender. I use an electric smoker because it easily maintains a steady temperature better than a charcoal smoker.*

The spice rub gives the meat a mildly hot taste. If you like yours more fiery, increase the amount of cayenne and use a hot paprika instead of a sweet one. The tamarind barbecue sauce is served with the brisket on the side. It is terrific with all sorts of barbecued meats. Tamarind is a tropical legume and is one of the ingredients that gives Worcestershire sauce its distinctive taste. I buy it in moist pulp form loaded with seeds in 8-ounce or 1-pound packages in Asian or Latin American markets. It is easy to prepare your own tamarind puree, and it is best to do so before you start with the brisket. Be sure to allow time for the brisket to marinate overnight.

1 (8-ounce) package moist tamarind
    pulp with seeds

2 cups boiling water

1/3 cup sweet paprika

1/4 cup firmly packed light brown
    sugar

2 tablespoons ground cumin

2 tablespoons plus 2 teaspoons salt

1 tablespoon plus 2 teaspoons freshly
    ground black pepper

2 teaspoons ground cinnamon

2 teaspoons ground cayenne pepper

7- to 8-pound beef brisket

36 to 40 hickory chunks

2 tablespoons vegetable oil

3 large yellow onions, coarsely
    chopped

10 cloves garlic, coarsely chopped

3 jalapeño chiles, seeded and
    coarsely chopped

1 teaspoon ground cloves

1/2 cup distilled white vinegar

1 cup unsulphured molasses

1/4 cup granulated sugar

3 (14 1/2-ounce) cans peeled whole
    tomatoes in juice

1 tablespoon dried whole thyme
    leaves

1. Break the tamarind pulp into walnut-sized pieces and place them in a bowl. Pour the boiling water over and let the mixture stand undisturbed for 1 hour. Break up the tamarind with your fingers to separate the pulp from the seeds and let it soak for 3 hours more. Press the mixture through a coarse sieve, reserving the puree. You will have about 1 1/2 cups of puree. Cover and refrigerate until needed. (It keeps well for several days.)

2. Combine the paprika, brown sugar, cumin, 2 tablespoons salt, 1 tablespoon black pepper, the cinnamon, and cayenne in a small bowl. Pat the brisket dry with paper towels and rub all of the spice mixture over it. Cover the brisket with plastic wrap and refrigerate overnight. Wrap the brisket in heavy-duty aluminum foil and let it stand at room temperature while you soak the hickory chunks and prepare the smoker.

3. Soak the hickory chunks in cold water for at least 2 hours.

4. Prepare the smoker, preheating the chamber to 200° to 220°. Add 3 or 4 hickory chunks and some water to the smoker, according to the manufacturer's instructions, and place the brisket on the top rack. Smoke for 3 hours, adding 3 or 4 chunks and additional water as needed while maintaining the smoker temperature between 200° and 220°. Unwrap the brisket and return it to the smoker fat side up. Continue cooking until the meat is very tender and pulls apart easily with a fork, about 5 to 7 hours. Test the temperature of the brisket occasionally with an instant-read thermometer. It should be about 165°. The brisket will look black but will be fine.

5. While the brisket cooks, prepare the barbecue sauce. Heat the oil in a heavy 4-quart saucepan over medium heat. Add the onions, cover the pan, and cook for 10 minutes without browning, stirring once. Add the garlic and jalapeños. Cover and cook for 5 minutes. Stir in the cloves, the remaining 2 teaspoons of black pepper, and 2 teaspoons salt. Cover and cook 5 minutes more over medium heat. Add the reserved tamarind puree, vinegar, molasses, granulated sugar, tomatoes, and thyme. Stir well. Break the tomatoes up with a spoon, pressing them against the side of the pan. (If you taste the sauce

now it will seem very sour and you will be tempted to add more sugar. Don't. Long, slow cooking will mellow the acidity.) Cover the saucepan and simmer the sauce over medium heat for 10 to 15 minutes. Set the lid askew on the pan and regulate the heat so that the sauce simmers very slowly for about 3 hours. Stir occasionally. At the end of cooking, the sauce will be slightly thickened. Cool it slightly and purée until smooth with a food processor. The sauce will have a deep brown color and be the consistency of a thick tomato puree. You'll have about 6 cups of sauce.

6. To serve the brisket, slice it thinly with a sharp knife at a 45-degree angle across the grain. Pass the sauce separately.

Note: The sauce keeps in the refrigerator for 4 to 6 weeks and improves with time. It can also be frozen in an airtight container.

HICKORY-SMOKED CHICKENS

Chicken is particularly tender, moist, and tasty when rubbed with a mixture of spices and smoked. I like to eat it warm, and I love using the leftovers in salads or in sandwiches. Hot-smoked foods can be refrigerated for about a week. Freeze them for longer storage.

Despite the variety of spices in the following rub, the flavor imparted to the chicken is fairly subtle. It's terrific on turkey, too.

1 tablespoon freshly ground black
   pepper
2 teaspoons salt
1 tablespoon ground cardamom
1 tablespoon ground ginger
2 teaspoons ground cinnamon
2 tablespoons sweet paprika
1 tablespoon ground cumin
2 teaspoons ground allspice
1 teaspoon ground cayenne pepper
1 teaspoon ground cloves
1 tablespoon ground coriander
2 large chickens (4 to 4½ pounds
   each)
12 hickory chunks, or 3 cups
   hickory chips

1. Combine all the ingredients except the chickens and hickory chunks thoroughly. If your smoker is large enough, you may want to double the spice mixture and smoke four chickens. Rinse the chickens inside and out and pat them dry with paper towels. Without tearing the skin, carefully separate it from the breast and thighs with your fingers. Rub some of the spice mixture onto the meat and press the skin back in place. Rub the remaining spice mixture over the outside of the chickens and in the cavities. Cover and refrigerate for 1 hour or longer.

2. Soak the hickory chunks or chips in water for at least 30 minutes. Prepare a charcoal grill or an electric smoker according to the manufacturer's directions. (Although some foods such as fish fillets can be smoked in a conventional large charcoal grill, I don't recommend smoking large food items this way. You'll spend so much time adding preheated briquets to the fire and lowering the temperature of the cooking chamber that the project won't be any fun.) When the smoker is ready, drain the hickory chunks and add half or, if using the chips, add one-third of the chips. Place the chickens on one of the cooking racks, cover the smoker and smoke for about 4 hours, or until the chickens are completely cooked. Test by wiggling a leg; it should move freely in its socket. Add more hickory chunks about halfway during cooking or add wood chips after 1 hour or so. Add the remaining drained wood chips about 1 hour before the chickens are cooked.

3. When done, the chickens will have a dark mahogany color. Remove the skin after carving the birds. Serve hot or warm. Cover and refrigerate if not serving within 1 hour.

   Note: When the chickens are set on a platter and refrigerated, you'll notice some jelled chicken juices sticking to the skin the next day. Save this and use to flavor salad dressings or soups.

SPAGHETTI WITH SMOKED CHICKEN AND WILD MUSHROOM SAUCE

Smoked chicken and wild mushrooms were made for each other. The first time I prepared this dish, I used fairy ring mushrooms, Marasmius oreades, *which pop up in June all over lawns in Missoula. It's too bad most people don't know how tasty fairy ring mushrooms are or they wouldn't waste so much time treating them as pests and trying to rid their lawns of them. Since this mushroom species has such a short season, and since it takes an experienced mushroom hunter to identify it, I've suggested morels as a substitute.*

1 pound fairy ring mushrooms or
    morels
2 tablespoons butter
¼ cup finely chopped shallots
½ teaspoon salt
¼ teaspoon freshly ground black
    pepper
¼ cup Calvados
⅔ cup rich chicken stock (page 5)
1 cup whipping cream
3 tablespoons finely chopped fresh
    thyme
1½ cups (8 ounces) diced smoked
    chicken (page 171)
1 pound uncooked spaghetti
Freshly squeezed lemon juice to taste
Freshly grated Parmesan cheese

1. Rinse the fairy ring mushrooms well in a basin of cold water, stirring them with your hands to remove any grasses. Carefully remove the cleaned mushrooms from the water and squeeze them gently to remove excess water. Wrap the mushrooms in paper towels to absorb excess moisture. If using morels, look over them carefully and wash and dry as above. If morels are 1 inch or so big, use them whole; if they are larger, cut them into 1-inch pieces.

2. Heat the butter in a large skillet over medium-high heat. Add the shallots and stir for a few seconds. Add the mushrooms and stir well, cooking a few minutes until mushrooms release their juices. Add the salt and pepper and continue cooking until most of the mushroom juices have evaporated. Add the Calvados and cook 1 minute more. Stir in the chicken stock and boil the mixture until the liquid is reduced by about half. Add the cream, thyme, and chicken. Stir the sauce well and remove it from the heat. Cook the spaghetti according to package directions. While the spaghetti cooks, return the sauce to high heat and cook, stirring frequently, until it is slightly reduced and has thickened a bit. Remove the pan from heat.

3. When the spaghetti is al dente, drain it well and add it to the skillet with the sauce. Stir to coat well. Add lemon juice, salt, and pepper to taste. Divide among four pasta bowls and serve immediately, passing the Parmesan at the table.

HICKORY-SMOKED STURGEON

YIELD: 1 TO 1 1/2 POUNDS

Smoked sturgeon is succulent and delicious all by itself or may be used as an ingredient in quiches, omelets, sandwiches, or in the Smoked Sturgeon Frittata with Fried Beets (page 174). I use a charcoal grill and hot-smoke the fish, which cooks and smokes it simultaneously.

1½ cups hickory chips

1 (1½- to 2-pound) sturgeon fillet, with skin

¼ cup sugar

¼ cup kosher salt

1. Soak the hickory chips in cold water for at least 2 hours.

2. Place the sturgeon in a glass or ceramic dish slightly larger than the fish. Combine the sugar and salt well. Coat the sturgeon completely with the mixture, patting it in place. Let marinate for at least 30 minutes, but no longer than 1 hour. (The texture of the fish changes if it sits in the salt-sugar mixture too long.)

3. Prepare a charcoal grill, preferably using hardwood charcoal. When the coals are ready, remove the grill rack and pour the coals to one side in a pile. Cover the grill.

4. Wipe off any remaining sugar-salt mixture from the fish and place skin side down on a piece of heavy-duty aluminum foil slightly larger than the fish. Poke a few holes in the foil with a metal skewer before setting the fish on it. Quickly uncover the grill, drain the wood chips, and scatter them over the coals. Replace the grill rack, place the fish on the side of the rack where there are no coals, and cover the grill. Keep the holes on the grill cover closed and cook for 1 to 1½ hours. When smoked, the fish will be golden brown to light brown in color and look and feel juicy. Serve hot, or let it cool completely and serve at room temperature. To store, cover and refrigerate for up to 1 week or freeze in an airtight container for up to 3 months.

SMOKED STURGEON FRITTATA WITH FRIED BEETS   YIELD: 4 TO 6 SERVINGS

This is a wonderful way to use smoked sturgeon. It's best to mix all of the frittata ingredients together and let them stand about 30 minutes before cooking, so that the smokiness permeates the eggs. Prepare the beets ahead of time.

3 beets

5 tablespoons butter

6 large eggs

½ teaspoon salt

¼ teaspoon freshly ground
    black pepper

4 ounces fresh mozzarella cheese, cut
    into small cubes

4 to 6 ounces smoked sturgeon
    (page 173), cut into small cubes

½ cup loosely packed fresh basil
    leaves, coarsely chopped

1. Preheat the oven to 350°. Wash the beets and wrap them in aluminum foil. Bake them in the preheated oven for about 1 hour 15 minutes, or until tender. Leave them wrapped in the foil and let cool slightly. Trim the ends and peel the beets with a small sharp knife, then slice ⅛ inch thick. Heat 2 tablespoons of the butter in a 12-inch ovenproof nonstick skillet over medium heat. When hot, place the beets in the skillet in a single layer. Cook the beets until golden brown and a crust develops on both sides, about 10 minutes. Remove and drain on paper towels. (This step may be done hours ahead.)

2. In a large bowl, whisk together the eggs, salt, and pepper until well combined. Stir in the mozzarella, sturgeon, and basil. Set aside for 30 minutes to 1 hour.

3. Melt the remaining 3 tablespoons of butter over medium heat in the same skillet used to cook the beets. When the butter is foamy, quickly arrange the browned beets in the pan in a single layer and add the egg mixture, spreading the sturgeon and cheese to distribute them evenly. Decrease the heat to the lowest setting.

4. Cook the frittata without disturbing the eggs until it is almost completely set. Only the top should be a bit runny. This takes about 15 minutes, but watch carefully to avoid overcooking. Meanwhile, place an oven rack 5 to 6 inches below the broiler, and preheat the broiler. To set the top of the frittata, place the skillet under the broiler until the top is set but not browned, usually 30 seconds to 1 minute. Remove immediately from the oven, cut into wedges, and serve.

VEGETABLES, GRAINS, AND SIDE DISHES

In Montana, some of the most successful small farmers are new immigrants, such as the Hmong who moved to this country from Southeast Asia after the Vietnam War. They farm organically and offer crops such as broccoli and carrots at our local farmers' market long before anyone else. And they've become expert huckleberry collectors. They inspire those of us who are less adroit kitchen gardeners, supplying the goods that enable us to relish the gifts of our landscape.

Near Great Falls, east of the Rockies, lentils, garbanzos, wheat, barley, and oats thrive. Quinoa grows nearby in Colorado, where the long, warm days and cool nights of the high-altitude San Luis Valley mimic the Andes, birthplace of this most nutritious high-protein grain.

If—and it can be a big if—we have been blessed with consistent, warm sunshine, abundant amounts of vine-ripened tomatoes, eggplant, corn, and peppers are ready for the picking by the end of summer. Because these crops don't always succeed, we relish them all the more when they do, and Montana cooks like me get a special kick from finding new ways to use them.

QUINOA DRESSING

Try this for a different dressing to serve with chicken or turkey. It is so good you'll be glad you made a lot. Cook this in a casserole or use it as a stuffing. The nutty taste of quinoa might keep you reaching for more.

3 cups quinoa

5½ cups chicken stock (page 5)

2 teaspoons salt

½ teaspoon freshly ground black pepper

¼ cup butter

1 large onion, finely chopped

1 large leek, washed well and diced

2 large celery stalks, washed and diced

½ pound oyster mushrooms, coarsely chopped

8 cloves garlic, finely chopped

½ cup chopped flat-leaf parsley

1 tablespoon chopped fresh thyme

1 tablespoon chopped fresh sage

1 tablespoon chopped fresh oregano

1 tablespoon chopped fresh tarragon

¾ cup pine nuts

1. Rinse the quinoa in a fine-mesh strainer under cold running water for about 1 minute to rinse off any acrid-tasting saponin. Shake to remove excess water. Combine the quinoa, chicken stock, salt, and pepper in a 4- to 5-quart saucepan. Bring to a boil over medium-high heat, cover the pan, and reduce heat to low. Cook 15 to 20 minutes, until the liquid is absorbed. Remove the pan from the heat and let stand, covered, while you prepare the rest of the stuffing.

2. Preheat the oven to 350°.

3. Melt the butter in a 5-quart sauté pan over medium heat. When hot, add the onion, leek, and celery and cook until tender but not browned, 6 to 8 minutes. Add the mushrooms and garlic and cook 2 to 3 minutes, stirring occasionally, until the mushrooms are cooked. Add the remaining ingredients and the cooked quinoa and combine well. Taste and adjust seasoning with salt and pepper, if necessary.

4. Use as a stuffing or transfer to a buttered 3- to 4-quart baking dish, cover with foil, and bake about 45 minutes.

QUINOA AND BASMATI RICE PILAF

This is an excellent side dish to serve with all sorts of game, poultry, or meats. Pine nuts add a roastiness, and the cardamom pods contribute an intriguing and exotic taste.

⅓ cup quinoa

⅔ cup chicken stock (page 5)

1 cup basmati rice

1 quart cold water

1 tablespoon olive oil

1 onion, finely chopped

1 clove garlic, finely chopped

⅓ cup pine nuts

1¼ cups hot water

1 teaspoon salt

4 cardamom pods

1. Rinse the quinoa in a fine-mesh strainer under cold running water for about 1 minute to remove the acrid-tasting saponin. Shake the strainer to remove excess water. Bring the chicken stock to a boil in a small saucepan and stir in the quinoa. When the mixture returns to a boil, cover the pan, and decrease the heat to very low. Cook 15 to 20 minutes, or until the liquid is absorbed. Remove the pan from the heat and set aside, uncovered.

2. Rinse the basmati rice in a fine strainer under cold running water for about 1 minute. Combine the rice with cold water in a bowl and let stand 30 minutes. Drain well and set aside. Both the quinoa and the rice may be prepared hours in advance.

3. Heat the olive oil in a 3-quart saucepan over medium heat. Add the onion, garlic, and pine nuts. Cook, stirring with a wooden spoon, until the pine nuts are lightly browned. Add the rice, raise the heat to high, and stir continuously to evaporate excess moisture, about 1 minute. Add the hot water, salt, and cardamom pods. Give the rice a stir and return the mixture to a boil. Cover the pan and decrease the heat to very low. Cook 20 minutes, or until the rice is tender. Add the quinoa to the rice and fluff with a fork. Cover and reheat over low heat. Serve hot.

QUINOA TABBOULEH

YIELD: 6 TO 8 SERVINGS

I created this recipe to help use up the mint forest growing outside our house where a dripping faucet waters the plants quite efficiently. One summer I made lots of mint juleps, convincing myself that the drink contained the four basic food groups. By fall, our mint supply appeared undiminished. Then a healthier idea struck. Why not make tabbouleh, the classic Lebanese salad? It uses lots of mint and parsley, which we also had in abundant supply. Tabbouleh is traditionally made with bulgur (cracked wheat). Here I've combined it with quinoa, which has a nutty, slightly acid taste, for a different texture. Because cooked quinoa is slightly moist, this tabbouleh is wetter than most.

½ cup quinoa

¾ cup plus 2 tablespoons water

⅓ cup fine bulgur

3 cups cold water

1 bunch scallions, thinly sliced

2 cups chopped flat-leaf parsley

¾ cup chopped fresh mint

1 cucumber, peeled, cut in half,
   seeded, and finely diced

1 teaspoon salt

½ teaspoon freshly ground black
   pepper

¼ cup freshly squeezed lemon juice

¼ cup extra-virgin olive oil

4 plum tomatoes, preferably 2
   red and 2 yellow, cut in half
   crosswise, seeded, and diced

6 to 8 large red lettuce leaves,
   washed and dried

1. Rinse the quinoa in a fine-mesh strainer under cold running water for about 1 minute to remove the acrid-tasting saponin. Shake the strainer to remove excess water. Bring the ¾ cup and 2 tablespoons of water to a boil in a small saucepan and stir in the quinoa. When the mixture returns to a boil, cover the pan and decrease the heat to very low. Cook 20 minutes, or until the liquid is absorbed. Remove from the heat and set aside, uncovered, to cool.

2. Soak the bulgur in 3 cups of cold water for 15 minutes. Drain well and squeeze the bulgur dry. Combine the bulgur, cooled quinoa, scallions, parsley, mint, cucumber, salt, pepper, lemon juice, and olive oil in a large bowl, tossing with a fork. Mix in the tomatoes. Cover and refrigerate 1 or 2 hours before serving. Place one lettuce leaf on each salad plate. Divide the tabbouleh among the lettuce leaves and serve cold.

Quinoa

Quinoa (pronounced KEEN-wah) is an annual plant that has been cultivated for thousands of years in the Andes. The tiny grains, about the size of millet, were a staple food of the ancient Incas. In fact, quinoa was so important to the diet of the Incas that they called it the "Mother Grain." Quinoa is exceptionally high in protein and in the amino acids lysine, methionine, and cystine, which are especially important for vegetarian diets. Quinoa is so nutritious that it helped sustain Thor Heyerdahl and his crew on their trans-Pacific voyage on the *Kon Tiki*. Quinoa's appeal stems from its rich, nutty taste and its ability to be substituted for almost any grain. Quinoa can also be processed into flour and used in a variety of pastries and bread recipes for a unique flavor and a protein boost.

Quinoa seedheads grow atop stalks 3 to 7 feet tall. They are dazzlingly beautiful in the field when they turn brilliant shades of red, white, yellow, or black. The leaves of the plant are also edible; quinoa is closely related to spinach and beets and even more closely to a worldwide weed known as lamb's-quarters. Each summer our underweeded garden is overrun with this delicious green, and the lamb's-quarters leaves looked remarkably like the quinoa leaves. Quinoa, along with amaranth and buckwheat, is probably best referred to as a leafy grain.

Until the mid-1980s, all quinoa came from South America. Since then, quinoa has been grown commercially in various parts of North America, including Washington, Oregon, Colorado, and western Canada.

FETTUCCINE WITH BUTTERNUT SQUASH, SWISS CHARD, WILD MUSHROOMS, AND GARLIC

YIELD: 4 SERVINGS

This is a perfect fall dish. I made it for the first time when we had an abundance of butternut squashes ripening in our garden. Our Swiss chard was also at its peak, so I decided to combine the two. Fresh shiitake mushrooms are a good addition. You could also use oyster mushrooms.

1 bunch red Swiss chard, stems and
    ribs removed
2 cups peeled and diced butternut
    squash
¼ pound fresh shiitake mushrooms
1 pound dried fettuccine
3 tablespoons extra-virgin olive oil
4 cloves garlic, minced
1½ cups chicken stock (page 5)
Salt and freshly ground black pepper

1. Rinse the chard well in cold water to remove any dirt and drain briefly. Place the chard in a 4-quart saucepan with about ½ cup water. Cover the pan and set over high heat. Boil, covered, 2 to 3 minutes, or until the chard is wilted. Drain and plunge the chard into a large bowl of cold water. Let stand several minutes or until cool. Transfer the chard to a colander and allow it to drain further, then gently squeeze it to remove most of the remaining moisture. Chop the chard coarsely and set aside. (The chard may be prepared several hours ahead and refrigerated.)

2. Place the squash in 2 quarts of rapidly boiling water. Cover and cook about 5 minutes, or until just tender. The tip of a sharp knife should meet a little resistance when inserted in the center. Drain in a wire strainer.

3. Remove the stems from the shiitake mushrooms and slice the caps into ¼-inch strips. Cook the fettuccine according to the directions on the package. The pasta should be al dente when the sauce is finished (next step).

4. Heat the olive oil in a large skillet over medium-high heat. Add the mushrooms, squash, and garlic. Stir and cook 1 to 2 minutes, or until the mushrooms are almost tender and the squash is hot. Add the chard, chicken stock, salt, and pepper. Stir well and cook another minute or so to be sure the sauce is hot. Adjust the seasoning, if desired.

5. Drain the fettuccine and add it to the skillet. Toss to combine well and divide the pasta among four warmed pasta bowls. Serve immediately.

BUTTERNUT SQUASH FLANS

Cooked butternut squash, pureed and mixed with a spiced custard, makes a wonderful accompaniment for steaks, roast beef, or pork chops. You can get it ready hours ahead and pop it into the oven when needed. Evaporated skim milk, besides containing no fat, gives these custards an attractive two-toned look. You'll need 6-ounce ramekins.

3 cups peeled, seeded, and diced
    butternut squash (½-inch cubes)

2 cups water

½ cup evaporated skim milk

3 eggs

½ teaspoon salt

⅛ teaspoon freshly ground black
    pepper

⅛ teaspoon freshly grated nutmeg

1. Butter six 6-ounce ovenproof glass or porcelain ramekins.

2. Place squash and water in a 3-quart saucepan over high heat. Bring mixture to the boil and cover the pan. Lower the heat to medium-high and cook until squash is very tender, 10 to 15 minutes. Drain well and return squash to saucepan on medium-high heat. Use a portable electric mixer to beat squash until smooth, about 1 minute. Continue cooking, stirring with a wooden spoon another minute or so, to drive off excess moisture. Set squash aside, uncovered, to cool to room temperature.

3. In blender jar, place evaporated skim milk, eggs, salt, pepper, nutmeg, and squash. Cover and blend on high speed for 30 seconds. Divide evenly among the buttered ramekins, and place ramekins into a shallow baking dish. (May be prepared to this point several hours ahead; cover with plastic wrap and refrigerate.)

4. When ready to bake, adjust oven rack to lower-third position and preheat oven to 325°. Bring kettle of water to the boil. Pour boiling water around ramekins to come 1 inch up the sides. Place pan in oven and bake 20 to 30 minutes. The custards are done when the tip of a paring knife inserted into the center of each custard comes out clean. Remove pan from oven and remove ramekins from the water. Let stand 5 minutes. Run a small, sharp knife around the sides of the ramekins to release the flans and invert them onto plates.

OYSTER MUSHROOM, ASPARAGUS, AND SWEET ONION SAUTÉ

YIELD: 4 SERVINGS

In late spring or early summer in the inland Mountain West, we get our first shipments of Walla Walla sweet onions from Washington. If we've had a good rain, the oyster mushrooms suddenly pop up at about the same time. And the asparagus, whether homegrown or bought, is in abundance. When all are cooked together, you have a major hit on your hands. The dish goes well with just about any poultry, fish, or meat.

1 pound asparagus

2 tablespoons extra-virgin olive oil

1 large sweet yellow onion, thinly sliced

½ pound oyster mushrooms, sliced ¼ inch thick

Salt and freshly ground black pepper to taste

1. If the asparagus spears are thin, use only their tips. About 4 inches from the tip, slice the asparagus into 2 pieces at an angle. Save the rest of the stalk for another use. If you have thick spears, peel the stalks and cut them at an angle into 2-inch lengths. You should have about ½ pound of prepared asparagus whether using whole spears or tips. Place the asparagus in a large pot of lightly salted boiling water and cook for 1 minute. Drain, then plunge the asparagus into a large bowl of cold water. Let stand a few minutes until cool, and drain well in a colander until needed. (The recipe may be prepared hours ahead up to this point and refrigerated.)

2. Heat 1 tablespoon of the olive oil in a 10-inch skillet over medium heat. Add the onion and cook, stirring occasionally, until the onion is tender and lightly browned, about 10 minutes. Transfer the onion to a bowl.

3. Heat the remaining 1 tablespoon of oil in the skillet over medium heat and add the mushrooms. Sauté until the mushrooms are cooked and lightly browned, about 5 minutes. Add the asparagus and onions and cook briefly to heat through. Add salt and pepper to taste. Serve hot or warm.

GREEN BEAN, SWEET ONION, AND YELLOW BEET SAUTÉ WITH VINEGAR

YIELD: 4 SERVINGS

In late summer, my wife and I harvest our green beans. Besides simply steaming them and enjoying them with butter, here is another way we like to eat them. This is a sweet-sour dish that tastes both homey and sophisticated. Yellow beets do not "bleed" and I like using them in sautés for both their sweetness and color. Summer savory is the herb of choice, but if you don't have any you may substitute fresh thyme.

1 pound (4 medium) yellow beets

½ pound (3- to 4-inch-long pods)
    green beans

2 tablespoons extra-virgin olive oil

1 large sweet yellow onion,
    thinly sliced

2 tablespoons red wine vinegar

1 tablespoon sugar

1 tablespoon chopped fresh summer
    savory or chopped fresh thyme

Salt and freshly ground black pepper

1. Preheat the oven to 350°.

2. Wash the beets and wrap them in aluminum foil. Bake them for 1 hour 15 minutes in the preheated oven, or until tender. (Test by piercing a beet through the foil with the tip of a sharp knife.) Remove the beets from the oven and let cool for 30 minutes. Trim the ends and peel the beets, and cut them into strips about 1½ inches long and 1/4 inch wide. (The beets may be made hours ahead and refrigerated.)

3. Snap the ends off the beans, leaving the beans whole. Place them in a large pot of lightly salted boiling water. Cover and return the water to a boil then cook, uncovered, until the beans are slightly tender but still have a bit of crunch, about 3 minutes. Drain and plunge beans into a large bowl of cold water. Let stand several minutes until the beans are completely cool. Drain well in a colander, and pat dry with paper towels. (The beans also may be made hours ahead and refrigerated.)

4. Heat 1 tablespoon of the oil in a 12-inch skillet over medium heat. Add the beets and sauté for several minutes to brown lightly on all sides, then remove the beets and set aside. Heat the remaining 1 tablespoon oil in the skillet over medium heat and add the onion. Cook, stirring occasionally, until the onion is tender and lightly browned, about 10 minutes. Add the beans and continue cooking and stirring for several minutes until the beans are tender. Add the beets and cook briefly to heat them through. In a small bowl, combine the vinegar with the sugar and add it to the skillet, stirring well. Add the summer savory, salt, and pepper. Toss well and continue cooking 1 minute, or until the vinegar is absorbed. Serve hot or warm.

BEANS WITH FRIED SWEET ONIONS

In mid- to late August, depending on how much of a summer we've had, green beans, yellow wax beans, and sweet Walla Walla onions mature at about the same time. I like to pair the beans with the fried onions; frying brings out a caramel taste in the onion that helps the sweetness of the beans to shine through. I like using a mixture of the yellow and green beans not only because the combination is pretty, but because they have slightly different tastes—the yellow wax beans being milder and less assertive than the green. Use slim pods about 4 inches long or slightly longer. You can serve this with just about anything, or eat a plateful all by itself, as I do. Incidentally, do not be alarmed by the large amount of oil used to fry the onions; if the temperature is right, hardly any oil is absorbed.

2 pounds green beans or a mixture of green and yellow wax beans

2 large Walla Walla or Vidalia onions

1 cup olive oil

3 tablespoons butter

2 teaspoons chopped fresh summer savory or fresh thyme

Salt and freshly ground black pepper

1. Snap both ends off the beans, discard, and rinse the beans in a colander. In a large pot, bring about 8 quarts water and 2 tablespoons salt to a boil over high heat. Drop in the beans, cover the pan, and return the water to a rapid boil as quickly as possible. Immediately uncover the pan and let the beans boil for about 3 minutes, until they're cooked but still have a bit of crunch. Taste frequently during the cooking to test. Drain the beans in a colander, then plunge them into a large bowl of cold water for a few minutes to stop the cooking process. Drain well and pat the beans dry on paper towels. This step is also important to maintain a fresh taste if you are going to refrigerate the beans for several hours or overnight.

2. Peel the onions and slice off the stem and root ends. Cut the onions into circles between $1/8$ and $1/4$ inch thick. Separate the circles into rings and pat them dry on paper towels. Heat the oil in a large skillet over medium-high heat. When the oil begins to smoke, drop in a few onion rings at a time, stirring, until about half have been added. Cook until the onions are a deep golden brown. Remove with a slotted spoon and transfer to paper towels to drain. Repeat with the remaining onion. (These may be prepared hours, or up to 1 day, ahead.) Wrap and refrigerate when cool.

3. When ready to serve, melt the butter in a large skillet over medium-high heat. Add the beans and summer savory, toss and cook to heat the beans through. Add salt and pepper. Add the browned onions and stir briefly to heat. Serve hot.

GREEN BEANS WITH GARLIC, MUSTARD, AND TARRAGON VINAIGRETTE

YIELD: 6 TO 8 SERVINGS

I made this for the first time when we had abundant crops of both green and yellow wax beans in our garden. The tarragon plants had reached their peak and a whiff of fresh anise drew me to them. With beans in hand I plucked a few tarragon sprigs and made for the kitchen. This salad will keep well for a day in the refrigerator. Longer storage will result in mushy beans. Serve with just about any grilled meat.

2 pounds green beans, or a mixture of green and yellow wax beans

1 tablespoon grained mustard

1 tablespoon red wine vinegar

1 tablespoon sherry vinegar

½ cup extra-virgin olive oil

1 large (1 ounce) shallot, finely chopped

2 cloves garlic, peeled and put through a garlic press

2 tablespoons finely chopped fresh tarragon

Salt and freshly ground pepper to taste

1. Snap both ends off the beans and rinse them in a colander. Bring about 6 quarts water and 2 tablespoons salt to the boil over high heat in a large pot. Drop in the beans, cover the pan, and return the water to a rapid boil as quickly as possible. Immediately uncover the pan and let the beans boil for 4 to 5 minutes, until they're cooked but still have a bit of crunch. Taste often during the cooking to be sure. Drain the beans in a colander and plunge them into a large bowl of cold water to cool them off for a few minutes. Drain well and pat the beans dry on paper towels. This step is also important to maintain a fresh taste if you are going to refrigerate the beans for a number of hours or overnight before using them.

2. Whisk together the mustard and both vinegars in a small bowl. Gradually whisk in the oil in a thin stream to make a creamy vinaigrette. Stir in the shallot, garlic, and tarragon. Taste and adjust seasoning with salt and pepper. About ¼ teaspoon of each should be enough. Combine the beans with the dressing, mixing them thoroughly. Cover and refrigerate, preferably not more than a few hours, before serving.

TOMATOES STUFFED WITH FRESH HERBS AND BREAD CRUMBS

YIELD: 4 TO 8 SERVINGS

These stuffed tomatoes are delicious late summer fare, when the vine-ripened globes are at their peak. Although you will have 8 tomato halves, one is often not enough for a serving. To be on the safe side, I recommend serving one whole tomato per person.

4 ripe but slightly firm tomatoes

¾ teaspoon salt

½ cup fresh fine bread crumbs, made from day-old French or Italian bread, trimmed of crusts

⅛ teaspoon freshly ground black pepper

1 clove garlic, minced

1 scallion, finely chopped

2 tablespoons finely chopped fresh oregano

2 tablespoons finely chopped fresh flat-leaf parsley

2 tablespoons melted butter

1. Remove the stems from the tomatoes and cut the tomatoes in half crosswise. Carefully remove the seeds with a small spoon or with the tip of your pinky finger and squeeze the halves gently to expel some of the juices. Sprinkle the cavities lightly with ½ teaspoon of the salt and set the tomatoes cut side down on a large plate for about 30 minutes to help draw out even more juice.

2. Meanwhile, combine the remaining ¼ teaspoon salt and remaining ingredients in a small bowl. Divide the filling evenly among the tomatoes and pack it down gently into the crevices. Place the tomatoes on a baking sheet; cover and refrigerate until ready to bake. (The tomatoes may be prepared several hours ahead.)

3. When ready to bake, adjust an oven rack to the upper-third position and preheat the oven to 400°. Bake, uncovered, 15 to 20 minutes, or until the crumbs are lightly browned and the tomatoes are thoroughly heated. Do not over-bake or the tomatoes will lose their shape. Serve immediately.

BULL'S-EYE BEETS AND BEET GREENS WITH FENNEL TOPS

YIELD: 6 SERVINGS

My wife, Dorothy, found these "bull's-eye" beets at our local farmers' market. The vendor had cut open a couple of them to reveal pink and white concentric circles. Hence, my name for them. (The beets are commonly known as striped beets and are a cross between Detroit red and sugar beets, which makes them extra sweet.) As we paid and turned to leave, the vendor said, "Here, take some fennel tops, too. They're great with beets." She was right. I've added a bit of balsamic vinegar to them so that the sweet beet taste doesn't overwhelm the mild greens. For the optimal taste, eat a bite of beet with a bit of greens.

2 bunches striped beets with greens

¼ cup butter

1 tablespoon chopped fresh
    fennel tops

2 teaspoons balsamic vinegar

Salt and freshly ground black pepper

1. Preheat the oven to 350°.

2. Cut the beets off the greens, leaving about an inch of stems attached. Wash the beets and arrange them in a single layer on a sheet of aluminum foil. Wrap the beets tightly in the foil and bake for 1 hour 15 minutes, or until beets are tender. Test by piercing a beet through the foil with the tip of a sharp knife. Remove from the oven and cool in the foil for 30 minutes. Trim the ends of the beets, peel, and slice them into ¼-inch-thick circles. Pat the beets dry with paper towels and set aside. (The beets may be prepared hours ahead and refrigerated.)

3. Strip away any tough stems from the beet greens and rinse the leaves in a colander under cold running water. Bring a large pot of water to a boil and add the greens. Boil the greens, partially covered, for 2 minutes. Drain well and plunge the greens into a large bowl of cold water to stop the cooking process. Drain in a colander and set aside.

4. Melt 2 tablespoons of the butter in a 12-inch nonstick skillet over medium-high heat. When the butter is hot, add the beets in a single layer and cook until the slices are lightly browned on both sides. When all the beets are cooked, sprinkle the fennel tops over them. Remove the beets from the pan. Cover and keep warm.

5. Melt the remaining 2 tablespoons butter in the same skillet and set the pan over medium-high heat. Gently squeeze the beet greens to remove most of the water and add them to the pan. Season with the balsamic vinegar, salt, and pepper. Stir and cook until the greens are hot. To serve, pile the greens onto a serving platter and encircle with the beet slices or arrange them on individual dinner plates.

RUSSIAN BEET, POTATO, AND GREEN PEA SALAD WITH HORSERADISH DRESSING

As part of Easter celebrations, my Russian grandmother made a salad called "vinigrette." Although the name is similar to the French "vinaigrette," there is no other similarity. This salad typically contains red beets, but it is wonderful with yellow beets. The yellow beets don't bleed like the red ones do, so the colors of the vegetables remain distinct. All the vegetables may be cooked a day ahead, wrapped separately, and refrigerated. The dressing may also be made a day ahead and refrigerated. Simply assemble everything about 1 hour before serving. Be sure to buy the freshest, salmonella-free eggs from a reliable vender when making this dish or any other that uses raw eggs.

4 yellow beets

1 pound yellow Finn or Yukon gold
    potatoes, peeled and cut into
    ½-inch cubes

1 tablespoon plus ½ teaspoon salt

2 carrots, peeled and cut into
    ½-inch cubes

2 cups fresh shelled peas, or 1
    (10-ounce) package frozen peas

1 large egg

3 tablespoons corn oil

1 tablespoon freshly squeezed
    lemon juice

2 teaspoons Dijon-style mustard

1 teaspoon prepared horseradish

¼ teaspoon freshly ground
    black pepper

3 tablespoons olive oil

⅓ cup sour cream

2 tablespoons chopped fresh dill,
    for garnish

1. Preheat the oven to 350°.

2. Wash the beets and wrap them in aluminum foil. Bake for about 1 hour 15 minutes, or until tender. Test by piercing a beet through the foil with the tip of a sharp knife. Remove from the oven and let cool in the foil for 30 minutes. Trim the ends of the beets, peel, and cut them into ½-inch cubes. (The beets may be prepared hours ahead and refrigerated.)

3. Place the potatoes and 1 tablespoon salt in 2 quarts of rapidly boiling water. Cook until the potatoes are just tender when pierced with the tip of a sharp knife, about 5 minutes. With a slotted spoon, transfer the potatoes to a large bowl of cold water to stop the cooking process; let stand 5 minutes, then drain well and set aside. Add the carrots to the boiling water and cook until just tender, about 5 minutes. With a slotted spoon, transfer the carrots to a bowl of cold water and let them stand 5 minutes. Drain well.

4. Add the fresh or frozen peas to the boiling water. If using fresh peas, cook them for 3 minutes. Cook frozen peas only until thawed, about 1 minute. Using a slotted spoon, transfer the peas to a bowl of cold water to stop the cooking process; let stand for 5 minutes, then drain well.

5. To make the dressing, combine the egg, 1 tablespoon of the corn oil, the lemon juice, mustard, horseradish, ½ teaspoon of the salt, and pepper in a food processor fitted with the metal blade for 1 minute. With the machine running, gradually add the remaining 2 tablespoons corn oil and the olive oil through the feed tube in a fine stream. Scrape down the inside of the work

bowl and add the sour cream. Process 10 seconds, then transfer to a mixing bowl. Cover and refrigerate until needed.

6. To assemble the salad, place the beets, potatoes, carrots, and peas in a 3-quart bowl. Add the dressing and gently fold together. Adjust the seasoning as desired. Cover and refrigerate 1 hour. Transfer to a serving dish and sprinkle with the dill.

ROASTED GARLIC MASHED POTATOES

The best potato for mashing, in my opinion, is a variety called Caribe. They grow well in our climate and mature early. The skin is purple but the flesh is pure white. The potato is rich tasting and has a very smooth texture. Because of that, you can dispense with the cream and use milk or buttermilk instead; I use a combination. If you can't find Caribe, use an Idaho russet.

2 heads garlic, separated into cloves
    and peeled

⅓ cup extra-virgin olive oil

1 tablespoon plus 1 teaspoon salt

3 pounds Caribe or russet potatoes,
    peeled and cut into 2-inch pieces

½ cup milk

½ cup buttermilk

¼ teaspoon freshly ground
    white pepper

⅛ teaspoon freshly grated nutmeg

Salt to taste

¼ cup snipped fresh chives (optional)

1. Adjust an oven rack to the center position and preheat the oven to 325°.

2. Combine the garlic with the olive oil in a baking dish small enough so that the garlic is completely covered with oil. Cover the dish and bake about 1 hour, or until garlic is very soft. Cool slightly, then transfer the garlic and oil to a small wire strainer placed over a bowl. Drain well. Save the oil for sautés or salad dressings.

3. Bring 2 quarts of water and the 1 tablespoon of salt to a rolling boil in a 4-quart saucepan over high heat. Add the potatoes and return the water to a boil. Cover the pan and cook over medium-high heat until the potatoes are tender when pierced with the tip of a sharp knife, 15 to 20 minutes. Be sure to cook the potatoes completely; slightly underdone potatoes do not mash well. Cut and taste one to test.

4. Drain the potatoes and return them to the pan. Stir 1 minute over medium heat to break up the potatoes and drive off excess moisture. Combine the milk and buttermilk in a small saucepan and set it over low heat. Do not allow the milk to boil. To mash the potatoes, pass them through a ricer and return them to the saucepan for the smoothest results. Or mash them in the pan with a handheld electric mixer or a conventional potato masher. When the potatoes are mashed, add the cooked, drained garlic, 1 teaspoon salt, the white pepper, nutmeg, and about half the milk mixture. Beat together well with a heavy wooden spatula or handheld electric mixer. Add more of the milk mixture to reach the consistency you like. Adjust the seasoning with salt and white pepper, if desired. Stir in the chives and serve immediately.

THAI SWISS CHARD WITH GARLIC

Vietnamese fish sauce, nuoc mam, adds an exotic and intriguing taste to cooked vegetables. The Southeast Asian influence on the new cooking of Montana is clearly shown in this spicy dish. Serve it with grilled chicken or fish.

2 bunches red Swiss chard

¼ pound fresh shiitake mushrooms

4 teaspoons nuoc mam (Vietnamese
     fish sauce)

2 teaspoons distilled white vinegar

1 teaspoon sugar

¼ teaspoon red pepper flakes

1 tablespoon Asian dark sesame oil

1 tablespoon corn oil

4 cloves garlic, minced

1. Remove stems and ribs from chard leaves. Rinse leaves well in cold water; drain and place in large pot with about ½ cup water. Cover pot and set over high heat. Boil, covered, about 5 minutes, until chard is wilted. Drain and plunge into large bowl of cold water. Let stand several minutes until completely cool and drain in a colander. Squeeze the chard gently between your hands to remove most, but not all, of the water. Chop the chard coarsely and set aside. (May be prepared several hours ahead and refrigerated.)

2. Remove stems from mushrooms. Slice the caps into thin strips and set aside. In a small bowl, combine the nuoc mam, vinegar, sugar, and red pepper flakes; cover until needed. (May be prepared several hours ahead.)

3. Place both oils in a 12-inch skillet and set pan over medium-high heat. Add the garlic and cook, stirring, for 30 seconds without browning. Add the mushrooms and sauté another minute. Add the chard. Stir and cook 2 to 3 minutes to heat through and to evaporate some of the excess moisture. Stir the sauce mixture well and add it to the pan. Toss well and serve hot.

BRAISED SAVOY CABBAGE AND CARROTS

This is an ideal fall dish to accompany game, a simple meat loaf, or grilled sausages.

2 tablespoons butter

2 medium yellow onions (¾ pound total), thinly sliced

2 medium carrots (½ pound total), peeled and thinly sliced

1 pound cored Savoy cabbage, cut into 1-inch chunks

2 bay leaves

⅓ cup dry white French vermouth

½ cup rich chicken stock (page 5)

¾ teaspoon salt

¼ teaspoon freshly ground black pepper

1. Melt the butter in a 12-inch skillet over medium-low heat. Add the onions and carrots. Stir well and cover the pan.

2. Cook until onions are wilted, about 10 minutes. Add the cabbage, bay leaves, vermouth, chicken stock, salt, and pepper.

3. Cook, covered, until cabbage is tender and liquid is almost completely absorbed, about 30 minutes. If there is too much liquid left, raise the heat and cook, while stirring, until liquid has evaporated. Taste and adjust seasoning with salt and pepper, if needed. Serve hot.

SCALLOPED POTATOES WITH LEEKS AND GARLIC

Leeks add a richness of flavor to an old favorite. This is delicious with anything, or on its own.

1¾ pounds boiling potatoes, such as
    yellow Finn
1 tablespoon butter
2 cloves garlic, minced
2 cups thinly sliced leeks, including
    some of the tender green part
1²/₃ cups milk
¾ teaspoon salt
¼ teaspoon freshly ground black
    pepper
⅛ teaspoon freshly grated nutmeg
1 egg
¼ cup grated Swiss, Gruyère, or
    Emmenthaler cheese

1. Adjust an oven rack to the center position and preheat the oven to 425°. Lightly butter a 12x8x1¾-inch ovenproof baking dish; set aside. Peel the potatoes and slice them thinly. (I like to use the 2mm slicing disc of a food processor.)

2. Melt the butter in a 2-quart saucepan over medium heat. Stir in the garlic and leeks. Cover the pan and cook 5 minutes. Remove pan from the heat. In a medium-sized bowl, whisk together the milk, salt, pepper, nutmeg, and egg to combine well. Arrange one-third of the potatoes in a single layer on the bottom of the prepared dish. Spoon half the leek mixture over the potatoes. Repeat the layering with half the remaining potatoes, the remainder of the leeks, and finish with the last of the potatoes. Carefully pour in the milk mixture, which should just come to the top of the potatoes. If not, add more milk.

3. Place the dish in the oven. After 30 minutes, remove the dish and press the top layer firmly with a large metal spatula to immerse the potatoes in the milk mixture. Sprinkle with the cheese and return the dish to the oven. Bake 15 to 20 minutes longer, or until browned on top and the potatoes are tender. Cut into squares and serve hot.

SWEET ONION TART

For this tart, slices of Walla Walla onions are dipped in flour and sautéed. The onions are arranged in a tart shell, bathed with a custard, and baked until golden brown. This serves 6 as a luncheon entree or makes 8 appetizer portions.

Pastry

1½ cups (6¾ ounces) unbleached
    all-purpose flour
½ cup (1¾ ounces) cake flour
½ teaspoon salt
¾ cup (1½ sticks) cold butter, cut
    into 8 pieces
⅓ cup ice water

Filling

3 large sweet yellow onions
Unbleached all-purpose flour, for
    coating
3 tablespoons butter
3 tablespoons olive oil
3 eggs
1 cup half-and-half
½ teaspoon salt
¼ teaspoon freshly ground black
    pepper
⅛ teaspoon freshly grated nutmeg
1 tablespoon chopped fresh oregano
5 tablespoons freshly grated
    Parmesan cheese

1. Measure the flours for the pastry by spooning them into metal measuring cups, filling the cups to overflowing, and sweeping off the excess with a metal spatula.

2. To make the pastry in a food processor, place the flours, salt, and butter in the work bowl of a food processor fitted with the metal blade. Pulse 4 times to chop the butter coarsely. Then, while pulsing very rapidly, gradually add the ice water through the feed tube in a steady stream. Pulse 20 to 30 times, or until the dough almost gathers into a ball. Carefully remove the dough from the work bowl and shape it into a 6-inch disc on waxed paper. Dust the dough lightly with flour if it is sticky. Wrap and refrigerate the dough 1 hour or longer.

3. To make the pastry by hand, place the flours, salt, and butter in a medium-size bowl. Cut in the butter with a pastry blender until the particles resemble coarse meal. Sprinkle the ice water over the dry ingredients while gently tossing the mixture with a fork. Continue mixing until the dough gathers into a ball. Shape, wrap, and refrigerate as directed.

4. Roll out the pastry on a lightly floured surface to form a 13-inch circle. Fit the dough loosely into a 10-inch tart pan 1-inch deep with a removable bottom. Gently work the pastry into the corners, but do not stretch it. Use scissors to trim the overhanging pastry to ½ inch beyond the edge of the pan. Fold the pastry onto itself, making the sides a double thickness by pressing the pastry firmly into place. While doing so, raise the edge of the pastry so that it extends about ¼ inch above the pan rim. Place the tart pan on a baking sheet and freeze, uncovered, for 20 to 30 minutes.

5. Meanwhile, adjust an oven rack to the center position and preheat the oven to 400°. Line the pastry shell with aluminum foil and fill it with dry beans

or rice. Bake 20 minutes, or until the edge of the pastry is lightly colored. Remove the foil and beans and return the pastry to the oven for 5 minutes, or until it appears set and is only very lightly browned. If the pastry puffs up during baking, prick it gently with a fork in a couple of places. Cool until ready to use.

6. To make the filling, peel the onions and slice them into circles about $1/3$ inch thick. You should have 15 to 16 slices. Spread the flour on a large sheet of waxed paper and dip the onion slices in the flour to lightly coat both sides. Combine $1^1/2$ tablespoons of the butter and $1^1/2$ tablespoons of the olive oil in a 12-inch skillet over medium heat. When the butter is hot, add half the onion slices in a single layer and cook until nicely browned on both sides, about 10 minutes. Turn the onions carefully with a wide metal spatula to keep the slices intact. Transfer the onions to paper towels and set aside to drain. Repeat with the remaining $1^1/2$ tablespoons butter and oil and the rest of the onions.

7. When ready to bake, adjust the oven rack to the center position and preheat the oven to 325°. In a medium-sized bowl, whisk together the eggs, half-and-half, salt, pepper, nutmeg, and oregano until well combined. Sprinkle the bottom of the pastry shell with 3 tablespoons of Parmesan. Arrange the onion slices, slightly overlapping, in the shell to cover the bottom. Pour in the egg mixture and sprinkle with the remaining 2 tablespoons of Parmesan. Bake the tart for 45 to 50 minutes, or until it is puffed and browned and the filling is set. Cool 5 minutes. Set the tart on an inverted 8-inch round cake pan. The sides should drop away easily. Slip a wide metal spatula between the tart and the base of the pan to remove the pastry, and slide it onto a serving platter. Serve hot or warm.

TWICE-BAKED POTATOES WITH PARSNIPS AND GOAT CHEESE

YIELD: 6 SERVINGS

Although goat cheese is not normally associated with the Mountain West, it has become very popular here. Several local dairies make wonderful goat cheeses, as excellent as any I've tried. In this recipe, the goat cheese gives a richness to the filling while adding a tanginess that accentuates the sweetness of the parsnip. You can prepare this dish a day ahead and bake it just before serving.

3 large russet potatoes

1 large parsnip, peeled and cut in
    ½-inch pieces

1 small carrot, peeled and cut in
    ½-inch pieces

3 cloves garlic, peeled and thinly
    sliced

2 ounces goat cheese

¼ teaspoon Tabasco sauce

½ cup buttermilk

¾ teaspoon salt

¼ teaspoon freshly ground black
    pepper

⅛ teaspoon freshly grated nutmeg

1 egg white

2 scallions, thinly sliced

2 tablespoons grated Romano cheese

¼ teaspoon sweet paprika

1. Adjust an oven rack to the center position and preheat the oven to 450°. Wash the potatoes, pierce them well with a fork, and place them on the oven rack. Bake until tender, about 50 minutes. Remove from the oven and let cool 30 minutes.

2. Meanwhile, bring 2 quarts of water to a boil in a 4-quart saucepan over high heat. Add the parsnip, carrot, and garlic. Cook, uncovered, about 20 minutes, or until the vegetables are tender. Drain well. Transfer the vegetables to the work bowl of a food processor fitted with the metal blade. Process until smooth, about 1 minute. Scrape down the inside of the work bowl. Crumble the goat cheese into the bowl and add the Tabasco. Process again until smooth.

3. Cut the warm potatoes in half lengthwise and scoop out the pulp, leaving a ¼-inch thick shell. Place the pulp in a medium-sized bowl and mash with a potato masher or handheld electric mixer. Add the buttermilk, salt, pepper, nutmeg, and egg white and beat together well. Stir in the scallions, then add the parsnip mixture. Stir well and adjust the seasoning, if necessary. Spoon the potato mixture into the shells, mounding the filling slightly in the center. Combine the Romano cheese and paprika in a small bowl and sprinkle about ½ teaspoon over each potato.

4. To bake, preheat the oven to 400°. Place the potatoes on a baking sheet and bake, uncovered, 15 to 20 minutes, or until the filling is very hot and the tops are lightly browned.

RUTABAGA AND POTATO CASSEROLE WITH CREAM CHEESE

Here is another casserole for a winter's meal. Julienned rutabagas and potatoes are baked in a white sauce enriched with Neufchâtel cheese, cream cheese with one-third less fat than its regular counterpart. I guarantee you won't miss the excess fat. Serve this with hamburger patties, buffalo burgers, roast beef or lamb, or with roast chicken.

1¼ pounds (2 medium) rutabagas

1¼ pounds (2 large) white boiling
   potatoes

2 tablespoons flour

1½ cups milk

1 teaspoon salt

¼ teaspoon freshly ground
   black pepper

4 ounces Neufchâtel cheese, cut into
   4 pieces

1 tablespoon Worcestershire sauce

2 tablespoons dry unseasoned fine
   bread crumbs

2 tablespoons finely chopped parsley

1 tablespoon melted butter

1. Adjust an oven rack to center position and preheat oven to 350°. Lightly butter a 1½-quart shallow ovenproof baking dish.

2. Bring 4 quarts of water to a rolling boil over high heat in an 8-quart pot. Meanwhile, peel rutabagas and potatoes and cut them into ¼-inch strips. Drop the rutabagas into the water, cover the pot, and return the water to a boil. Uncover the pot and boil 2 minutes. Add the potatoes, cover the pot, and bring the water back to the boil. Remove lid and cook at a rapid boil 1 minute longer. Drain vegetables in a large colander.

3. Place the flour in a 2- to 3-quart saucepan. Gradually whisk in the milk to make a smooth texture. Add the salt and pepper and bring mixture to the boil, whisking constantly over medium-high heat. Continue whisking and cooking for 1 minute after the mixture boils and thickens. Remove pot from heat and add the cream cheese. Stir with wire whisk until cheese is melted and mixture is smooth. Mix in the Worcestershire sauce.

4. In a large bowl, combine the rutabagas and potatoes with the sauce, folding together gently. Transfer to prepared dish and cover tightly with foil. Bake 45 minutes. Combine the bread crumbs, parsley, and butter in a small bowl. Remove dish from oven, uncover and sprinkle with the crumb mixture. Bake uncovered 15 to 20 minutes longer. Serve hot or warm.

GRATIN OF WINTER SQUASH WITH PARSNIPS

This is definitely a dish to serve on a cold winter's day. Cubes of winter squash and parsnips are tossed with seasoned bread crumbs, topped with cheddar cheese, and baked. English Double Gloucester and aged Wisconsin or Vermont white cheddar are excellent choices.

⅓ cup dry unseasoned fine bread crumbs

½ teaspoon dried oregano leaves, crumbled

½ teaspoon dried whole thyme leaves, crumbled

1 teaspoon salt

¼ teaspoon freshly ground black pepper

½ cup finely chopped fresh flat-leaf parsley

6 cups peeled, cubed winter squash, such as Hubbard

2 cups peeled, cubed parsnips

3 tablespoons extra-virgin olive oil

1 cup shredded sharp cheddar cheese

1. Adjust an oven rack to the center position and preheat the oven to 325°. Lightly butter a shallow 2-quart ovenproof baking dish. (I use a 10-inch glass dish that is 2 inches deep).

2. In a large bowl, combine the bread crumbs, oregano, thyme, salt, pepper, and parsley. Add the squash and parsnips and toss to coat well. Add the olive oil and toss to combine well. Transfer to the prepared dish and cover tightly with foil. Bake 1½ hours. Uncover the pan and sprinkle evenly with the cheese. Return the pan to the oven and bake, uncovered, another 15 minutes. Serve hot or warm.

BARLEY, CORN, AND DRY JACK CHEESE BAKE

This is my version of a barley and corn side dish that I devoured in Red Lodge, Montana, at the Pollard Hotel. The chef at the time, Scott Greenlee, served it with ostrich steaks (for more information about ostrich meat, see page 125), and the combination was sensational. Barley is so tasty, it deserves more attention. The two most common forms of barley available are whole hulled barley, which you are most likely to find in health food stores, and pearl barley, which is available in supermarkets and in health food stores. Whole hulled barley needs to be soaked overnight in water before cooking; even pearl barley, which can be cooked without soaking, will have a fluffier texture if presoaked. I believe it is improper cooking that has limited the appeal of this tasty, nutritious grain. According to Bert Greene in The Grains Cookbook, *heating the cooking liquid to boiling before adding the barley will prevent the grains from sticking to each other. Another of his recommendations to achieve a fluffy texture is to parboil the barley and then steam it. This dish may be made several hours ahead and refrigerated before baking. Dry Monterey Jack cheese has a firm, compact texture and a nutty flavor. If unavailable, use regular Jack cheese.*

1 cup whole hulled or pearl barley

2 tablespoons plus 1 teaspoon salt

2 tablespoons butter

1 large sweet yellow onion, chopped

2 ears sweet yellow corn, kernels cut off the cob

1 small red bell pepper, cored, seeded, and diced

¼ teaspoon freshly ground black pepper

3 tablespoons chopped fresh flat-leaf parsley

1 tablespoon chopped fresh thyme leaves

1 cup grated dry Monterey Jack cheese

1. If using whole hulled barley, soak it overnight in 5 cups cold water. It isn't necessary to soak the pearl barley, but you can if you want to. The next day, bring 4 quarts of water and the 2 tablespoons of salt to a rolling boil in an 8-quart pot. If presoaked, drain the barley in a wire strainer. Add the barley to the pot and stir once or twice to prevent it from sticking. Cover briefly until the water returns to a boil, then uncover and boil the whole hulled barley for 1 hour, or boil pearl barley for 20 minutes. Drain in a colander.

2. Fill a steamer with several inches of boiling water and bring the water to a boil. Add the barley to the top of the steamer, cover it loosely with a damp kitchen towel, and steam for 30 minutes. (Presoaked pearl barley will probably be ready in 15 minutes.) The barley should be fluffy and tender.

3. Butter a 12x8x2-inch ovenproof dish.

4. Melt the butter in a large skillet over medium heat. When hot, add the onion and corn. Cook, stirring often, until the onion and corn are almost tender, 6 to 8 minutes. Do not brown the vegetables. Add the red bell pepper and cook 2 to 3 minutes. Stir in the steamed barley, remaining 1 teaspoon of salt, the pepper, parsley, and thyme. Transfer half of the mixture to the prepared pan. Sprinkle with $1/2$ cup of the cheese and spread the remaining barley mixture over the cheese. Sprinkle the remaining cheese over the top.

5. Adjust an oven rack to the center position and preheat the oven to 350°. Cover the dish tightly with aluminum foil and bake for 45 minutes, or until the barley is very hot. Serve immediately.

Variations: Remove and discard stems from $1/4$ pound fresh shiitake mushrooms. Slice the mushroom caps thin and sauté them in 1 tablespoon butter until tender; season with salt and freshly ground black pepper and stir into barley-corn mixture. Proceed with the recipe as described above.

For a smoky taste, cook 4 slices of bacon until crisp. Drain well and crumble the bacon or chop it into small pieces. Stir it into the barley-corn mixture and proceed with the recipe as described above.

For a Southwestern flavor with a bit of heat, roast, peel, seed, and dice 2 poblano chiles and add them to the barley-corn mixture. You can also add red bell pepper both for color and for its sweet taste. Proceed with the recipe as described above.

DESSERTS

In Montana, fresh fruits take center stage in desserts. We lavish attention on wild huckleberries, strawberries, and raspberries. Our locally grown cherries, especially the sour Montmorency variety, are used in pies, tarts, and turnovers. The sweet cherries are mostly eaten as is, preserved whole in brandy, or stewed into a sauce for game.

Rhubarb, which thrives in the cool mountain air, is especially appreciated here, where the warm weather takes its time to come; it is the first of summer's "fruit," ready to be picked in early May. Rhubarb, which is really a vegetable, needs a lot of sugar to temper its acidity. When using rhubarb, I do not skimp on sugar, but I also try to avoid overwhelming its natural taste. Vanilla, for example, adds a sweetness of its own, which allows me to use less sugar. You'll find recipes here for unusual uses of rhubarb—such as rhubarb ice cream and rhubarb curd.

In July, the strawberries ripen (provided the robins and voles haven't claimed them first), followed by raspberries, blueberries, and huckleberries. I am inspired by nature's bounty to make pies, tarts, sorbets, ice creams, sauces, chutneys, and jams. So much fruit, and so little time!

I've worked on the pastry recipes for the pies and tarts in this chapter over many years, until I felt I couldn't make them any better. During this process, I've come to prefer making pastry dough with a food processor. The food processor gives me excellent results quickly, and I can make batch after batch if I'm pressed for time.

I have not included chocolate recipes because I wanted to celebrate the foods that grow in the region. For surefire success with these recipes, use the freshest ingredients of the highest quality, and follow the instructions closely. You will be delighted with your results.

RHUBARB PUREE

Rhubarb is like zucchini—one plant will give you more than you can use in a season. Rhubarb grows exceptionally well in Montana. The cool nights and long days provide us with luxuriant rhubarb plants with bright-red stalks from early May through August. Spring rhubarb is less fibrous and more tart than summer rhubarb, and I prefer it in this rhubarb puree. Rhubarb Ice Cream (page 211), and Rhubarb Curd (page 217) are just a couple uses of this versatile preparation.

2 pounds trimmed rhubarb stalks

2²/₃ cups sugar

1. Cut the rhubarb stalks into 1-inch pieces. Combine the rhubarb and sugar in a heavy 4-quart stainless steel or enamelware saucepan. Cover and cook over medium-low heat, stirring occasionally, until the rhubarb is very tender and falling apart, about 1 hour.

2. Let it cool slightly, then either pass the mixture through the finest holes of a food mill or through the power strainer attachment of a food processor.

3. If using early-season rhubarb, you should have about 4 cups of puree; late-season rhubarb will give you about 3 cups puree. In either case, return the puree to the saucepan and cook, stirring frequently over medium-low heat, until thickened and reduced to 2½ cups. Remove from the heat, and cool completely; cover and refrigerate. This keeps well in the refrigerator for about 1 week.

BITTERROOT VALLEY STRAWBERRY PIE

YIELD: 8 SERVINGS

The Bitterroot Valley, just south of my home in Missoula, is one of the best strawberry-growing areas in the country. The berries are small, tender, juicy, and loaded with flavor. Besides tasting great plain with a bit of sugar, they are excellent baked in this pie. This recipe is based on a prizewinner from the Tenth Pillsbury Bake-Off. I was a teenage finalist in the same contest and didn't make the pie until many years later. The small amount of pineapple in the filling works wonderfully with the strawberries. This pie is delicious plain or with whipped cream, ice cream, or vanilla frozen yogurt.

Pastry

1¼ cups (5½ ounces) unbleached
    all-purpose flour

⅓ cup (1¼ ounces) cake flour

½ teaspoon salt

½ cup (1 stick) butter, chilled and cut
    into 6 pieces

¼ cup vegetable shortening, chilled

¼ cup ice water

Strawberry-Pineapple Filling

1 cup plus 1 tablespoon sugar

5 tablespoons cornstarch

¼ teaspoon salt

5 cups hulled and sliced strawberries

1 (8-ounce) can pineapple tidbits in
    juice, very well drained

2 tablespoons butter, chilled and cut
    into small pieces

1. Measure the flours for the pastry by spooning them into measuring cups, filling the cups to overflowing, and sweeping off the excess with a metal spatula.

2. To make the pastry in a food processor, place both flours in the work bowl of a food processor fitted with the metal blade. Add the salt, butter, and shortening. Pulse the machine 4 times, about 1 second each. Then, while pulsing rapidly, gradually add the ice water through the feed tube. Keep pulsing very rapidly until the dough almost gathers into a ball. Remove the dough from the work bowl and place it on a sheet of plastic wrap. Pat the dough gently to form a 6-inch disc.

3. To make the pastry by hand, place both flours in a large mixing bowl and stir in the salt. Add the butter and shortening and cut them in with a pastry blender until the particles resemble small peas. Sprinkle in the ice water while tossing the mixture lightly with a fork. Keep tossing until the mixture is moistened and gathers into a ball. Remove the dough from the bowl, place it on a sheet of plastic wrap, and pat it gently to form a 6-inch disc.

4. Cut one-quarter of the pastry circle away and bring the cut ends of the larger piece together to form a new, smaller circle. Wrap both pieces of pastry in plastic and refrigerate at least 1 hour.

5. Adjust two oven racks with one rack in the lowest position and one rack in the center. Place a heavy baking sheet on the lower rack and preheat the oven to 450°. On a lightly floured surface, roll the larger piece of pastry into a 13-inch circle. Fit it loosely into a 9-inch pie pan. Trim away excess pastry with scissors, leaving $1/2$ inch of overhang. Reserve the pastry scraps. Fold the pastry edge back on itself and press together to form a high-standing rim. Flute the edge. (Even with a high rim, the filling may bubble over if the berries are especially juicy.) Place the crust in the freezer while you prepare the filling.

6. In a large mixing bowl, combine the 1 cup sugar, the cornstarch, and salt. Add the strawberries and pineapple and fold them in until the mixture is moistened. Add the pastry scraps to the wedge of pastry and roll it into an 8-inch circle on a lightly floured surface. Prick the pastry generously with a fork and cut it into 8 wedges.

7. Remove the crust from the freezer and pour the filling into it. Dot the top with the butter and set the pastry wedges over the filling, leaving a little space between the wedges. Lightly brush cold water over the pastry and sprinkle it with the remaining 1 tablespoon sugar. Immediately place the pie on the baking sheet on the lower shelf and bake for 15 minutes. Transfer the pie, still on the baking sheet, to the center shelf, reduce the oven temperature to 350°, and continue baking 50 to 60 minutes, or until the filling is very bubbly and the top crust is golden brown. Cool completely, cut into wedges, and serve.

Calamity Jane's 20 Year Cake

Calamity Jane, born Martha Jane Cannary, was a legendary frontiers-woman. She had many talents, one of which happened to be cooking. She also had a highly developed imagination and kept a diary addressed to her imaginary daughter Janey. She was a generous, good-hearted woman, and this is her "receipt" or recipe for fruitcake, which she calls "20 Year Cake."

"Mix together 25 eggs beaten separate, $\frac{1}{2}$ pounds each of sugar, flour and butter, $7\frac{1}{2}$ pounds seeded raisins, $1\frac{1}{2}$ pounds citron cut very fine, 5 pounds currants, $\frac{1}{4}$ ounce [ground] cloves, $\frac{1}{2}$ ounce cinnamon, 2 ounces mace, 2 ounces nutmeg, 2 teaspoons yeast powder [baking powder], or 2 teaspoons soda and 3 cream tartar. Bake.

This will make 3 cakes 8 pounds each. Pour a pint of brandy over the cakes while still warm. Seal in tight crock. This cake is unexcelled and will keep good to the last crum, even if it takes twenty years."

RHUBARB ICE CREAM

This is velvety smooth, rich, and creamy, much like a gelato. The addition of strawberry liqueur prevents the ice cream from becoming rock hard. This is excellent by itself or served with Rhubarb Pie (page 222), Gingered Apple Pie (page 224), or Rhubarb, Strawberry, and Hazelnut Crisp (page 212).

4 egg yolks

2 cups heavy cream

⅛ teaspoon salt

¼ cup sugar (optional)

1½ cups strained rhubarb puree
(page 206)

¼ cup strawberry liqueur

1. Whisk the yolks in a small bowl, just well enough to blend. Place the cream in a heavy 2-quart saucepan and set over medium-high heat until tiny bubbles form around the edges and steam rises from the surface. Very gradually, whisk about ½ cup of the cream into the egg yolks to warm them. Then, off heat, whisk the egg yolk mixture into the remaining cream in the saucepan. Stir in the salt and sugar. The amount of sugar you use, if any, will depend on the tartness of the rhubarb. Taste carefully and adjust the sweetness accordingly.

2. Return the pan to medium heat and stir continuously with a rubber spatula, going all around the side of the pan and along the bottom until the mixture thickens into a custard and is very hot. The temperature should be 175° to 180°. Do not allow it to boil. Place the pan in a large shallow pan filled with ice cubes and water, and stir occasionally with the rubber spatula until the mixture reaches room temperature. Stir in the rhubarb puree and liqueur. Chill well, about 2 hours. Freeze in an ice cream maker according to the manufacturer's directions.

RHUBARB, STRAWBERRY, AND HAZELNUT CRISP

The tartness of rhubarb and the sweetness of strawberries are a classic duo. Luckily, the two appear in markets at about the same time. But I have made this crisp without strawberries and think it is just as delicious, maybe because the hazelnuts add their own sweetness. Serve with Rhubarb Ice Cream (page 211), whipped cream, vanilla ice cream, or frozen vanilla yogurt.

Filling

¼ cup (1¼ ounces) unbleached
    all-purpose flour

½ cup granulated sugar

½ cup firmly packed dark
    brown sugar

½ teaspoon ground cinnamon

¼ teaspoon freshly grated nutmeg

⅛ teaspoon mace

½ pound ripe, juicy strawberries

1½ pounds trimmed rhubarb stalks,
    cut in ½-inch pieces (6 cups)

1 teaspoon pure vanilla extract

Topping

1 cup (5 ounces) unbleached
    all-purpose flour

⅓ cup firmly packed dark
    brown sugar

2 tablespoons granulated sugar

1 teaspoon ground cinnamon

½ cup (1 stick) chilled unsalted
    butter, cut into 6 pieces

½ cup toasted, skinned hazelnuts
    (see page 3)

1. Adjust an oven rack to the center position and preheat the oven to 375°.

2. Measure the flour for the filling by scooping a measuring cup into the flour container, filling the cup to overflowing, and sweeping off the excess with a metal spatula. In a large bowl, combine both sugars, the cinnamon, nutmeg, mace, and flour. Use your fingertips to break up any lumps of brown sugar. Rinse the strawberries and pat them dry on paper towels. Remove the hulls and cut the berries into ¼- to ½-inch-thick slices. (You should have about 2 cups.) Add the rhubarb, strawberries, and vanilla to the sugar mixture and fold gently with a rubber spatula until the mixture is well moistened. Turn into an ungreased 9x9x2-inch baking pan or a 10-inch round baking dish 2 inches deep.

3. Measure the flour for the topping by scooping a dry measuring cup into the flour container, filling the cup to overflowing, and sweeping off the excess with a metal spatula.

4. To make the topping in a food processor, place the flour in the work bowl of a food processor fitted with the metal blade. Add both sugars, the cinnamon, and butter. Pulse 3 or 4 times to begin breaking the butter up into smaller pieces. Add the hazelnuts and pulse rapidly about 10 times until both the butter and the nuts are finely chopped.

5. To make topping by hand, combine the flour, both sugars, and the cinnamon in a large bowl. Use your fingertips to break up any lumps in the brown sugar. Add the butter and cut it in with a pastry blender until the particles resemble small peas. Chop the hazelnuts medium-fine with a large knife and stir them in.

6. Turn mixture over the rhubarb filling and spread it gently with your hands, without packing it down, to cover the filling completely. Place the pan in the oven and bake 40 to 50 minutes, or until the filling is very bubbly and the topping is a rich brown color. Remove from the oven, cool, and serve warm or at room temperature.

SOUR CHERRY STREUSEL TART

Fresh sour pie cherries are as precious as rubies. Bright and shiny like the gems they resemble, the sour Montmorency cherries have a short season (only 2 to 3 weeks in July) where I live, so I always buy some to use fresh and some to freeze. A true luxury is popping a just-picked warm fresh cherry into my mouth, pulling away the stem, and eating the flesh off its pit. I shiver from the tartness, but I know summer is here at last.

This recipe is one of the best ways I know to celebrate the pie cherry. Please note that the filling mixture needs to sit at room temperature about 5 hours, so prepare it first. You could even start it the night before and leave it in the refrigerator. And be careful when eating this mouthwatering treat: Even though the cherries are pitted, I always warn people to beware of renegade pits. One or two often manage to escape the pitter.

Filling

2 pounds fresh sour pie cherries,
　　stemmed and pitted (4 cups)

1 cup sugar

3 tablespoons cornstarch

¼ teaspoon salt

Finely grated zest of 1 lemon

Pastry

1¼ cups (6¼ ounces) unbleached
　　all-purpose flour

⅓ cup (1½ ounces) cake flour

¼ teaspoon salt

1 tablespoon sugar

½ cup (1 stick) chilled unsalted
　　butter, cut into 6 pieces

2 tablespoons chilled vegetable
　　shortening

⅓ cup ice water

Streusel Topping

½ cup (2½ ounces) unbleached all-purpose flour

½ cup firmly packed light brown sugar

1 teaspoon ground cinnamon

¼ teaspoon mace

6 tablespoons (¾ stick) chilled unsalted butter, cut into 6 pieces

1. To make the filling, combine the cherries with the sugar in a large bowl and let the mixture stand for about 5 hours at room temperature, stirring occasionally, until the sugar is dissolved and the cherry juices are released. Drain well in a wire strainer set over a bowl. Transfer the juice to a 2-cup glass measure and add enough water to reach $1^{1}/4$ cups. In a heavy-bottomed 2-quart saucepan, whisk together the liquid, cornstarch, and salt. Bring to a boil over medium heat, stirring gently but continuously with a rubber spatula, and cook 2 to 3 minutes, or until the mixture is thick and translucent. Remove from the heat and stir in the grated lemon zest and the drained cherries.

2. Measure the flours for the pastry by scooping a dry measuring cup into the flour containers, filling the cup to overflowing, and sweeping off the excess with a metal spatula.

3. To make the pastry in a food processor, place both flours, the salt, sugar, butter, and shortening in the work bowl of a food processor fitted with the metal blade. Pulse rapidly 4 times to begin breaking up the fat. While pulsing very rapidly, gradually pour the ice water through the feed tube. Pulse 20 to 30 more times, or until the dough almost gathers into a ball. Carefully remove the dough from the work bowl, lightly dust it with flour, and shape it into a 6-inch disc. Wrap securely in plastic wrap and refrigerate at least l hour.

4. To make the pastry by hand, place both flours, the salt, sugar, butter, and shortening in a large mixing bowl. Cut in the fats with a pastry blender until the particles resemble small peas. While tossing with a fork, gradually sprinkle in the ice water until the dough gathers into a ball. Continue as directed above.

5. Roll out the pastry on a lightly floured surface into a 14-inch circle. Loosely fit it into an 11-inch tart pan 1 inch deep with a removable bottom and a fluted edge. Trim the overhanging pastry to within $1/2$ inch of the tart pan rim, then fold the overhang against the sides of the pastry in the pan, pressing firmly to join the two. There should be about $1/4$ inch of pastry extending above the tart rim. Place the tart pan in the freezer for 15 minutes.

6. Meanwhile, adjust an oven rack to the center position, place a heavy baking sheet on the rack, and preheat the oven to 400°. Remove the pastry from the freezer and line it with a square of aluminum foil, pressing the foil into the

corners and allowing the excess to extend upright above the rim. Fill the tart pan with dried beans or rice, place the pan on the baking sheet, and bake for about 20 minutes, or until pastry is lightly colored. Remove the pan from the oven, carefully remove the foil and beans or rice, and return the tart shell to the oven for 5 more minutes. Watch carefully to see if the pastry puffs; if it does, prick it in a few places with a cake tester or a narrow wooden skewer. Remove the pan from the oven and set aside to cool. (The crust may be made hours ahead.)

7. Measure the flour for the topping by scooping a measuring cup into the flour container, filling the cup to overflowing, and sweeping off the excess with a metal spatula.

8. To make the topping in a food processor, place the flour, brown sugar, cinnamon, mace, and butter in the work bowl of a food processor fitted with a metal blade. Pulse several times, or until the mixture is crumbly.

9. To make the topping by hand, combine the flour, brown sugar, cinnamon, and mace in a medium-size bowl, breaking up any lumps in the brown sugar with your fingertips. Add the butter and cut it in with a pastry blender until the mixture resembles coarse crumbs.

10. Preheat the oven to 400°.

11. Turn the cherry filling into the cooled partially baked crust, and spread it level. Sprinkle the topping evenly over the filling, patting it very gently in place without packing it down. The tart shell should be full. Place the tart pan on the baking sheet and place in the oven. Bake for 30 minutes, or until the filling is bubbly and the topping is nicely browned. Remove from the oven and place on a rack to cool. When the tart has cooled to room temperature, remove the side of the pan, cut the tart into wedges, and serve.

Note: To prepare pie cherries for freezing, combine 4 cups pitted cherries with 1 cup sugar and 4 level teaspoons of Fruit Fresh, stirring to mix well. Transfer to airtight freezer containers, seal, date, and freeze. The cherries will keep well for up to 1 year, but you'll probably want them during the winter to revive summer memories. To use, thaw thoroughly in a wire strainer set over a bowl to collect all the juices. Measure the juice and add enough water to reach 1¼ cups. Proceed as the recipe directs.

RHUBARB CURD

This is a tart and delicious spread to use on toast, English muffins, crumpets, hot biscuits, or waffles. You can also use it to fill pancakes or tart shells or as a base for a filling in cream puffs, cakes, or pies. It keeps well in the refrigerator for 2 weeks. The color is a bit odd, almost like coffee with a small amount of cream added. But don't be put off by its looks. The beauty, in this case, is most definitely in the taste.

3 eggs
¼ cup (½ stick) butter
1 cup rhubarb puree (page 206)

1. Whisk the eggs in a small bowl to combine well. Melt the butter in a heavy 2-quart saucepan over medium heat. Stir in the rhubarb puree. Cook, stirring continuously with a rubber spatula, until the mixture is warm. Remove the pan from the heat and quickly whisk in the eggs. Return the pan to the heat and cook, stirring continuously with the rubber spatula, until the mixture thickens to the consistency of lightly whipped cream, 8 to 10 minutes. Draw the flat tip of the spatula from side to side over the bottom of the pan. You should be able to see the bottom of the pan briefly before the curd flows together. When ready, the curd should register 180° on an instant-read thermometer.

2. Place the saucepan in a large shallow pan filled with ice cubes and water, and stir occasionally with the rubber spatula until the curd reaches room temperature. Transfer to a container, cover tightly, and refrigerate. The curd will thicken further and become like a soft pudding when chilled.

BLUEBERRY-RHUBARB PIE

In midsummer, when blueberries make their welcome appearance, I like to make this pie. Blueberries or huckleberries and rhubarb are an excellent combination.

Pie Crust Pastry

1¾ cups (8¾ ounces) unbleached
    all-purpose flour

¾ cup (3¼ ounces) cake flour

½ teaspoon salt

1 cup (2 sticks) chilled butter, cut into
    8 pieces

1 egg yolk

1 teaspoon cider vinegar

Ice water

Blueberry-Rhubarb Filling

¾ pound trimmed rhubarb stalks, cut
    into ½-inch pieces (3 cups)

1½ cups plus 1 tablespoon sugar

4 to 5 tablespoons quick-cooking
    tapioca

¼ teaspoon salt

¼ teaspoon ground cinnamon

¼ teaspoon mace

Finely grated zest of 1 orange

1½ pounds (5 cups) blueberries,
    picked over

2 tablespoons cold butter, cut into
    small pieces

1. Measure the flours for the pastry by scooping a measuring cup into the flour containers, filling the cup to overflowing, and sweeping off the excess with a metal spatula.

2. To make the pastry in a food processor, place both flours in the work bowl of a food processor fitted with the metal blade. Add the salt and butter. Pulse 4 times to break up the butter. In a glass measuring cup, combine the egg yolk, cider vinegar, and enough ice water to total ½ cup. Start pulsing very rapidly while adding the wet ingredients in a steady stream through the feed tube. It will take 25 to 30 quick pulses to thoroughly mix the pastry, but do not process until dough gathers into a ball; stop just before that happens. Remove the dough from the work bowl, press it gently into one mass and divide it in two, with one piece slightly larger than the other. (If you have a scale, one portion should weigh about 12 ounces and the other 10 ounces.) Shape each portion into a 6-inch disc, dusting it lightly with flour if necessary, and wrap securely in plastic wrap. Refrigerate 1 hour or longer.

3. To make the pastry by hand, place both flours in a large mixing bowl. Stir in the salt and add the butter, cutting it in with a pastry blender until the mixture resembles small peas. In a glass measuring cup, combine the egg yolk, cider vinegar, and enough ice water to total ½ cup. Gradually add the wet ingredients to the flour and butter mixture while gently tossing with a fork. Continue tossing until the mixture gathers into a ball. Shape and chill as directed above.

4. To prepare the filling, combine the rhubarb and ½ cup of the sugar in a 2- to 3-quart saucepan. Cover and cook over low heat, stirring occasionally, until the rhubarb begins to soften and its juices are released, about 20 minutes. Transfer to a wire strainer set over a bowl and set aside to cool. (You will not use the juice in this recipe, however, it makes an excellent drink when combined with mineral water or dry white wine.) In a large bowl, combine

the remaining 1 cup sugar, the tapioca, salt, cinnamon, mace, and orange zest. Add the blueberries and rhubarb and fold together gently but thoroughly. Let the mixture stand for 15 minutes.

5. Meanwhile, adjust two oven racks so that one is on the lowest shelf and the other is in the center. Place a heavy baking sheet on the lower rack and preheat the oven to 450°.

6. On a lightly floured surface, roll the larger pastry disc into a 13-inch circle. Fit the dough loosely into a 9-inch glass or metal pie pan, leaving excess pastry hanging over the edge. Spread the filling in the crust, mounding it slightly in the center, then pat it gently in place with your hands. Scatter the butter pieces over the blueberries and rhubarb.

7. On a lightly floured surface, roll the second pastry disc into a 12- to 13-inch circle. Brush the edge of the bottom crust lightly with water and cover it with the top crust, pressing the edges to seal. Trim away excess pastry with scissors, leaving $1/2$ inch of overhang. Fold the pastry edge back on itself to make a standing rim and flute. Brush the top of the pastry lightly with cold water and sprinkle it evenly with remaining 1 tablespoon of sugar. At right angles make 4 slits about $1^1/2$ inches long in the top crust to allow steam to escape during baking, and place the pie on the baking sheet on the lower rack. Bake for 15 minutes. Transfer the pie, still on the baking sheet, to the center shelf, reduce the temperature to 350°, and continue baking for 1 hour, or until the crust is well-browned and you can see the juices bubbling away in the slits. Cool for several hours before serving.

HUCKLEBERRY PIE

I've struggled over the years with huckleberry pies, attempting to find the best thickener and figuring out how much of it to use. I've tried quick-cooking tapioca, flour, cornstarch, and a combination of flour and cornstarch. Each batch of berries seemed to require a different amount of thickener and I never knew what to expect until I cut into the pie. Sometimes the berries would be perfectly set; other times, the filling would run all over. Lately, I've been getting fairly consistent results with quick-cooking tapioca. But even if your filling turns out runny, don't lose heart; the pie will still be delicious. If you can't get Rocky Mountain huckleberries, use ready-made huckleberry filling (see mail-order sources on pages 236–237) or blueberries and follow the directions for the variation that follows this recipe.

Pie crust pastry (page 218)

Huckleberry Filling

1 cup plus 1 tablespoon granulated sugar

¼ cup firmly packed light brown sugar

4 to 5 tablespoons quick-cooking tapioca

1 teaspoon ground cinnamon

½ teaspoon freshly grated nutmeg

1¾ pounds huckleberries, picked over (5 cups), fresh or frozen

1 tablespoon freshly squeezed lemon juice

2 tablespoons butter, chilled and cut into small pieces

1. Refrigerate the pastry dough for at least 1 hour.

2. On a lightly floured surface, roll out the larger disc into a 13-inch circle. Fit the dough loosely into a 9-inch glass or metal pie pan, leaving excess pastry hanging over the edge. Refrigerate until ready to fill.

3. Adjust two oven racks, placing one on the lowest shelf and the other in the center. Place a heavy baking sheet on the lower shelf. Preheat the oven to 450°.

4. In a large bowl, combine 1 cup of the granulated sugar, the brown sugar, tapioca, cinnamon, and nutmeg. Break up any brown sugar lumps with your fingertips and mix everything together thoroughly. Fold in the huckleberries (thaw them for 30 minutes if frozen) and lemon juice and let the mixture stand for 15 minutes.

5. Remove the pie shell from the refrigerator and pour the filling into the crust, mounding it slightly in the center. Dot with the butter and set aside. On a lightly floured surface, roll out the top crust into a 12-inch circle. Brush the edge of the lower crust lightly with water and place the top crust over the berries. Press the edges firmly to seal and trim away excess pastry to within ½ inch of the rim of the pan. Fold the pastry back on itself to form a standing

rim and flute. At right angles make four slits about $1\frac{1}{2}$ inches long in the top crust with the tip of a small sharp knife. Brush the top lightly with water and sprinkle with the remaining 1 tablespoon sugar. Place the pie in the oven on the baking sheet and bake for 15 minutes. Transfer the baking sheet to the center shelf, reduce the temperature to 350°, and continue baking for 45 to 60 minutes, or until the juices are thickened and bubbly and the crust is a rich brown color. Cool completely for several hours before cutting. Or refrigerate the cooled pie for a few hours before serving.

Blueberry Pie Variation: Combine 1 cup granulated sugar, 2 tablespoons firmly packed dark brown sugar, 1 teaspoon pumpkin pie spice, and 4 to 5 tablespoons quick-cooking tapioca in a large bowl. Add 2 pounds (6 cups) fresh blueberries (thaw for 30 minutes if frozen) and 2 tablespoons freshly squeezed lime juice. Fold together gently with a rubber spatula and let stand for 15 minutes. Continue with the directions for Huckleberry Pie, baking for 60 to 70 minutes once the oven temperature is reduced to 350°.

Huckleberry Heaven

"Once in the mouth . . . there can be no doubt: this is something else entirely. And here the trouble begins, because for those who have tasted mountain huckleberries, no description is needed; and for those who haven't description is impossible."

—Asta Bowen, *The Huckleberry Book*

RHUBARB PIE

Most rhubarb pies turn out soft and runny, but not this one. Mixing the cut rhubarb with sugar and letting the mixture stand overnight draws out the excess moisture from the rhubarb. Some of the liquid is then thickened with cornstarch, folded into the rhubarb, and baked in the pie. After the pie has cooled, the filling stays put when you cut it. This double-crust pie makes a great visual presentation—as good to look at as it is to eat.

Pie crust pastry (page 218)

Rhubarb Filling

2 pounds trimmed rhubarb stalks, cut into ½-inch pieces (about 8 cups)

2 cups sugar

3 whole cloves

Finely grated zest of 1 lemon

3 tablespoons freshly squeezed lemon juice

¼ cup cornstarch

1½ teaspoons pure vanilla extract

2 tablespoons chilled butter, cut into small pieces

1. Refrigerate the pastry dough overnight.

2. Combine the rhubarb, sugar, and cloves in a large mixing bowl. Cover and let stand at room temperature overnight. (If your kitchen is warm, refrigerate the mixture then bring it to room temperature before proceeding.) The next morning, the rhubarb will be sitting in a pool of juice. Drain well for about 1 hour in a large strainer set over a bowl and discard the cloves.

3. Measure 1¼ cups rhubarb juice and stir in the lemon zest, lemon juice, and cornstarch. Place in a 2-quart saucepan and cook over medium heat, stirring gently and continuously with a rubber spatula until the mixture boils and thickens. Cook and stir gently for another 2 minutes, scraping the bottom of the pan well with the rubber spatula, then cool to room temperature and stir in the vanilla.

4. Prepare the oven and roll out the pastry as described in the Blueberry-Rhubarb Pie recipe (pages 218–219).

5. Gently fold the drained rhubarb and cornstarch mixture together. Pour into the bottom crust and smooth the top, mounding it a bit in the center. Dot the filling with the chilled butter bits and cover with the top crust. Finish the crust and complete the baking as directed on page 219. Cool completely on a wire rack before serving. Refrigerate the pie for a few hours and serve it cold.

Apple Growing in Montana

At the turn of the twentieth century, apple growing lured many to come out West. In Montana, most apple ranches didn't succeed because of the extreme climate and blight, and commercial apple production eventually fell by the wayside. However, many apple varieties can be grown in certain parts of the state if one perseveres. Art and Nancy Callan grow many types of apples in the Bitterroot Valley. They tend about 1,200 trees on $2^1/_2$ acres, and they begin selling their apples at farmers' markets in early August. Every week the selection changes, depending on what's been harvested. Apples that do particularly well here are the disease-resistant varieties such as the all-purpose Liberty and William's Pride. For some reason, blight is more prevalent in Montana than in Idaho and Washington. If everything goes well, in a good year the annual crop may yield Vista Bella, Discovery, Jersey Mac, State Fair, Summer Red, William's Pride, Lyman's Large, Jonamac, McIntosh, Gala, Liberty, Kidd Orange, Sweet Sixteen, and Honey Crisp. Jonamac is their most dependable variety. It is a delicious all-purpose cooking and eating apple that can be harvested from early September to mid-October. Many of these varieties do not store well, so they must be used soon after picking.

GINGERED APPLE PIE

This makes a huge, gorgeous pie. Be sure to use a firm cooking apple in this recipe. You can't go wrong with Golden Delicious, but if you live in an apple-growing region, do ask about local varieties that are good to bake with.

Pie crust pastry (page 218)

Apple-Ginger Filling

Juice of 1 lemon

4 pounds firm cooking apples, peeled, cored, and cut in quarters

¾ cup plus 1 tablespoon granulated sugar

2 tablespoons dry unseasoned bread crumbs

¼ cup (1¼ ounces) unbleached all-purpose flour

½ cup firmly packed light brown sugar

1 teaspoon ground cinnamon

¼ teaspoon mace

¼ cup finely chopped crystallized ginger

3 tablespoons butter, chilled and cut into small pieces

1 egg

2 teaspoons water

1. Refrigerate the pastry dough for at least 1 hour.

2. Strain the lemon juice into a large mixing bowl. Slice each apple quarter into 3 or 4 wedges. Add to the lemon juice, tossing well as you go along. Add ½ cup of the granulated sugar and toss to combine thoroughly. Let stand 1 hour or longer to draw out excess juices. Drain well. (You will not need the juice for the recipe.)

3. Adjust two oven racks with one on the lowest shelf and the other in the center. Place a heavy baking sheet on the lower shelf and preheat the oven to 450°.

4. On a lightly floured surface, roll out the larger pastry disc into a 13-inch circle. Place the dough loosely in a 9-inch glass or metal pie pan, leaving the excess pastry hanging over the edge. Sprinkle the bread crumbs over the bottom of the pie shell.

5. Measure the flour by scooping a measuring cup into the flour container, filling the cup to overflowing, and sweeping off the excess with a metal spatula.

6. In a large bowl combine the flour, brown sugar, ¼ cup of the granulated sugar, the cinnamon, mace, and ginger. Add the apples and fold together until the mixture is moistened. Transfer the filling to the pie shell and dot the top with the butter. On a lightly floured surface, roll out the second pastry disc into a 12- to 13-inch circle. In a small bowl, beat the egg and water together with a fork just to combine well, and brush some onto the edge of the bottom crust. Place the second circle of pastry on top and press the edges firmly to seal. Trim away excess pastry to within ½ inch of the edge of the pie plate. Fold the pastry back on itself to form a standing rim and flute. At right angles cut four slits about 1½ inches long in the top of the pie and brush the crust with the egg wash.

7. Sprinkle with the remaining 1 tablespoon sugar and place the pie on the baking sheet. Bake 15 minutes, then transfer the pie, still on the baking sheet, to the center rack. Reduce the temperature to 350° and continue baking for 60 to 70 minutes, or until the crust is well-browned, the apples are tender (insert a sharp knife through one of the slits in the top crust to test), and the filling is bubbly. Cool completely before serving.

PEACH PIE

Juicy and flavorful peaches grow in Paradise, Montana, an hour northwest of Missoula. The 2,500-foot elevation and abundant sunshine conspire to produce outstanding peaches from late July through September. Tom and Lynn McCamant have been growing peaches since 2001, and they're some of the best peaches I've eaten anywhere. When buying peaches, select fruit that smell peachy and that feel firm but give a little when gently pressed. Choose freestone varieties, if possible, to make pitting easy work. Serve the pie plain or with frozen vanilla yogurt, vanilla ice cream, or Huckleberry Ice Cream (see page 230).

Pie crust pastry (page 218)

Filling

3½ pounds ripe peaches (about 9 medium to large)

½ cup firmly packed light brown sugar

½ cup plus 1 tablespoon granulated sugar

3 tablespoons cornstarch

1½ teaspoons pumpkin pie spice

¼ teaspoon salt

1 tablespoon fresh lime juice

2 tablespoons chilled butter, cut into small pieces

1. Prepare pastry as directed and refrigerate until needed.

2. Adjust two oven racks with one on the lowest shelf and the other in the center. Place a heavy baking sheet on the lower shelf and preheat oven to 450°.

3. Bring a large pot of water to the boil. Have a large bowl of cold water nearby. Add about half the peaches to the water with a slotted spoon and bring the water back to the boil. Cook 30 seconds and transfer peaches from the boiling water to the bowl of cold water with the slotted spoon. Repeat with the remaining peaches. Cool for 2 to 3 minutes, then remove the peaches from the water one at a time and peel them with a sharp paring knife. Cut the peaches in half at their seams, remove the pits, and slice the peach halves into ½-inch-thick wedges.

3. Combine brown sugar, ½ cup granulated sugar, cornstarch, pumpkin pie spice, and salt in a large bowl. Add peaches and lime juice and fold everything together gently and thoroughly with a rubber spatula. Roll out pastry as described in the Blueberry-Rhubarb Pie recipe (pages 218–219) and fit loosely into a 9-inch pie pan. Mound peaches into pastry, patting the filling down slightly with the rubber spatula; distribute butter pieces over the filling. Brush overhanging edge of pastry with water and place top crust over the filling. Press edges of top and bottom crusts together firmly to seal. Trim away excess pastry to within ½-inch from rim of pie pan. Fold pastry edge to form a standing rim. Flute. Brush top of pastry lightly with water and sprinkle with the 1 tablespoon granulated sugar. Cut four 1½-inch long slits at right angles to each other in the top crust. Place pie pan on baking sheet and bake 20 minutes.

4. Transfer pie pan on its baking sheet to the center shelf, reduce oven temperature to 350°, and continue baking about 75 minutes longer, until pie is a deep golden brown and the filling is bubbling up through the slits. Cool completely on a wire rack for several hours before serving.

RASPBERRY COBBLER

The entire Rocky Mountain West and Pacific Northwest are great raspberry-growing areas. The cool nights and long days make for exceptionally juicy and flavorful berries. In our garden, we grow thornless varieties of red and yellow berries, which are easy to pick. I've made this cobbler with both kinds, either combined or separately, and I can't tell which one I like best. Just use the plumpest and freshest berries you can find.

½ cup firmly packed dark brown sugar

4 teaspoons cornstarch

½ teaspoon ground cinnamon

¼ teaspoon freshly grated nutmeg

½ cup water

2 teaspoons pure vanilla extract

3 pints (6 cups) raspberries

1 cup (4½ ounces) unbleached
    all-purpose flour

¼ cup granulated sugar

1 teaspoon baking powder

¼ teaspoon baking soda

¼ teaspoon salt

6 tablespoons butter (¾ stick),
    chilled and cut into 6 pieces

⅔ cup buttermilk

1. Adjust an oven rack to the center position and preheat the oven to 400°.

2. In a large bowl, combine the brown sugar, cornstarch, cinnamon, nutmeg, water, and vanilla. Press the mixture against the side of the bowl with the flat side of a rubber spatula to break up any sugar lumps and dissolve the cornstarch; set aside. Pick over the raspberries.

3. Measure the flour by spooning it into a measuring cup, filling the cup to overflowing, and sweeping off the excess with a metal spatula. In a medium-size bowl, sift together the flour, granulated sugar, baking powder, baking soda, and salt. Cut in the butter with a pastry blender until the mixture resembles coarse meal. Add the buttermilk and stir with a fork just until the mixture gathers together to form a soft dough. Gently fold the raspberries into the cornstarch mixture with a rubber spatula. Pour the mixture into a shallow 2-quart baking dish. (I use a round ovenproof glass dish 10 inches in diameter and 2 inches deep.)

4. Place spoonfuls of batter over the raspberries in 8 mounds, leaving a bit of space between the mounds. Bake for about 35 minutes, or until the cobbler is well-browned and the juices are thickened and bubbly. Serve warm or cool.

HUCKLEBERRY SHAKE

This shake is a gorgeous purple color with that special tang only real huckleberries have.

¼ cup milk

⅓ to ½ cup huckleberries, fresh or
    frozen

½ cup premium vanilla ice cream or
    frozen yogurt

Pour the milk into a blender and add the berries (if frozen, thaw first). Blend at high speed 1 minute. Add the ice cream and blend until smooth. Pour into a tall frosted glass and drink immediately.

A Huckleberry by Any Other Name Is Not the Same

When my wife and I moved to Montana in 1972, it was almost the beginning of huckleberry season. Our neighbors kept talking about whether it would be a good year for the wild berries and their plans for their harvest. We had never heard of huckleberries, but within a few weeks we knew what all the fuss was about. Rocky Mountain huckleberries have a taste all their own: similar to blueberries, but much tarter and richer in flavor. Since then, we've also tasted huckleberries from the Cascade Mountains. The berries from the Cascades not only looked smaller and had larger seeds, they didn't have the depth of flavor of our Rocky Mountain berries. Botanically speaking, all huckleberries and blueberries belong to the genus *Vaccinium*, but sorting out the details of their relationships is very complicated.

What we call huckleberries in Montana may be referred to as whortleberries, bilberries, dewberries, or by some other name in another part of the country. The different varieties of huckleberries don't taste the same. The wild mountain huckleberries we eat range in color from light purple to almost black. One tiny specimen has a pronounced reddish tinge. If you can't get fresh huckleberries, the next best thing to do is to buy a jar of huckleberry jam, syrup, or pie filling made from wild Montana or Idaho berries. Then you will have some idea what all the fuss is about.

HAZELNUT PRALINE ANGEL FOOD CAKE

Hazelnuts, or filberts as they are sometimes called, grow abundantly in nearby Oregon. I decided to see how they'd work in an angel food cake, and this is the result. For years I had problems baking egg white–based cakes where I live. The altitude, about 3,500 feet, is not exceptionally high, but it is just high enough above sea level to make trouble. I found that putting the cake pan into a cold oven and then setting the thermostat to the desired temperature was the way to avoid disaster. The cakes always rose beautifully and stayed that way—no last-minute collapse, which happened if the oven was preheated. The reason the cold oven works is simple: As the bubbles in the batter expand, the air pushes against a protein network. If the expansion happens too quickly, as it does in a preheated oven, the proteins don't have enough time to set properly and to trap the air. Instead, they break down, the air escapes, and the cake falls. I have become so fond of this method that I even use it at sea level, where it works just as well for me. You'll need a 10x4-inch angel food pan with a removable bottom but without a nonstick finish. Also handy is a large (8-quart) stainless steel mixing bowl. Mine measures 13 ½ inches across and 5 inches deep. An extra-wide rubber spatula helps speed the folding process. Be sure all bowls and utensils are grease-free.

The cake needs no accompaniment, but it goes particularly well with blackberries mixed with a bit of sugar and allowed to stand for an hour or so. Or serve it with heavy cream flavored with hazelnut liqueur (use about 1 tablespoon liqueur for each cup of cream) and whipped to soft peaks.

Hazelnut Praline

1 cup sugar

¼ cup water

¼ teaspoon cream of tartar

*½ cup blanched, toasted hazelnuts
   (page 3)*

Cake Batter

*1 cup (4 to 4½ ounces) sifted
   unbleached all-purpose flour*

1 cup sifted confectioners' sugar

2 cups (14 to 16 large eggs) egg whites

½ teaspoon salt

1½ teaspoons cream of tartar

1½ teaspoons pure vanilla extract

⅔ cup granulated sugar

1. Line a 9-inch square baking pan with aluminum foil. To make the praline, combine the sugar, water, and cream of tartar in a heavy-bottomed 1-quart saucepan over high heat. Stir continuously with a wooden spatula until the sugar is dissolved and the mixture comes to a boil. Cover the pan and boil 3 minutes. (During this time, the condensing steam inside the pan will wash down any sugar crystals clinging to the side.) Uncover the pan and keep boiling, without stirring, for several minutes until the syrup turns a deep caramel color. Swirl the pan occasionally to keep the color even. Remove the pan from the heat and quickly add the nuts, swirling the pan to combine them with the syrup. Immediately pour the mixture into the prepared pan. Do not scrape the pan clean, just pour out what will come. Cool the praline completely, about 30 minutes, then break it up into chunks and pulverize it into a powder in a food processor fitted with the metal blade. Store in an airtight container. The praline powder keeps very well in the freezer for months.

2. To make the cake batter, adjust an oven rack to the lower-third position, but do not preheat the oven. Sift the flour with the confectioners' sugar four times.

3. In the large bowl of an electric mixer, beat the egg whites with the whip attachment on medium speed until foamy, about 1 minute. Add the salt, cream of tartar, and vanilla. Increase the speed to medium-high and continue beating until the egg whites form soft peaks. Test by dipping the tip of a rubber spatula in the beaten whites; the whites should curl over, not form stiff peaks, when the spatula is pulled away. Beat again at medium speed and add the granulated sugar 1 rounded tablespoon at a time, beating for 15 seconds between additions. When all of the sugar has been incorporated, increase the speed to high and beat just until the whites are glossy and hold a firm peak when the whip is raised (the peaks should stand up straight). This happens quickly.

4. Transfer the whites to the large mixing bowl. Measure ¾ cup of the hazelnut praline powder, and set aside. Return the dry ingredients back to the sifter and sift about ¼ cup at a time over the surface of the whites as you fold gently with a large rubber spatula. Work quickly, and remember to be gentle but thorough. Sprinkle the praline evenly over the whites and fold it in quickly with a few broad strokes. Immediately spoon the mixture into a grease-free 10x4-inch angel food cake pan. The pan will be almost full. Run a table knife through the batter in concentric circles to remove large air pockets, and smooth the top with a rubber spatula.

5. Place the pan in a cold oven. Set the thermostat to 350° and turn the oven on. Bake for 45 to 55 minutes, or until the top of the cake is well-browned and the cake springs back when gently pressed with a fingertip. The top of the cake may crack during baking.

6. Cool the cake in its pan, upside down, with plenty of air circulation underneath. Even if the pan has "feet," it must still be supported with more space. I use a metal funnel or a narrow-necked wine bottle. The cake must be completely cool before you remove it from the pan. To do that, use a sharp, serrated knife, with a long blade. Holding the knife vertically, insert it between the cake and the side of the pan. Use a slow up-and-down sawing motion as you rotate the pan and work your way all around it to release the cake from the sides. Lift the cake out of the pan by its central tube and run a small sharp knife under the cake to release it from the bottom of the pan. Carefully invert onto a rack, remove the pan bottom, and invert the cake again onto a dessert platter. Cut with a serrated knife to serve.

HUCKLEBERRY ICE CREAM

YIELD: 1 QUART

The first dessert I make with the season's first huckleberries is Huckleberry Pie (page 220–221). I also make this ice cream to serve with it. It may be overkill, but nothing succeeds like excess. This ice cream does not freeze brick hard.

3 cups huckleberries

1 cup sugar

2 cups heavy whipping cream

4 egg yolks

¼ teaspoon salt

1. Combine the huckleberries and sugar in a heavy-bottomed 3-quart nonreactive saucepan. Cover and cook over medium-low heat, stirring occasionally, until the berries are cooked and very soft and the sugar is dissolved, about 20 minutes. Uncover the pan, increase the heat to medium-high, and boil the mixture for 5 minutes, stirring often. Remove from the heat and break up the berries in the pan with a potato masher. Pass through a fine strainer, pressing on the pulp to extract as much liquid as possible. You should have about 1½ cups of huckleberry syrup.

2. Heat the cream in a heavy 1-quart saucepan over medium heat until bubbles form around the edges and the cream is very hot but not boiling. Set aside. Meanwhile, whisk the yolks and salt together in a medium-sized bowl just to combine well. Very gradually whisk in the hot cream, adding droplets at first then adding it in a thin stream as the yolks warm up. Transfer the mixture to the 3-quart saucepan and cook over medium-low to low heat, stirring continuously with a rubber spatula until the mixture thickens into a custard and coats the spatula with a thin layer. When cooked, the mixture should register between 175° and 180° on an instant-read thermometer. Remove from the heat and stir in the huckleberry syrup.

3. Place the saucepan in a larger pan filled with ice cubes and water and stir occasionally until the mixture feels cold. It will thicken as it chills. Freeze in an ice cream maker according to the manufacturer's directions. Transfer to an airtight container and freeze. It keeps well for about 1 week.

FRESH APRICOT-BLUEBERRY CRISP

YIELD: 8 SERVINGS

We have two beautiful apricot trees in our backyard. Every five years—if we're lucky—we get a crop. Each year, the trees bloom at the end of April. The bees come by the hundreds to pollinate the flowers, then we hold our breath, hoping a late frost won't kill our expectations. If we can just make it to the end of May, we're safe. The problem with apricots is that they do bloom early. In fact, the name "apricot" is derived, like the word "precocious," from the Latin praecox. There is nothing like the taste of a homegrown apricot, warmed by the sun and bursting with flavor. Fortunately, store-bought apricots taste better baked than fresh and work perfectly well in this crisp. In supermarkets, apricot season is very short, lasting from late May to the beginning of July.

1 cup (4½ ounces) unbleached all-
　　purpose flour

½ cup firmly packed dark brown
　　sugar

1 teaspoon ground cinnamon

¼ teaspoon mace

¼ teaspoon freshly grated nutmeg

¼ teaspoon salt

½ cup (1 stick) butter, chilled and cut
　　into 6 pieces

2 pounds fresh apricots, cut in half,
　　pitted, and cut into 1-inch pieces

1 cup blueberries

½ cup granulated sugar

2 teaspoons pure vanilla extract

1 pint vanilla frozen yogurt (optional)

1. Adjust an oven rack to the center position and preheat the oven to 350°. Butter a 9x9x2-inch baking dish.

2. Measure the flour by spooning it into a dry measuring cup, filling it to overflowing, and sweeping off the excess with a metal spatula.

3. In a medium-sized bowl, stir together the flour, brown sugar, cinnamon, mace, nutmeg, and salt. Add the butter and cut in with a pastry blender until the mixture resembles small peas. In a large bowl, combine the apricots, blueberries, granulated sugar, and vanilla until the mixture is moistened. Turn into the prepared pan and sprinkle with the crumb mixture, patting it gently in place without packing it down. Bake 40 to 45 minutes, or until the topping is browned, the filling is bubbly, and the apricots are tender. Cool. Serve warm or at room temperature with the frozen yogurt, if desired.

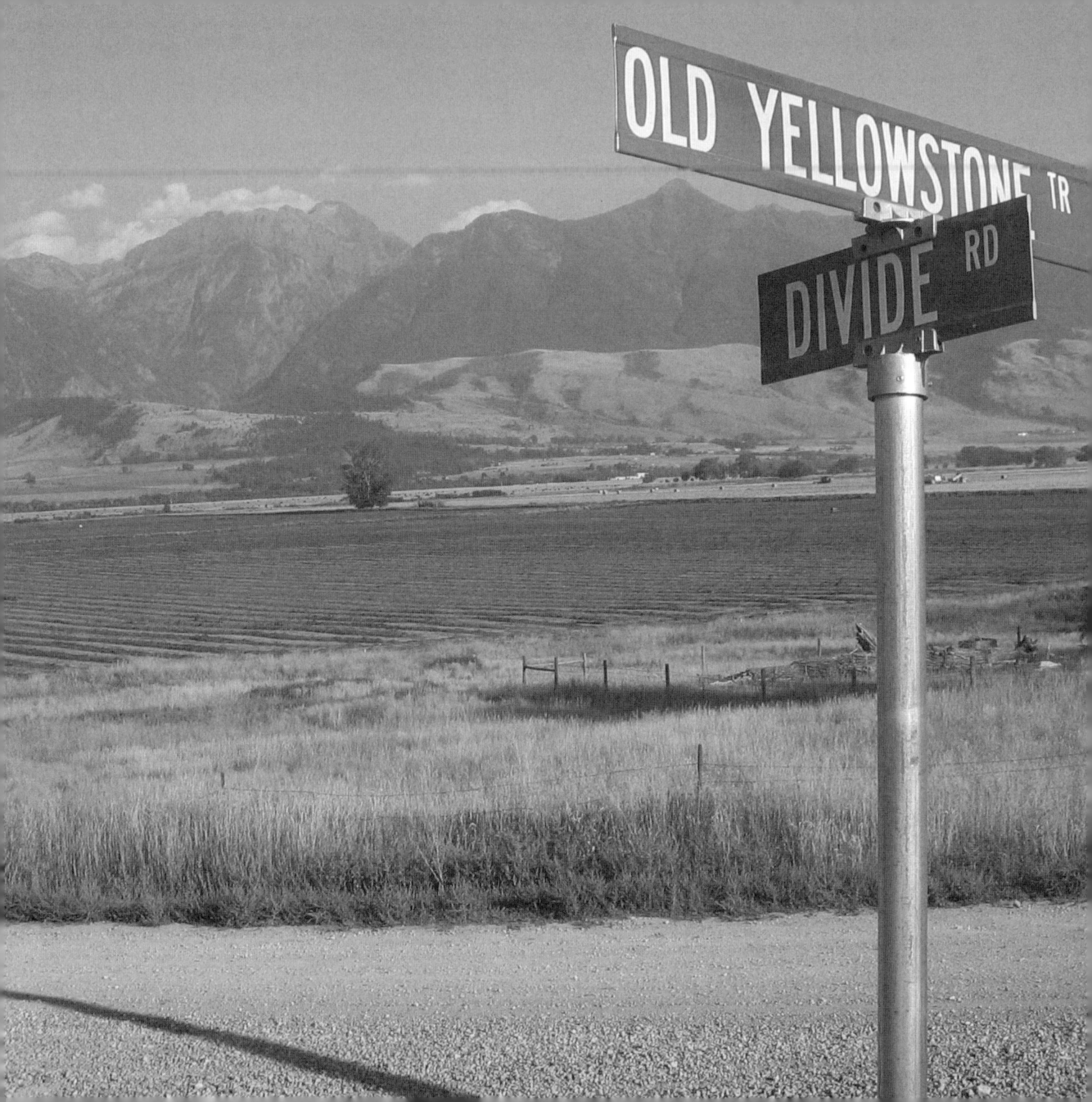
OLD YELLOWSTONE TR
DIVIDE RD

HUCKLEBERRY LIME SAUCE

YIELD: 2 TO 3 CUPS

I often freeze huckleberries and make this sauce throughout the winter to serve with sponge cake, cheesecakes, pancakes, waffles, or ice cream. It keeps in the refrigerator for 2 weeks.

4 to 5 cups huckleberries, fresh or
    frozen
1½ cups sugar
2 tablespoons freshly squeezed
    lime juice
2 teaspoons cornstarch
2 tablespoons water

1. Place 3 cups of the huckleberries (if frozen, measure the 3 cups first, then thaw) and the sugar in the work bowl of a food processor fitted with the metal blade. Process 2 minutes, then transfer to a 3-quart saucepan. Stir in the lime juice.

2. Dissolve the cornstarch in the water and add it to the berry mixture. Cook over medium heat, stirring gently but continuously with a rubber spatula, until the mixture thickens and comes to a boil. Decrease heat to low and cook, stirring, 2 minutes more.

3. Remove from the heat and pass through a fine-mesh strainer set over a large bowl, pressing to extract as much juice as possible. Discard the pulp. Stir the remaining 1 to 2 cups berries into the sauce (if frozen, add them unthawed). Cool completely, then cover and refrigerate. Serve cold.

TREASURE STATE TROPICAL CAKE

YIELD: 12 TO 16 SERVINGS

Montana is known as the Treasure State, and we who live in western Montana, where the climate is strongly influenced by Pacific coastal weather systems, tend to have milder winters compared to the rest of the state. Because of this, a very popular bumper sticker appeared several years ago, proclaiming "Native of Tropical Montana." Whenever I traveled by car to points south, people always commented on that message. Montana is, of course, far from tropical. But I make this cake to honor the sentiment on the bumper sticker and to use up all the egg yolks left over from the Hazelnut Praline Angel Food Cake (pages 228–229).

Cake Batter

Unseasoned dry fine bread crumbs,
   for dusting

3 cups (13½ ounces) unbleached all-
   purpose flour

½ cup cornstarch

¼ teaspoon salt

1¼ cups (about 14) egg yolks

1½ cups butter, softened

4 cups (12 ounces) sifted
   confectioners' sugar

Grated zest of 1 lemon

Grated zest of 1 orange

Grated zest of 1 lime

2 teaspoons pure vanilla extract

3 tablespoons freshly squeezed
   lime juice

1 cup nonfat plain yogurt

1 teaspoon baking soda

Tropical Icing

1 ⅓ cups (4 ounces) sifted confectioners' sugar

1 tablespoon freshly squeezed lemon juice

½ teaspoon pure orange extract

1½ teaspoons hot water

1. For the cake, butter a 10-inch, 3½-inch-deep nonstick bundt pan and dust it generously with the bread crumbs. Tap out excess crumbs and set the pan aside. Adjust the oven rack to the lower-third position and preheat the oven to 350°.

2. Measure the flour by spooning it into a dry measuring cup, filling the cup to overflowing, and sweeping off the excess with a metal spatula. Transfer the flour to a sifter set over a square of waxed paper. To measure the cornstarch, place a ½-cup measure on waxed paper and pour cornstarch into the cup, filling it to overflowing and sweeping off the excess with a metal spatula. Sift the flour, cornstarch, and salt together 3 times and set aside.

3. In the large bowl of an electric mixer, beat the egg yolks at high speed with the whip attachment until they are more than triple in volume and are very pale and thick, about 5 minutes. Transfer the yolks to another bowl and set aside. In the mixer bowl, beat the butter on high speed about 1 minute until it is smooth and creamy. Add the confectioners' sugar, fruit zest, and vanilla.

Beat several minutes on high speed until the mixture is fluffy and almost white. Scrape the side of the bowl once or twice. On medium or medium-high speed, beat in the lime juice, then add the beaten yolks. At first the mixture may appear curdled, but continued beating will make it smooth.

4. In a medium-sized bowl, stir together the yogurt and baking soda. The mixture will become very foamy. With the mixer set on the lowest speed, add the flour mixture to the egg mixture in four additions, alternately adding the yogurt mixture in three additions, beginning and ending with the dry ingredients; stop periodically to scrape down the bowl well between additions. Pour the batter into the prepared pan and spread it level with a rubber spatula. The batter will fill the pan halfway. Bake for 50 to 60 minutes, or until the cake is a rich golden brown and a cake tester or wooden skewer comes out clean when inserted in the center. When baked, the cake will fill the pan by three fourths and may have a few cracks on the top.

5. Let the cake cool in the pan set on a rack for 30 minutes, then cover it with a cake rack, invert the two, and remove the pan. Cool completely.

6. Prepare the icing by whisking together all of the ingredients in a small bowl until smooth. The icing will be the consistency of medium-thick cream. Adjust the consistency with a little more sugar or hot water if necessary. Spoon and spread the icing on the top of the cake to cover it completely, letting some drip unevenly down the sides. When the icing has set, carefully transfer the cake with a wide metal spatula to a dessert platter. Cover and let the cake stand a few hours before serving. Store, covered, at room temperature for up to 4 days.

MAIL-ORDER SOURCES FOR SPECIALTY INGREDIENTS AND EQUIPMENT

D'Artagnan
399-419 St. Paul Ave.
Jersey City, NJ 07306
1-800-327-8246
Web site: www.dartagnan.com
Huge selection of game meats, including New Zealand venison and red deer (elk), ostrich, duck, quail, and a variety of smoked and cured meats. Also source for lamb.

Eva Gates
P.O. Box 696
Bigfork, MT 59911-0696
1-800-682–4283
Web site: www.evagates.com
Wide range of homemade preserves and syrups, including huckleberry, raspberry, black cap, and cherry. Huckleberry topping for ice cream contains whole berries.

Game Sales International
P.O. Box 7719
Loveland, CO 80537
1-800-729–2090
Web site: www.gamesalesintl.com
Large selection of game meats, pheasant, quail, ostrich, dried wild mushrooms, and many more wild products.

Giusto's Specialty Foods Inc.
344 Littlefield
South San Francisco, CA 94080
1-866-972-6879
Web site: www.giustos.com
High-performance organic baking flours, spices, sea salts, oils, and baking equipment.

Gourmet Mushrooms
2901 Gravenstein Highway North
Sebastopol, CA 95472
1-707-823–1743
Web site: www.gourmetmushroomsinc.com
Fresh and dried cultivated mushrooms and wild mushrooms.

Indian Harvest Specialitifoods, Inc.
P.O. Box 428
Bemidji, MN 56601
1-800-346–7032
Web site: www.Indianharvest.com
Specialty heirloom dried beans, wild rice, lentils, and other hard-to-find items.

Jamison Farms
171 Jamison Ln.
Latrobe, PA 15650
1-800-237–5262
Web site: www.jamisonfarm.com
Lamb in all forms, including whole dressed lambs. Most orders are shipped frozen, but fresh shipments can be arranged.

King Arthur Flour Company
P.O. Box 876
Norwich, VT 05055-0876
1-800-827–6836
Web site: www.bakerscatalogue.com
An outstanding source for many kinds of organic and inorganic flours; baking equipment, including scales, baking stones, and specialty baking pans; high-quality bulk yeast; books; and much more.

Manchester Farms
P.O. Box 97
Dalzell, SC 29040
1-877-669-4669
Web site: www.manchesterfarms.com
Specializes in quail.

Meco Corporation
1500 Industrial Rd.
Greenville, TN 37743-8222
(800) 346–3256
Web site: gasgrillsnow.com/Meco.asp
Excellent electric water smokers, grills, grill accessories, and wood chunks and chips. The water smoker model to check out is SKU: 5029-MECO, catalog number 7926.

Mountain Lake Fisheries
P.O. Box 1067
Columbia Falls, MT 59912
1-888-809–0826
Web site: www.whitefishcaviar.com
Whitefish filets, whitefish caviar, and other products.

Rocky Mountain Natural Meats, Inc.
P.O. Box 16668
Denver, CO 80216
1-800-327–2706
Web site: www.greatrangebison.com
Wide range of buffalo cuts and sausages. Will do special orders.

Weber-Stephen Products Co.
1-800-446-1071
Web site: http://weber.com
Outstanding selection of charcoal and gas grills and accessories.

White Mountain Farms, Inc.
5305 State Highway 17
Mosca, CO 81146
1-800-364-3019
Web site: whitemountainfarm.com
Offers organically grown standard quinoa, black quinoa, quinoa flour, and several varieties of exotic potatoes.

Williams-Sonoma
1-877-812-6235
Web site: www.Williams-Sonoma.com
Large selection of cookware, baking equipment, specialty foods, and much more.

CREDITS FOR QUOTES

Page 2: Bryan, Lettice. *The Kentucky Housewife*. Columbia, SC: University of South Carolina Press, 1839.

Pages 2–3: Marcy, Randolph. *The Prairie Traveler*. Bedford, MA: Applewood Books, 1859 (original), 1988 (facsimile).

Page 117: Arnold, Samuel P. *Eating Up the Santa Fe Trail*. Niwot, CO: University Press of Colorado, 1990.

Page 129: Author's interview with Tony Grace in May, 1992, in Hamilton, MT.

Page 210: Butruille, Susan G. *Women's Voices from the Oregon Trail: The Times That Tried Women's Souls and A Guide to Women's History Along the Oregon Trail*, 2nd ed. Boise, ID: Tamarack Books, 1994.

SELECTED BIBLIOGRAPHY

Arnold, Samuel P. *Eating Up the Santa Fe Trail*. Niwot, CO: University Press of Colorado, 1990. Recipes, lore, and anecdotes, with an extensive bibliography.

————. *Fryingpans West*. Denver: Arnold and Company, 1985. Historically accurate recipes and history of food and drink of the Western frontier.

Arora, David. *Mushrooms Demystified*, rev. ed. Berkeley, CA: Ten Speed Press, 1990. Comprehensive guide to wild mushroom identification with delicious recipes.

Ash, John, and Sid Goldstein. *American Game Cooking: A Contemporary Guide to Preparing Farm-Raised Game Birds & Meats*. New York: Addison-Wesley, 1993. Covers all types of game, how to cook them, and what wines to serve with them; includes extensive list of sources.

Bertolli, Paul, and Alice L. Waters. *Chez Panisse Cooking: New Tastes & Techniques*. New York: Random House, 1988. Excellent general cookbook, with exemplary chapter on breads (including various sourdoughs).

Bittman, Mark. *Fish: The Complete Guide to Buying and Cooking*. New York: Macmillan, 1994. Everything you need to know about fish from anchovies to wolffish, including how to clean and fillet a fish properly.

Butruille, Susan G. *Women's Voices from the Oregon Trail: The Times That Tried Women's Souls and A Guide to Women's History Along the Oregon Trail*, 2nd ed. Boise, ID: Tamarack Books, 1994. Quotes from diaries relating what life was like on the trail; includes photos and an extensive bibliography.

————. *Women's Voices from the Western Frontier*. Boise, ID: Tamarack Books, 1995. Women settlers' quotes about their new life in the West; includes photos and extensive bibliography.

Cox, Beverly, and Martin Jacobs. *Spirit of the Harvest: North American Indian Cooking*. New York: Stewart Tabori & Chang, 1991. Detailed history and survey of Native American cookery, with recipes and color photographs.

Gilliss, Julia. *So Far From Home: An Army Bride on the Western Frontier 1865–1869*. Eugene, OR: Oregon Historical Society Press, 1993. One pioneer woman's collection of letters.

Greenberg, Judith E., and Helen Carey McKeever. *A Pioneer Woman's Memoir*. New York: Franklin Watts, 1995. Based on the journal of Arabella Clemens Fulton, who first settled in the Idaho Territory in 1864. Authors' historical information provides the framework for Fulton's recollections. Archival photos and sketches included.

Holmes, Kenneth L., ed. *Covered Wagon Women: Diaries and Letters from the Western Trails, 1840–1890*. Glendale, CA/ Spokane, WA: Arthur H. Clark, 1983–1991. Ten volumes in a series that is an indispensable source for historians.

Hooker, Richard J. *Food and Drink in America*. Indianapolis: Bobbs-Merrill, 1981. An essential reference with a comprehensive bibliography.

Jamison, Cheryl A., and Bill Jamison. *Smoke & Spice: Cooking with Smoke, the Real Way to Barbecue on Your Charcoal Grill, Water Smoker, or Wood Burning Pit*. Boston, MA: Harvard Common Press, 1994. A useful all-purpose guide to smoking with delicious recipes.

Knote, Charlie, and Ruthie Knote. *Barbecuing & Sausage Making Secrets,* rev. ed. Cape Girardeau, MO: Culinary Institute of Smoke Cooking, 1993. Detailed discussions of smokers and sausage formulas. To order, write The Culinary Institute of Smoke Cooking, 2323 Brookwood Dr., Box 163, Cape Girardeau, MO 63702-0163.

Leader, Daniel, and Judith Blahnik. *Bread Alone: Bold Fresh Loaves from Your Own Hands.* New York: William Morrow, 1993. Most of the recipes are for hearty whole-grain breads; includes excellent discussion of grains, fermentation, and various kinds of starters.

Lucchetti, Cathy. *Home on the Range: A Culinary History of the American West.* New York: Villard Books, 1993. Hundreds of black-and-white archival photos along with a detailed, lively text summarizing the culinary history of a vast region.

Marcy, Randolph B. *The Prairie Traveler.* Bedford, MA: Applewood Books, 1988. A facsimile of the handbook originally published in 1859. Includes information on routes, first aid, clothing, provisions, wagon maintenance, and much more. Used by many pioneers on their way West.

Niethammer, Carolyn. *American Indian Food & Lore.* New York: Simon & Schuster, 1974. Describes dozens of plant foods used by Native Americans and how to cook with them. About 150 vegetarian recipes with large, clear pencil sketches of the plants described.

Oppenneer, Betsy. *The Bread Book.* New York: Harper Collins, 1994. Yeast and quick breads for the home cook described by a professional baker in clear, no-nonsense language. Nice discussion of various starters.

Ortiz, Joe. *The Village Baker: Classic Regional Breads from Europe and America.* Berkeley, CA: Ten Speed Press, 1993. Insights from a master baker. Includes helpful photos and sketches. No quick breads.

Patent, Dorothy Hinshaw, and Diane E. Bilderback. *The Harrowsmith Country Life Book of Garden Secrets.* Charlotte, VT: Camden House, 1991. Describes organic vegetable gardening by climatic zones; especially helpful to gardeners in the Rocky Mountain West.

Rainbolt, Jo. *The Last Cowboy: Twilight Era of the Horseback Cowhand, 1900–1940.* Helena, MT: American & World Geographic Publishing, 1992. Profiles the lives of seven cowboys, including Tony Grace.

Root, Waverley. *Food.* New York: Simon and Schuster, 1980. Encyclopedic dictionary of the world's foods, with history, sketches, and photos. An invaluable reference.

Root, Waverley, and Richard de Rochemont. *Eating in America: A History.* New York: Ecco Press, 1994. A comprehensive social history of American gastronomy from the time of the earliest explorers to the present. An essential volume for serious cooks.

Sharpe, J. Ed, and Thomas B. Underwood. *American Indian Cooking and Herb Lore.* Cherokee, NC: Cherokee Publications, 1973. A 32-page booklet with recipes, illustrations, and stories. To order, write Cherokee Publications, P.O. Box 430, Cherokee, NC 28719, or call (704) 488-8856.

Silverton, Nancy, and Laurie Ochoa. *Nancy Silverton's Breads from the La Brea Bakery: Recipes for the Connoisseur.* New York: Random House, 1996. Offers the most detailed and clear descriptions for making successful starters from wild yeasts, making terrific breads with the starters, and keeping the starters alive; for absolutely devoted home bread makers.

Sunset editors. *The Sunset Cookbook of Breads.* Menlo Park, CA: Lane Book Company, 1963. Excellent collection of yeast and quick breads, with an easy-to-follow description of making a milk-based wild yeast starter that really works.

von Bremzen, Anya, and John Welchman. *Please to the Table: The Russian Cookbook.* New York: Workman, 1990. Winner of the 1990 James Beard Food and Beverage Book Award, this is a fun and enthusiastic collection of 400 recipes gleaned from one end of Mother Russia to the other.

Webber, Bert. *The Oregon Trail Diary of Twin Sisters, Cecelia Adams and Parthenia Blank in 1852.* Medford, OR: Webb Research Group, 1994. Two sisters' accounts of their wagon train journey. Illustrated with photographs and a map. To order, write Webb Research Group, Publishers, P.O. Box 314, Medford, OR 97501.

The Web-Foot Cookbook. Portland, OR: W. B. Ayer, 1994. A facsimile edition of the original, which was published by the First Presbyterian Church of Portland, Oregon, in 1885. This is perhaps the first cookbook to come out of the Pacific Northwest. Essential reading for food historians.

Williams, Jacqueline. *Wagon Wheel Kitchens: Food on the Oregon Trail.* Lawrence, KS: University Press of Kansas, 1993. Vivid descriptions of life and cooking on the Oregon Trail. Lively prose and illustrations.

Wood, Rebecca. *Quinoa the Supergrain: Ancient Food for Today.* New York: Farrar, Strauss, & Giroux, 1989. A history of quinoa with lots of recipes.

Zumbo, Jim. *Amazing Venison Recipes.* Cody, WY: Wapiti Valley Publishing, 1994. Everything you need to know about venison, with recipes also for elk, moose, antelope, and other big-game animals. To order, write Wapiti Valley Publishing Co., P.O. Box 2390, Cody, WY 82414, or call (307) 587-5486.

RECIPE INDEX

ABOUT THE AUTHOR

Greg Patent is a food writer and cookbook author whose most recent cookbook, *A Baker's Odyssey: Celebrating Time-Honored Recipes from America's Rich Immigrant Heritage,* which includes a companion DVD, was published in December 2007, by John Wiley & Sons. His previous cookbook, *Baking in America: Traditional and Contemporary Favorites from the Past 200 Years* (Houghton Mifflin), won the 2003 James Beard Award for Best Baking Book of the Year and the World Gourmand Cookbook Award for Best Baking Book in the English Language. He is also the author of *A Is for Apple,* co-authored with his wife, Dorothy (Broadway Books, 1999), and numerous other cookbooks. Greg was a regular contributor to *Cooking Light* magazine for thirteen years and served on its editorial board. For many years, he had his own cooking show, which aired on The Learning Channel, and he has also been a chef in two Montana restaurants.